Dungeon

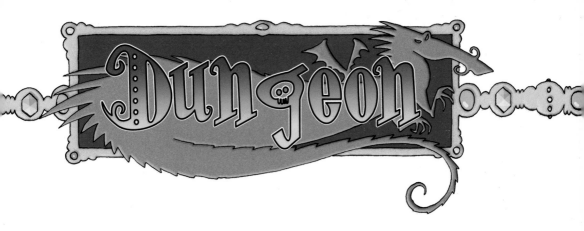

Little Guide to Dungeon

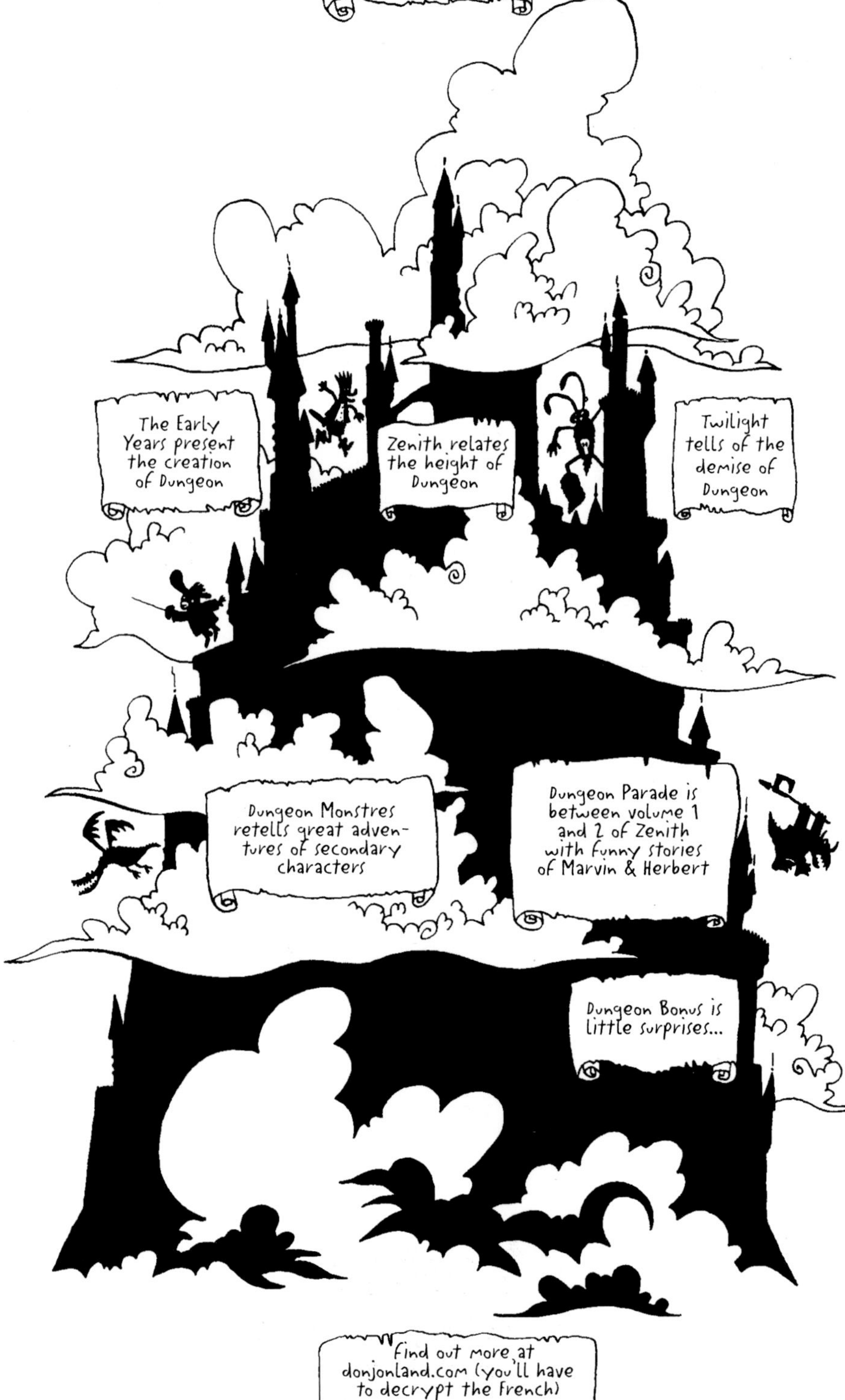
The Early Years present the creation of Dungeon
Zenith relates the height of Dungeon
Twilight tells of the demise of Dungeon
Dungeon Monstres retells great adventures of secondary characters
Dungeon Parade is between volume 1 and 2 of Zenith with funny stories of Marvin & Herbert
Dungeon Bonus is little surprises...

Find out more at donjonland.com (you'll have to decrypt the French)

G N
SFA

Twilight
Volume 1:
Dragon Cemetery

Joann SFAR, Lewis TRONDHEIM

NANTIER • BEALL • MINOUSTCHINE
Publishing inc.
new york

Also available
Dungeon, Zenith, vols. 1, 2: $14.95 each, 3: $14.99
Dungeon Early Years, vols. 1: $14.99, 2: $12.95
Dungeon, Twilight, vols. 1, 2, 4: $14.99, 3: $12.99
Dungeon, Parade, vol. 2: $9.95
Dungeon, Monstres, vols. 2: $12.95, 3: $12.99, 4: $14.99
Also by Trondheim:
Little Nothings, vols. 2, 3, 4: $14.95 each
with Thierry Robin:
Happy Halloween, Li'l Santa, $14.95

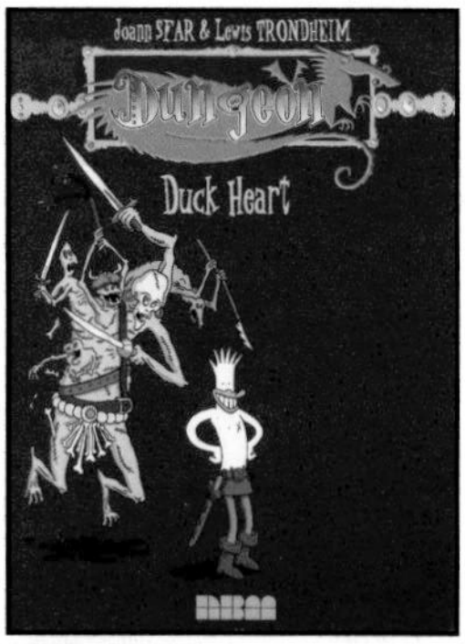
Joann SFAR & Lewis TRONDHEIM
Dungeon
Duck Heart

See previews, get exclusives and order from:
NBMPUB.COM

we have over 200 titles available
Catalog upon request
NBM
160 Broadway, Suite 700, East Wing
New York, NY 10038
If ordering by mail add $4 P&H 1st item,
$1 each addt'l

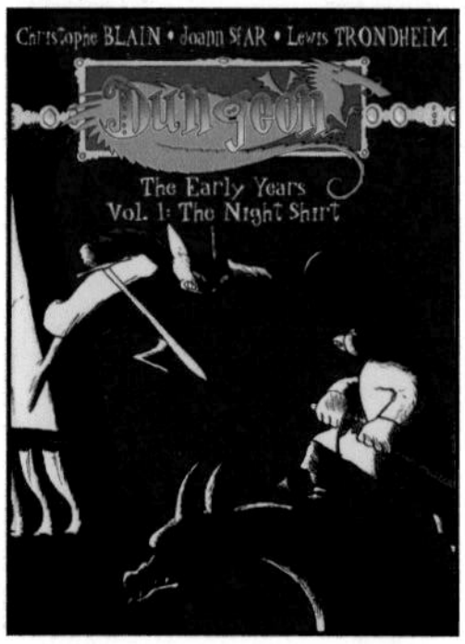
Christophe BLAIN • Joann SFAR • Lewis TRONDHEIM
Dungeon
The Early Years
Vol. 1: The Night Shirt

Originally published in French in 2 books:
Donjon Crepuscule:
Le Cimetiere des Dragons and
Le Volcan des Vaucanson
ISBN-10: 1-56163-460-3
ISBN-13: 978-1-56163-460-6

Translation by Joe Johnson
Lettering by Ortho
Printed in China

2nd printing December 2014

T 108496

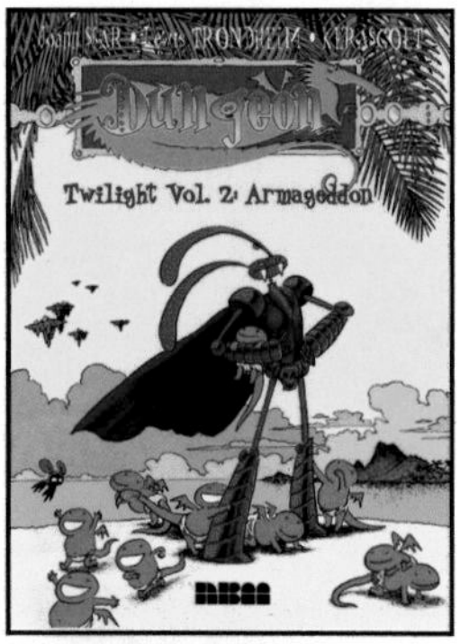
Dungeon
Twilight Vol. 2: Armageddon

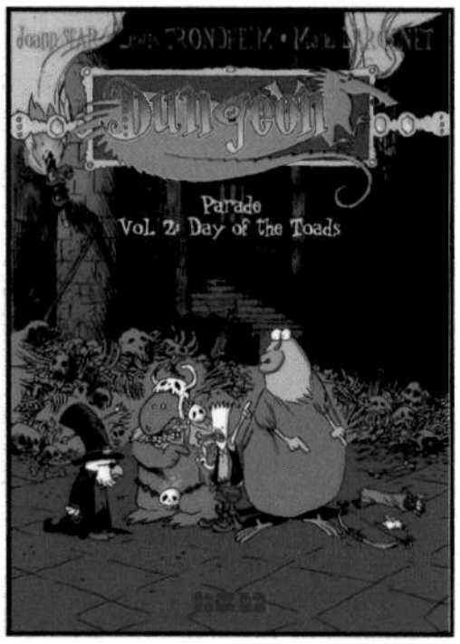
Dungeon
Parade
Vol. 2: Day of the Toads

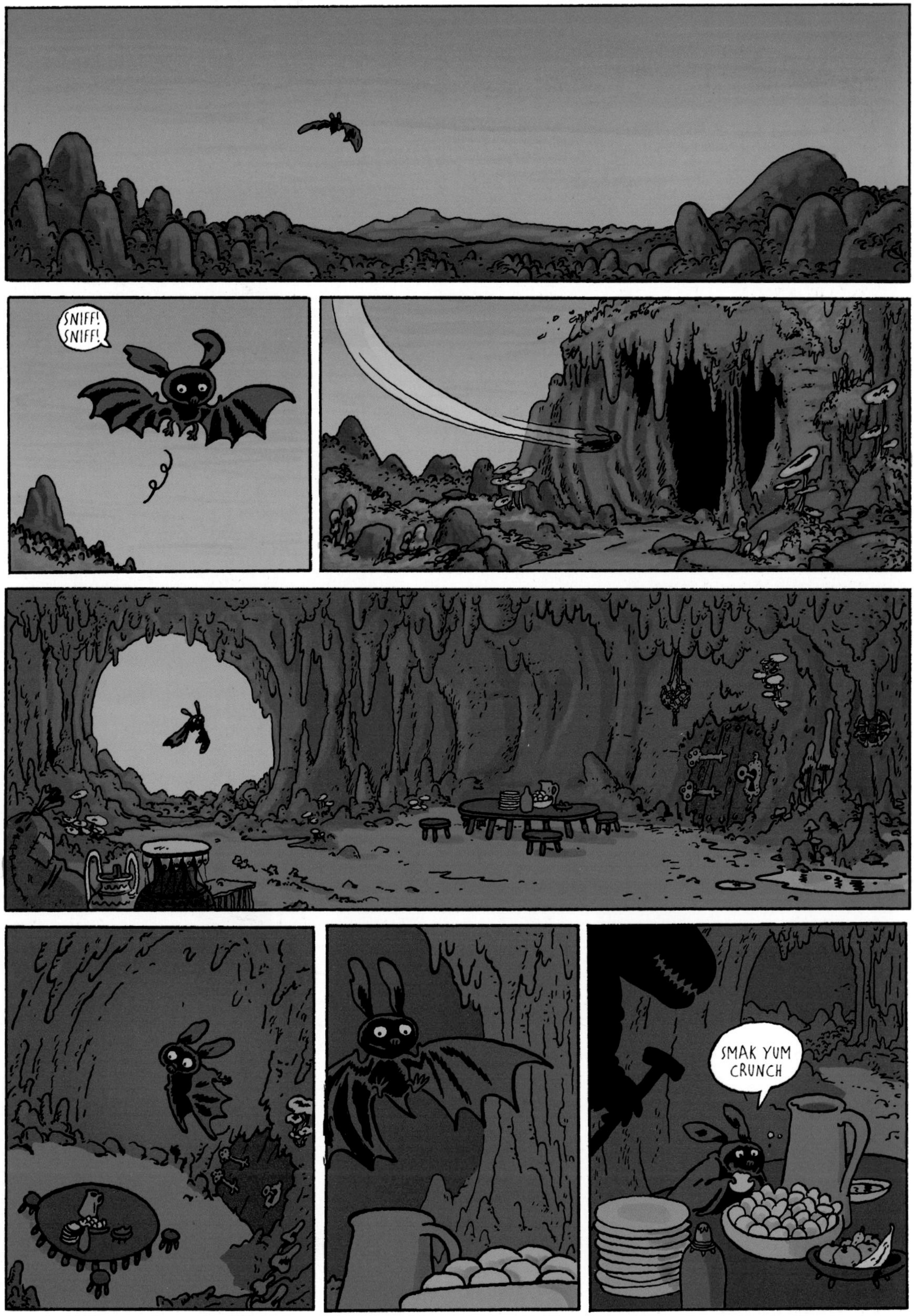
SNIFF!
SNIFF!
SMAK YUM
CRUNCH

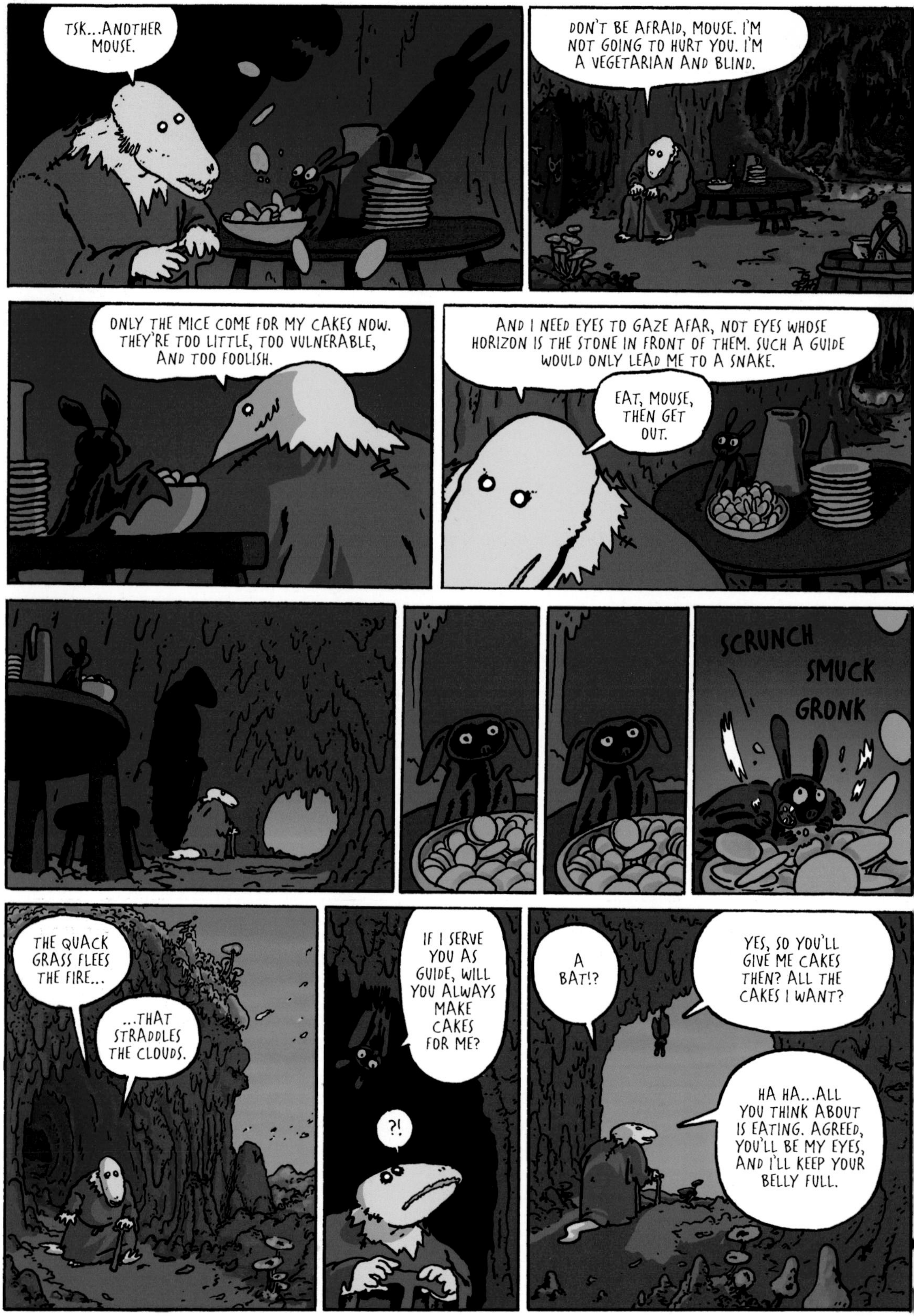
TSK...ANOTHER MOUSE.
DON'T BE AFRAID, MOUSE. I'M NOT GOING TO HURT YOU. I'M A VEGETARIAN AND BLIND.
ONLY THE MICE COME FOR MY CAKES NOW. THEY'RE TOO LITTLE, TOO VULNERABLE, AND TOO FOOLISH.
AND I NEED EYES TO GAZE AFAR, NOT EYES WHOSE HORIZON IS THE STONE IN FRONT OF THEM. SUCH A GUIDE WOULD ONLY LEAD ME TO A SNAKE.
EAT, MOUSE, THEN GET OUT.
SCRUNCH
SMUCK
GRONK
THE QUACK GRASS FLEES THE FIRE...
...THAT STRADDLES THE CLOUDS.
IF I SERVE YOU AS GUIDE, WILL YOU ALWAYS MAKE CAKES FOR ME?
?!
A BAT!?
YES, SO YOU'LL GIVE ME CAKES THEN? ALL THE CAKES I WANT?
HA HA...ALL YOU THINK ABOUT IS EATING. AGREED, YOU'LL BE MY EYES, AND I'LL KEEP YOUR BELLY FULL.

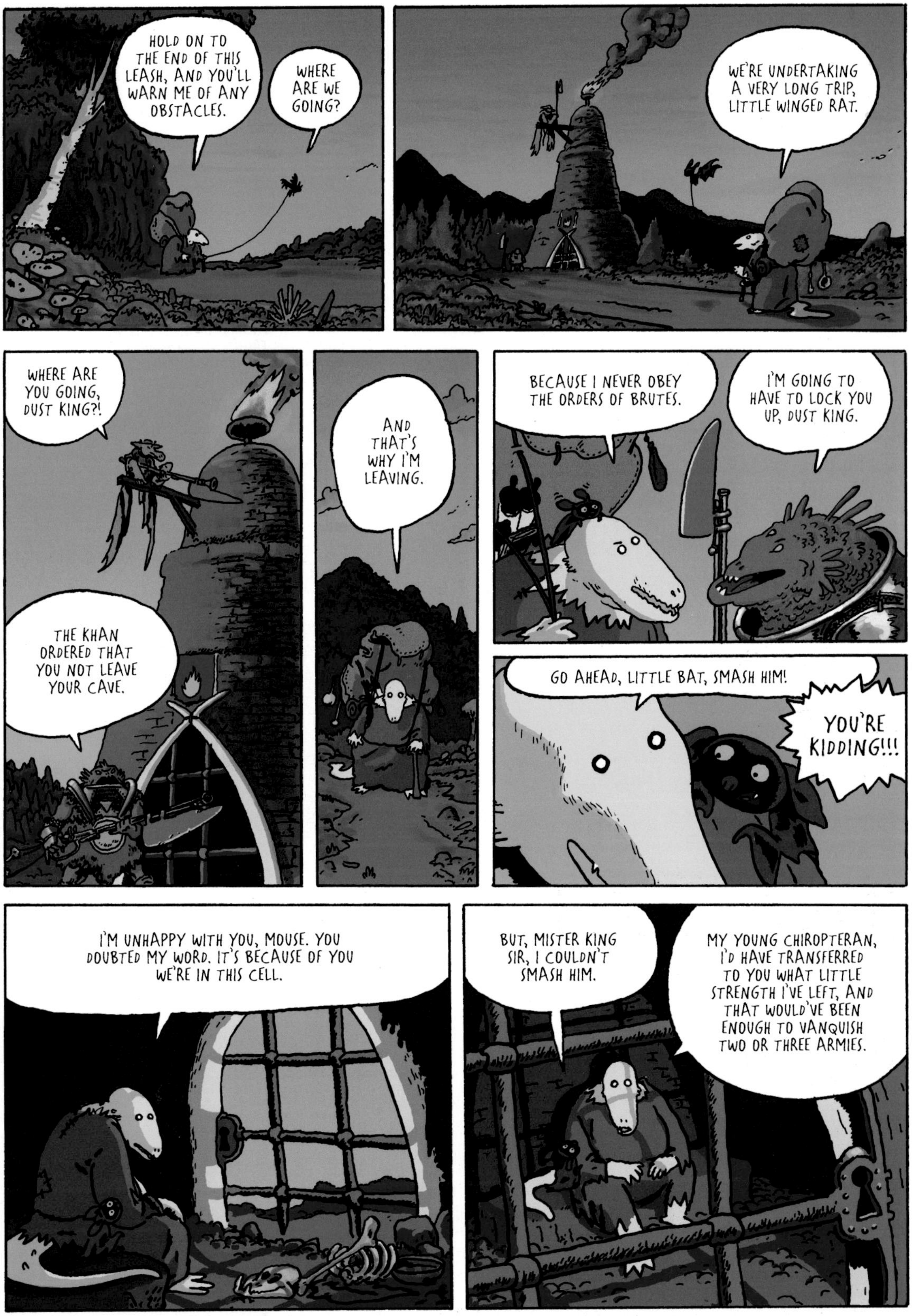
HOLD ON TO THE END OF THIS LEASH, AND YOU'LL WARN ME OF ANY OBSTACLES.
WHERE ARE WE GOING?
WE'RE UNDERTAKING A VERY LONG TRIP, LITTLE WINGED RAT.
WHERE ARE YOU GOING, DUST KING?!
THE KHAN ORDERED THAT YOU NOT LEAVE YOUR CAVE.
AND THAT'S WHY I'M LEAVING.
BECAUSE I NEVER OBEY THE ORDERS OF BRUTES.
I'M GOING TO HAVE TO LOCK YOU UP, DUST KING.
GO AHEAD, LITTLE BAT, SMASH HIM!
YOU'RE KIDDING!!!
I'M UNHAPPY WITH YOU, MOUSE. YOU DOUBTED MY WORD. IT'S BECAUSE OF YOU WE'RE IN THIS CELL.
BUT, MISTER KING SIR, I COULDN'T SMASH HIM.
MY YOUNG CHIROPTERAN, I'D HAVE TRANSFERRED TO YOU WHAT LITTLE STRENGTH I'VE LEFT, AND THAT WOULD'VE BEEN ENOUGH TO VANQUISH TWO OR THREE ARMIES.

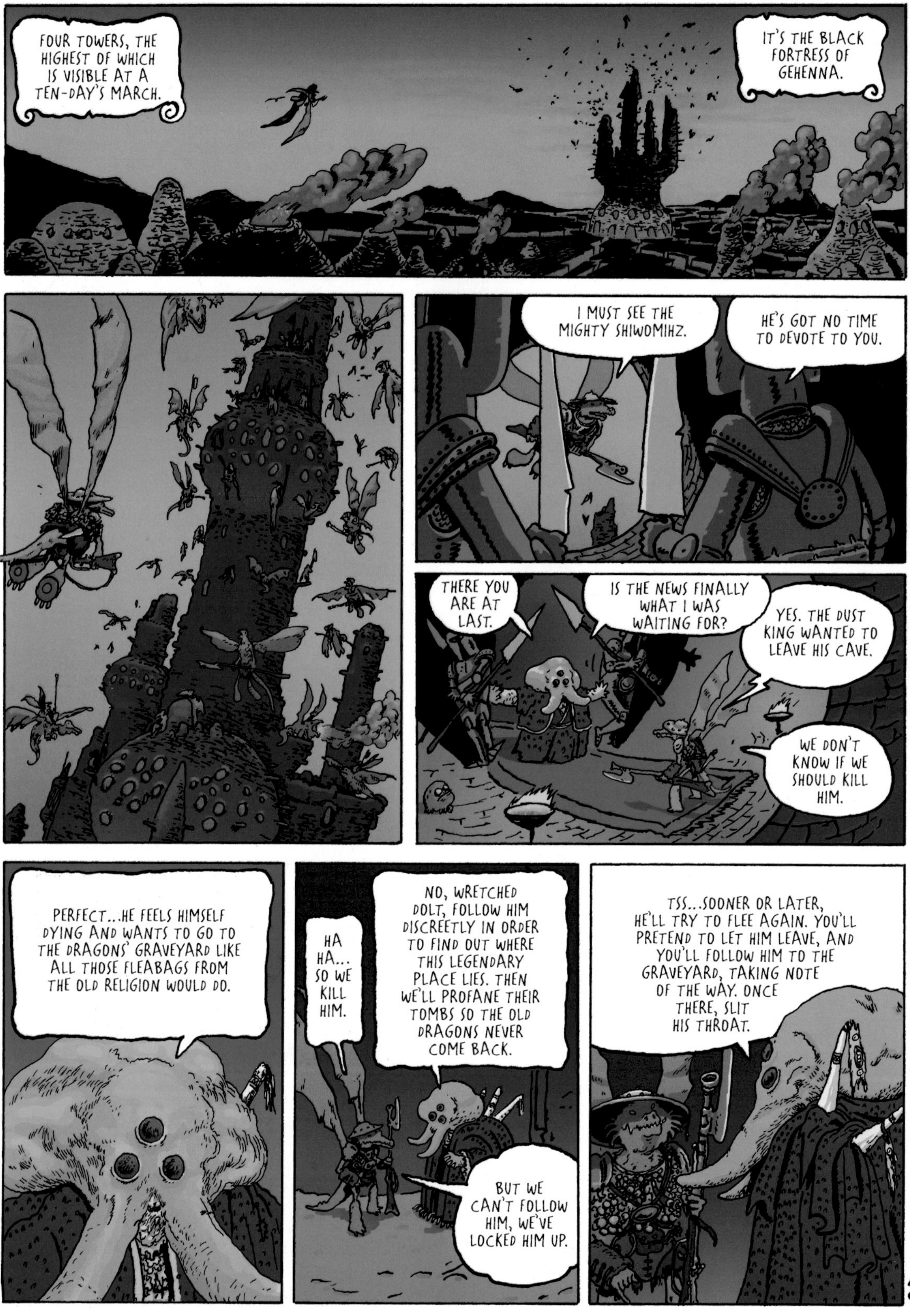
FOUR TOWERS, THE HIGHEST OF WHICH IS VISIBLE AT A TEN-DAY'S MARCH.
IT'S THE BLACK FORTRESS OF GEHENNA.
I MUST SEE THE MIGHTY SHIWOMIHZ.
HE'S GOT NO TIME TO DEVOTE TO YOU.
THERE YOU ARE AT LAST.
IS THE NEWS FINALLY WHAT I WAS WAITING FOR?
YES. THE DUST KING WANTED TO LEAVE HIS CAVE.
WE DON'T KNOW IF WE SHOULD KILL HIM.
PERFECT...HE FEELS HIMSELF DYING AND WANTS TO GO TO THE DRAGONS' GRAVEYARD LIKE ALL THOSE FLEABAGS FROM THE OLD RELIGION WOULD DO.
HA HA... SO WE KILL HIM.
NO, WRETCHED DOLT, FOLLOW HIM DISCREETLY IN ORDER TO FIND OUT WHERE THIS LEGENDARY PLACE LIES. THEN WE'LL PROFANE THEIR TOMBS SO THE OLD DRAGONS NEVER COME BACK.
BUT WE CAN'T FOLLOW HIM, WE'VE LOCKED HIM UP.
TSS...SOONER OR LATER, HE'LL TRY TO FLEE AGAIN. YOU'LL PRETEND TO LET HIM LEAVE, AND YOU'LL FOLLOW HIM TO THE GRAVEYARD, TAKING NOTE OF THE WAY. ONCE THERE, SLIT HIS THROAT.

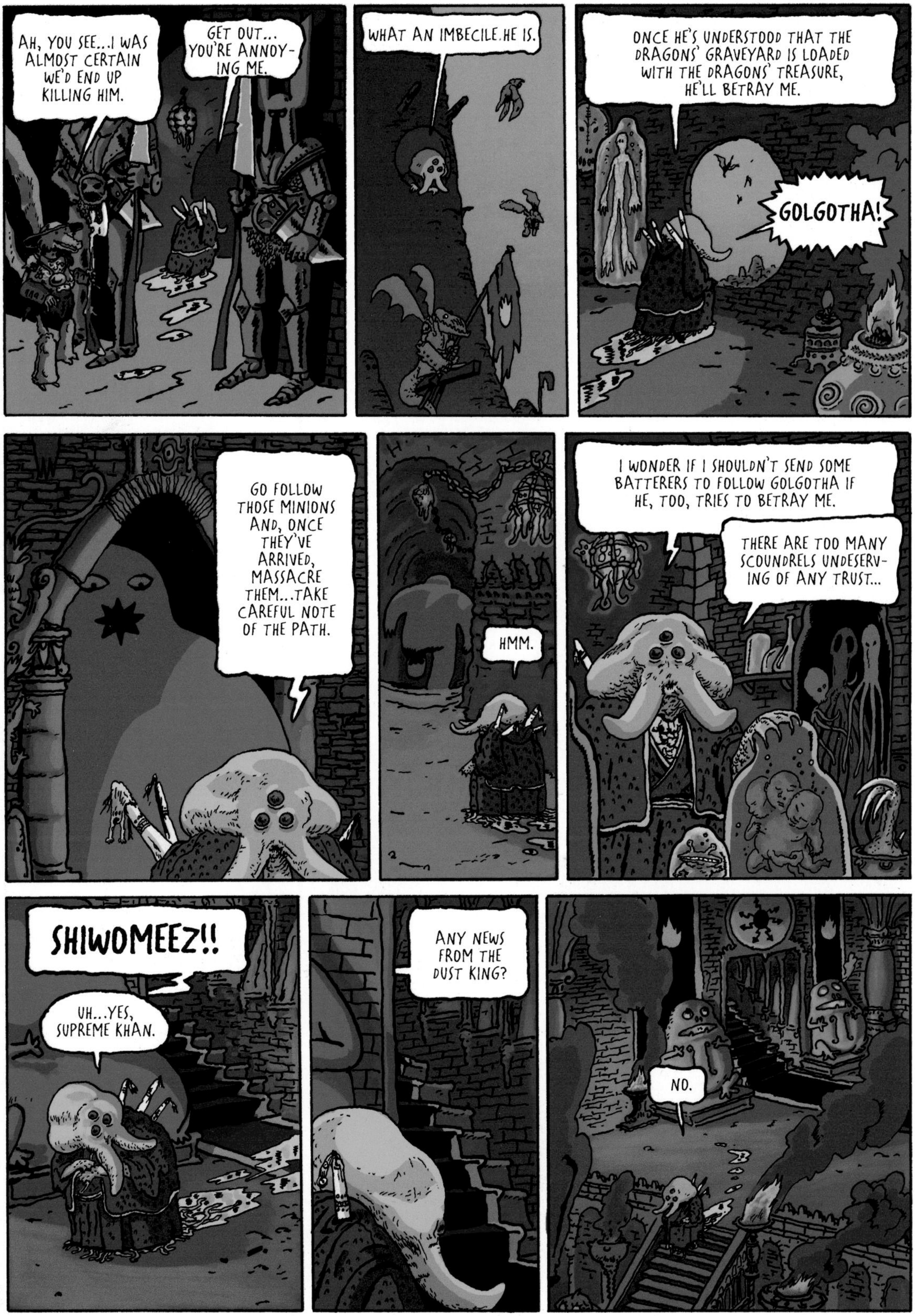

AH, YOU SEE...I WAS ALMOST CERTAIN WE'D END UP KILLING HIM.
GET OUT... YOU'RE ANNOYING ME.
WHAT AN IMBECILE HE IS.
ONCE HE'S UNDERSTOOD THAT THE DRAGONS' GRAVEYARD IS LOADED WITH THE DRAGONS' TREASURE, HE'LL BETRAY ME.
GOLGOTHA!
GO FOLLOW THOSE MINIONS AND, ONCE THEY'VE ARRIVED, MASSACRE THEM...TAKE CAREFUL NOTE OF THE PATH.
HMM.
I WONDER IF I SHOULDN'T SEND SOME BATTERERS TO FOLLOW GOLGOTHA IF HE, TOO, TRIES TO BETRAY ME.
THERE ARE TOO MANY SCOUNDRELS UNDESERVING OF ANY TRUST...
SHIWOMEEZ!!
UH...YES, SUPREME KHAN.
ANY NEWS FROM THE DUST KING?
NO.

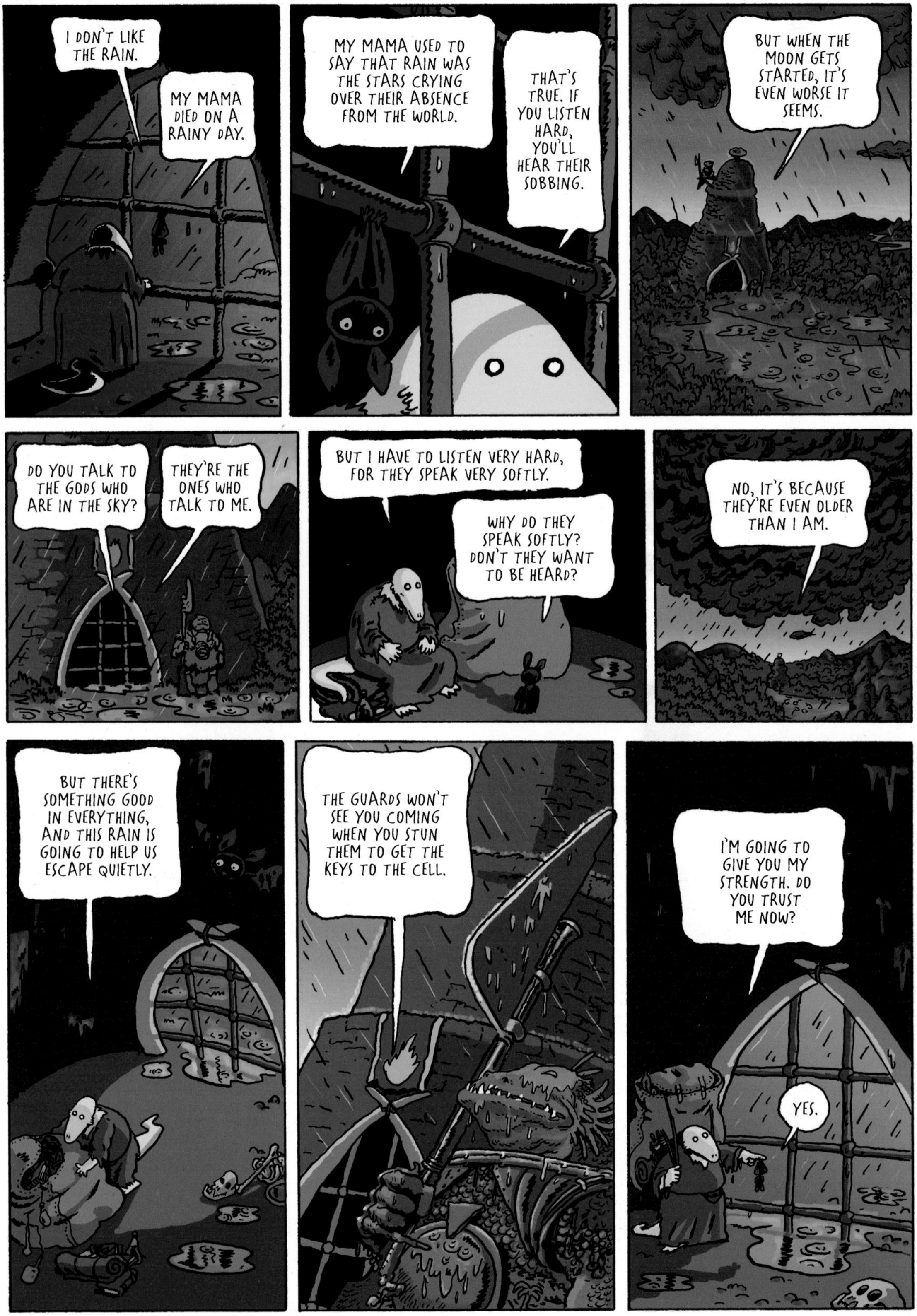
I DON'T LIKE THE RAIN.
MY MAMA DIED ON A RAINY DAY.
MY MAMA USED TO SAY THAT RAIN WAS THE STARS CRYING OVER THEIR ABSENCE FROM THE WORLD.
THAT'S TRUE. IF YOU LISTEN HARD, YOU'LL HEAR THEIR SOBBING.
BUT WHEN THE MOON GETS STARTED, IT'S EVEN WORSE IT SEEMS.
DO YOU TALK TO THE GODS WHO ARE IN THE SKY?
THEY'RE THE ONES WHO TALK TO ME.
BUT I HAVE TO LISTEN VERY HARD, FOR THEY SPEAK VERY SOFTLY.
WHY DO THEY SPEAK SOFTLY? DON'T THEY WANT TO BE HEARD?
NO, IT'S BECAUSE THEY'RE EVEN OLDER THAN I AM.
BUT THERE'S SOMETHING GOOD IN EVERYTHING, AND THIS RAIN IS GOING TO HELP US ESCAPE QUIETLY.
THE GUARDS WON'T SEE YOU COMING WHEN YOU STUN THEM TO GET THE KEYS TO THE CELL.
I'M GOING TO GIVE YOU MY STRENGTH. DO YOU TRUST ME NOW?
YES.

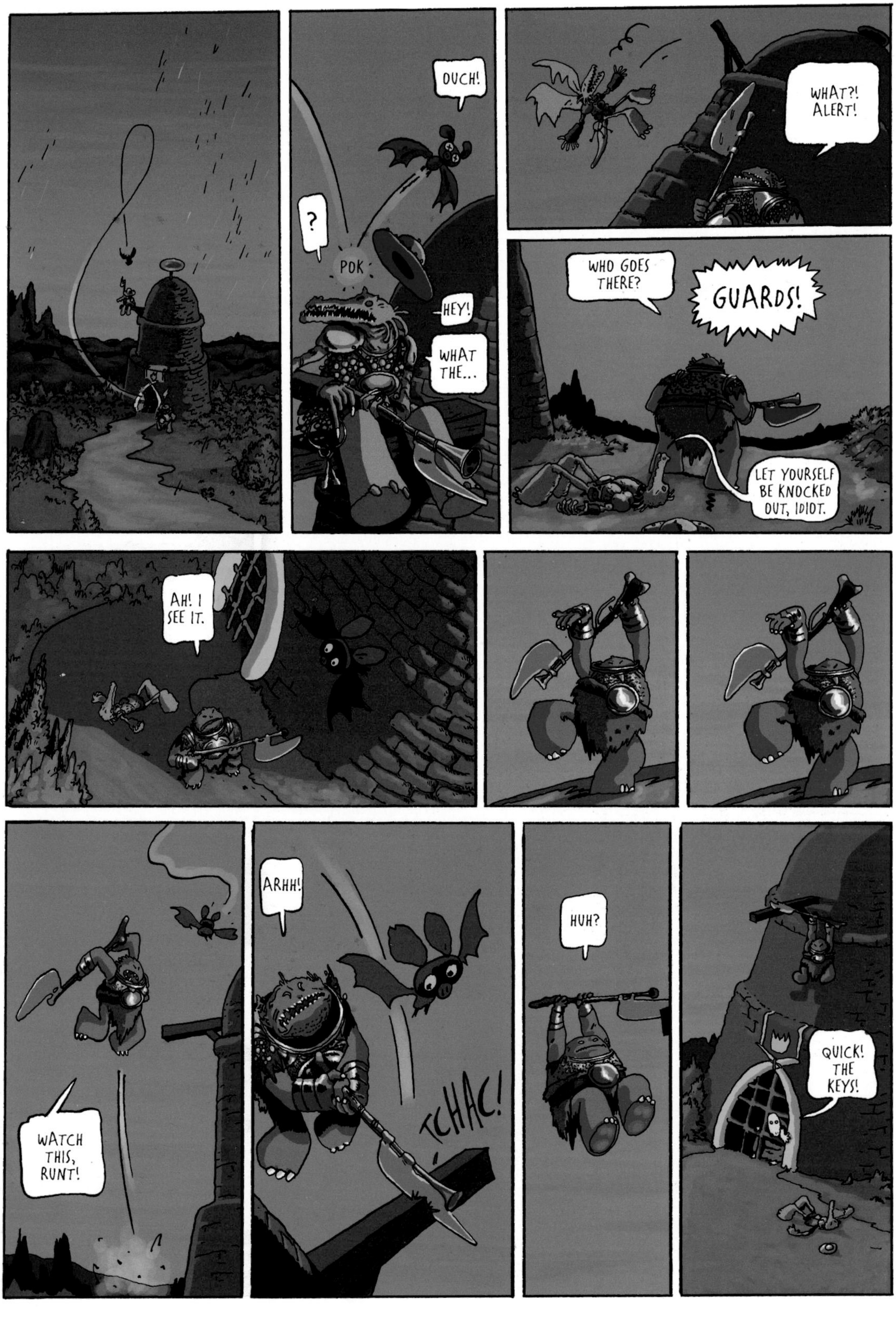
OUCH!
?
POK
HEY!
WHAT THE...
WHAT?! ALERT!
WHO GOES THERE?
GUARDS!
LET YOURSELF BE KNOCKED OUT, IDIOT.
AH! I SEE IT.
WATCH THIS, RUNT!
ARHH!
TCHAC!
HUH?
QUICK! THE KEYS!

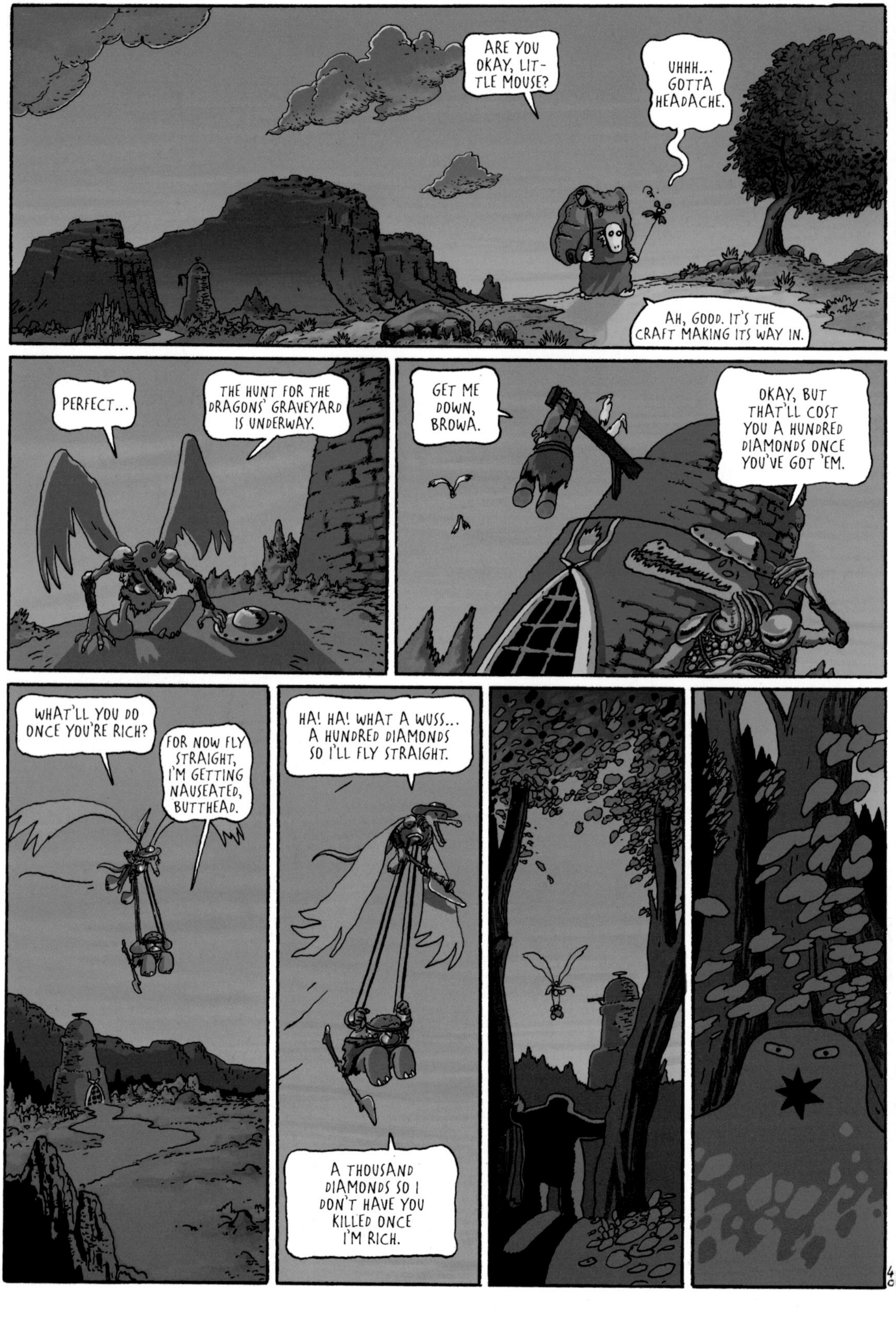
ARE YOU OKAY, LITTLE MOUSE?
UHHH... GOTTA HEADACHE.
AH, GOOD. IT'S THE CRAFT MAKING ITS WAY IN.
PERFECT...
THE HUNT FOR THE DRAGONS' GRAVEYARD IS UNDERWAY.
GET ME DOWN, BROWA.
OKAY, BUT THAT'LL COST YOU A HUNDRED DIAMONDS ONCE YOU'VE GOT 'EM.
WHAT'LL YOU DO ONCE YOU'RE RICH?
FOR NOW FLY STRAIGHT, I'M GETTING NAUSEATED, BUTTHEAD.
HA! HA! WHAT A WUSS... A HUNDRED DIAMONDS SO I'LL FLY STRAIGHT.
A THOUSAND DIAMONDS SO I DON'T HAVE YOU KILLED ONCE I'M RICH.

A FEW DAYS LATER, IN A BURG UNAFFECTED BY TIME...

YES, GENTLEMEN, THE BLIND ONE AND THE BAT WERE HERE YESTERDAY EVENING.

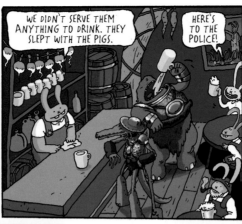

WE DIDN'T SERVE THEM ANYTHING TO DRINK. THEY SLEPT WITH THE PIGS.

HERE'S TO THE POLICE!

HE ASKED IS ORLANDOH STILL LIVED ON THE HEIGHTS AT VAUGRANIA.

I CAN SHOW YOU VERY EXACTLY THEIR PATH. WE LOVE TO ASSIST GEHENNA HERE.

IN ZEDOTAMAXIM, WE LIKE THINGS TO BE ORDERLY. SEE YOU SOON, GENTLEMEN.

MARVIN!

YOU'RE NOT SUPPOSED TO SHOW YOUR FACE IN THE VILLAGE, MARVIN. GET OUT AND I WON'T TURN YOU IN.

TRAITOR!

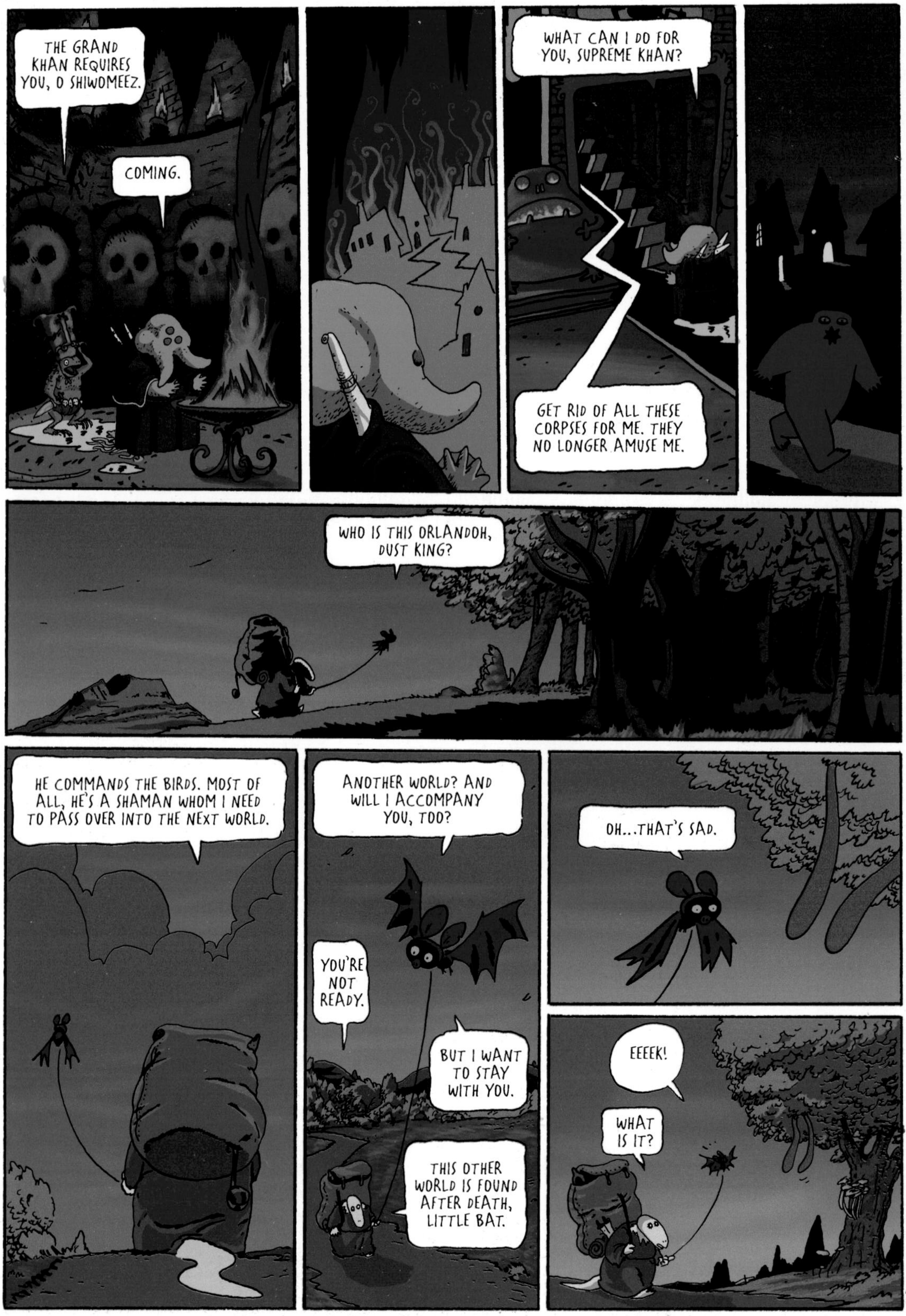
THE GRAND KHAN REQUIRES YOU, O SHIWOMEEZ.
COMING.
WHAT CAN I DO FOR YOU, SUPREME KHAN?
GET RID OF ALL THESE CORPSES FOR ME. THEY NO LONGER AMUSE ME.
WHO IS THIS ORLANDOH, DUST KING?
HE COMMANDS THE BIRDS. MOST OF ALL, HE'S A SHAMAN WHOM I NEED TO PASS OVER INTO THE NEXT WORLD.
ANOTHER WORLD? AND WILL I ACCOMPANY YOU, TOO?
YOU'RE NOT READY.
BUT I WANT TO STAY WITH YOU.
THIS OTHER WORLD IS FOUND AFTER DEATH, LITTLE BAT.
OH...THAT'S SAD.
EEEEK!
WHAT IS IT?

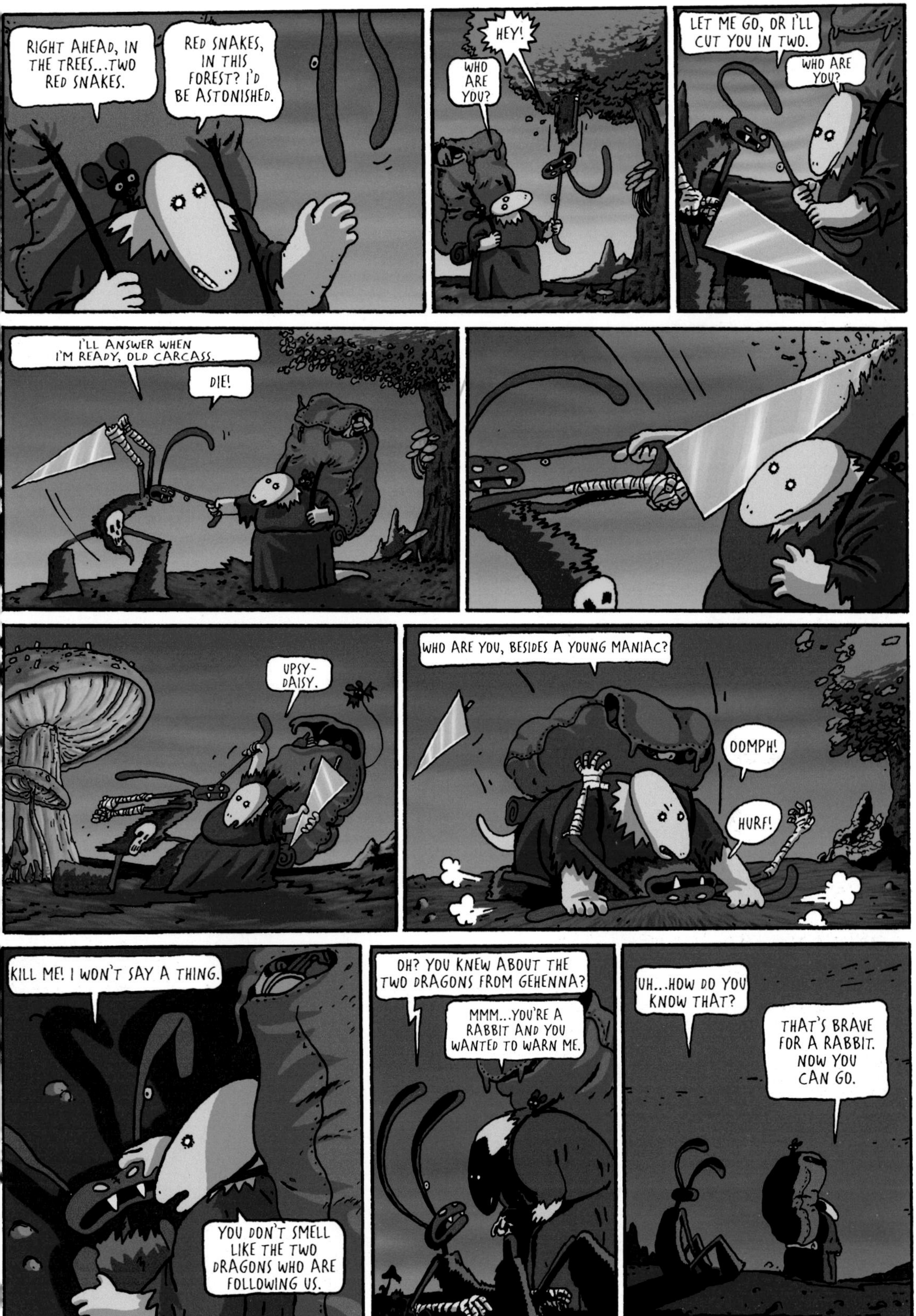
RIGHT AHEAD, IN THE TREES...TWO RED SNAKES.
RED SNAKES, IN THIS FOREST? I'D BE ASTONISHED.
HEY!
WHO ARE YOU?
LET ME GO, OR I'LL CUT YOU IN TWO.
WHO ARE YOU?
I'LL ANSWER WHEN I'M READY, OLD CARCASS.
DIE!
UPSY-DAISY.
WHO ARE YOU, BESIDES A YOUNG MANIAC?
OOMPH!
HURF!
KILL ME! I WON'T SAY A THING.
YOU DON'T SMELL LIKE THE TWO DRAGONS WHO ARE FOLLOWING US.
OH? YOU KNEW ABOUT THE TWO DRAGONS FROM GEHENNA?
MMM...YOU'RE A RABBIT AND YOU WANTED TO WARN ME.
UH...HOW DO YOU KNOW THAT?
THAT'S BRAVE FOR A RABBIT. NOW YOU CAN GO.

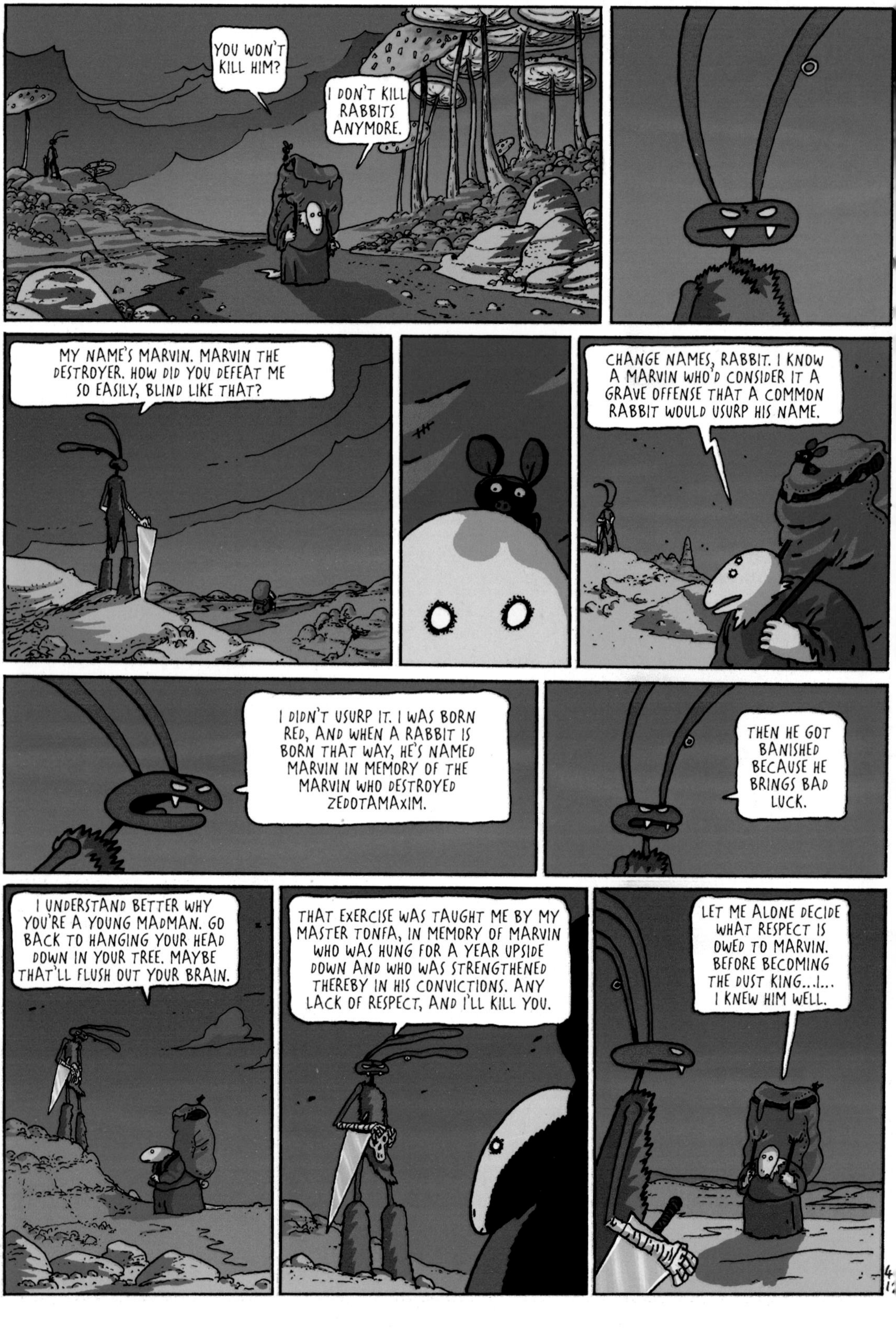
YOU WON'T KILL HIM?
I DON'T KILL RABBITS ANYMORE.
MY NAME'S MARVIN. MARVIN THE DESTROYER. HOW DID YOU DEFEAT ME SO EASILY, BLIND LIKE THAT?
CHANGE NAMES, RABBIT. I KNOW A MARVIN WHO'D CONSIDER IT A GRAVE OFFENSE THAT A COMMON RABBIT WOULD USURP HIS NAME.
I DIDN'T USURP IT. I WAS BORN RED, AND WHEN A RABBIT IS BORN THAT WAY, HE'S NAMED MARVIN IN MEMORY OF THE MARVIN WHO DESTROYED ZEDOTAMAXIM.
THEN HE GOT BANISHED BECAUSE HE BRINGS BAD LUCK.
I UNDERSTAND BETTER WHY YOU'RE A YOUNG MADMAN. GO BACK TO HANGING YOUR HEAD DOWN IN YOUR TREE. MAYBE THAT'LL FLUSH OUT YOUR BRAIN.
THAT EXERCISE WAS TAUGHT ME BY MY MASTER TONFA, IN MEMORY OF MARVIN WHO WAS HUNG FOR A YEAR UPSIDE DOWN AND WHO WAS STRENGTHENED THEREBY IN HIS CONVICTIONS. ANY LACK OF RESPECT, AND I'LL KILL YOU.
LET ME ALONE DECIDE WHAT RESPECT IS OWED TO MARVIN. BEFORE BECOMING THE DUST KING...I... I KNEW HIM WELL.

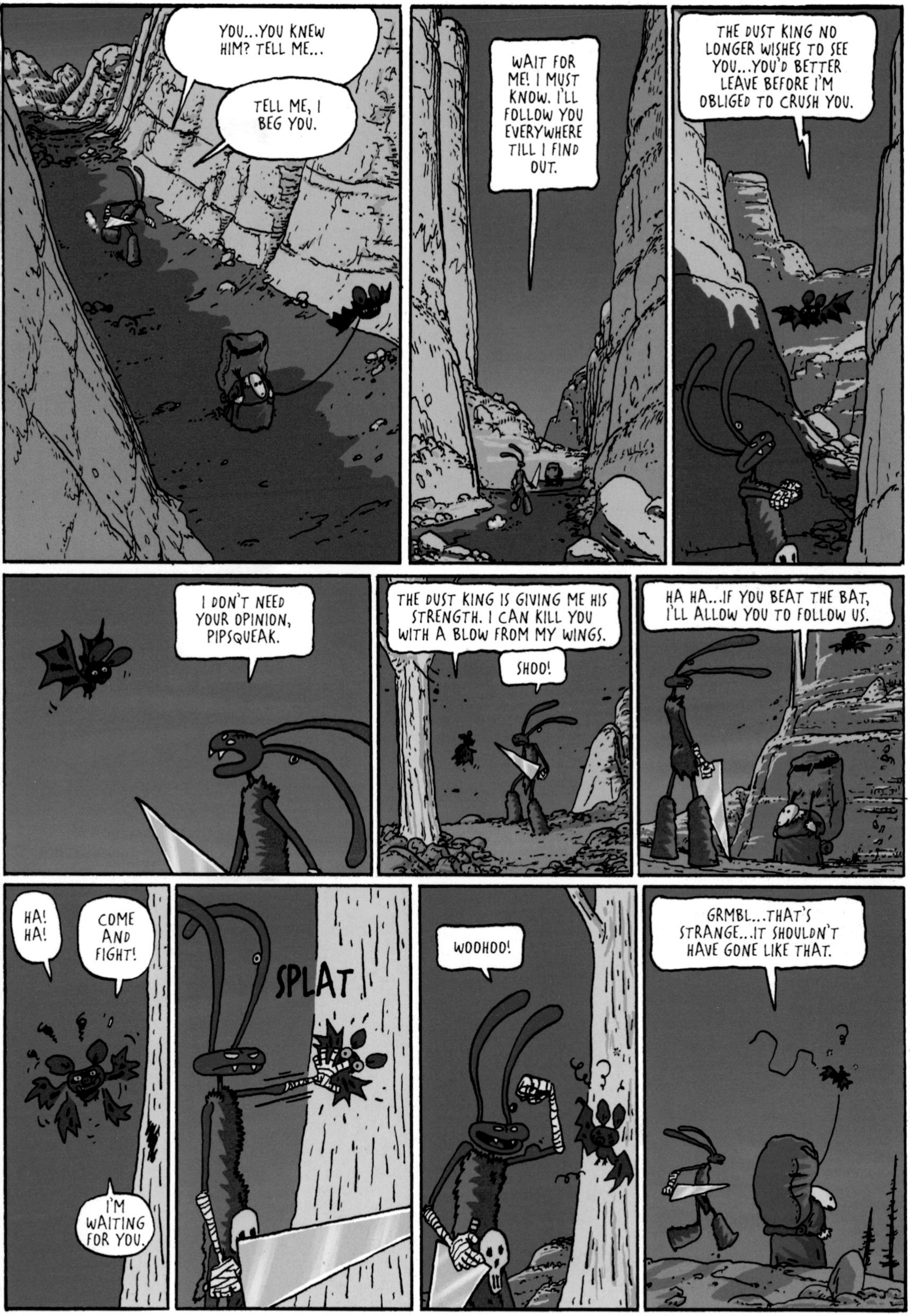
YOU...YOU KNEW HIM? TELL ME...
TELL ME, I BEG YOU.
WAIT FOR ME! I MUST KNOW. I'LL FOLLOW YOU EVERYWHERE TILL I FIND OUT.
THE DUST KING NO LONGER WISHES TO SEE YOU...YOU'D BETTER LEAVE BEFORE I'M OBLIGED TO CRUSH YOU.
I DON'T NEED YOUR OPINION, PIPSQUEAK.
THE DUST KING IS GIVING ME HIS STRENGTH. I CAN KILL YOU WITH A BLOW FROM MY WINGS.
SHOO!
HA HA...IF YOU BEAT THE BAT, I'LL ALLOW YOU TO FOLLOW US.
HA! HA!
COME AND FIGHT!
I'M WAITING FOR YOU.
SPLAT
WOOHOO!
GRMBL...THAT'S STRANGE...IT SHOULDN'T HAVE GONE LIKE THAT.

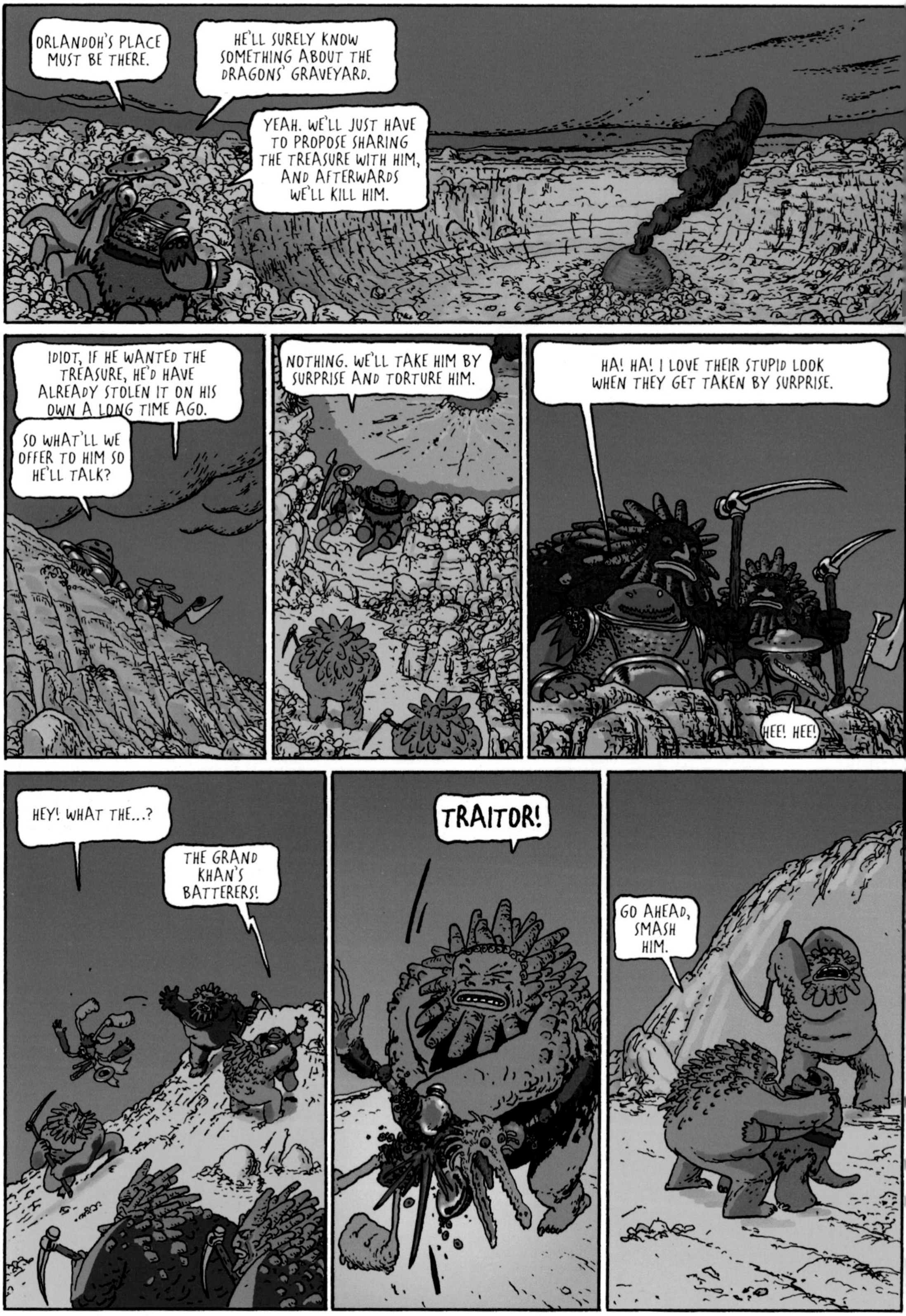
ORLANDOH'S PLACE MUST BE THERE.
HE'LL SURELY KNOW SOMETHING ABOUT THE DRAGONS' GRAVEYARD.
YEAH. WE'LL JUST HAVE TO PROPOSE SHARING THE TREASURE WITH HIM, AND AFTERWARDS WE'LL KILL HIM.
IDIOT, IF HE WANTED THE TREASURE, HE'D HAVE ALREADY STOLEN IT ON HIS OWN A LONG TIME AGO.
SO WHAT'LL WE OFFER TO HIM SO HE'LL TALK?
NOTHING. WE'LL TAKE HIM BY SURPRISE AND TORTURE HIM.
HA! HA! I LOVE THEIR STUPID LOOK WHEN THEY GET TAKEN BY SURPRISE.
HEE! HEE!
HEY! WHAT THE...?
THE GRAND KHAN'S BATTERERS!
TRAITOR!
GO AHEAD, SMASH HIM.

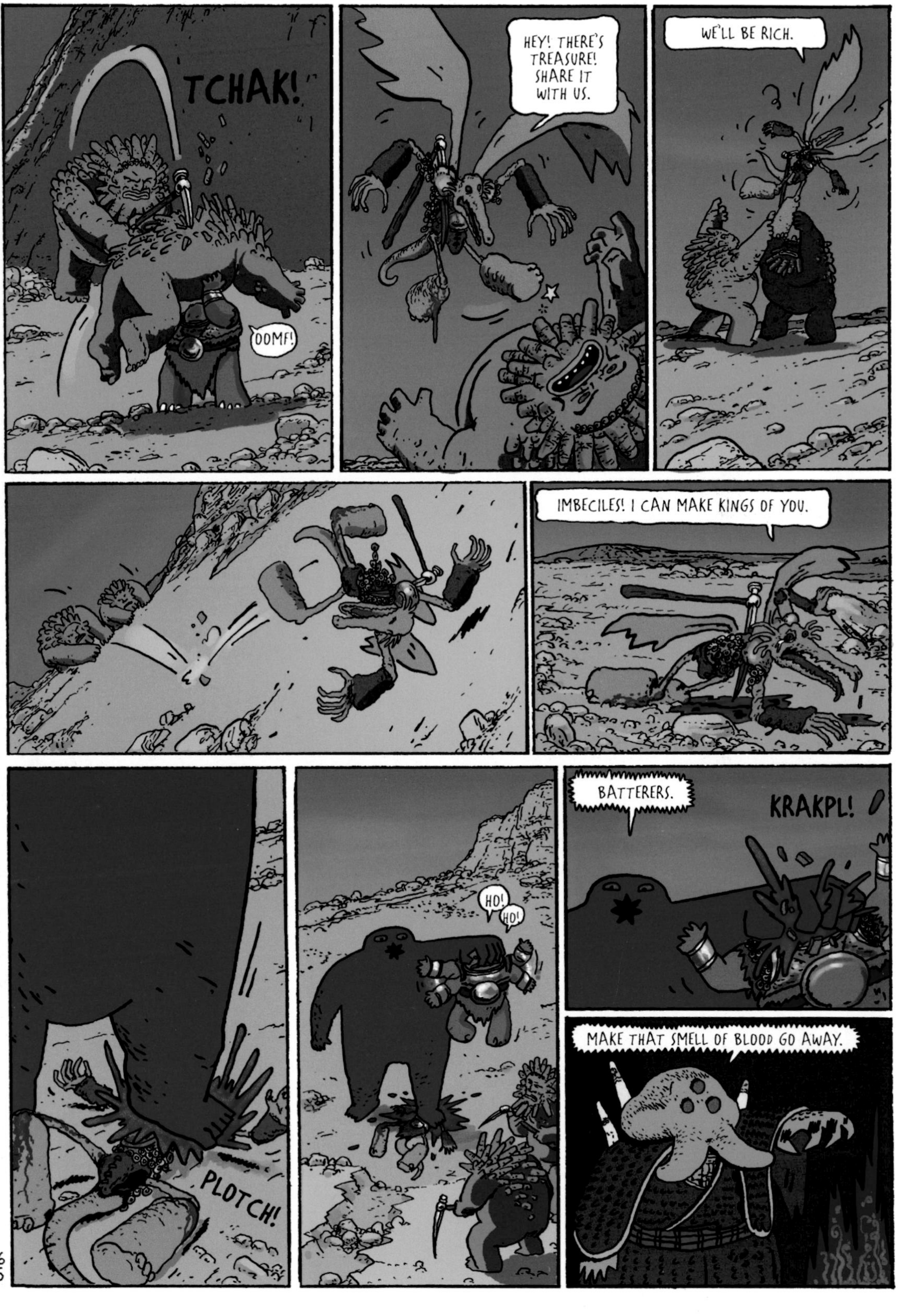
TCHAK!
OOMF!
HEY! THERE'S TREASURE! SHARE IT WITH US.
WE'LL BE RICH.
IMBECILES! I CAN MAKE KINGS OF YOU.
PLOTCH!
HO!
HO!
BATTERERS.
KRAKPL!
MAKE THAT SMELL OF BLOOD GO AWAY.

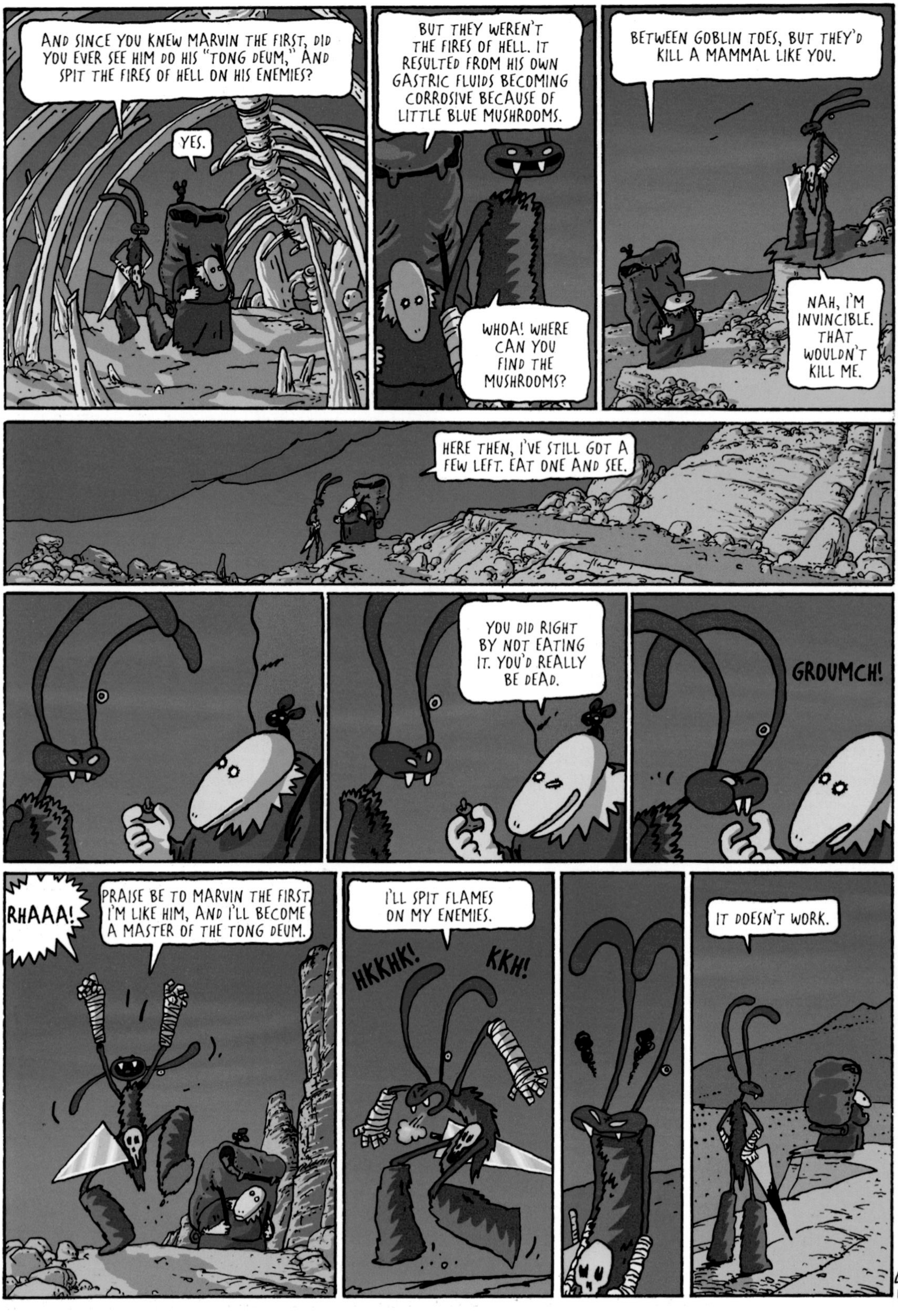
AND SINCE YOU KNEW MARVIN THE FIRST, DID YOU EVER SEE HIM DO HIS "TONG DEUM," AND SPIT THE FIRES OF HELL ON HIS ENEMIES?
YES.
BUT THEY WEREN'T THE FIRES OF HELL. IT RESULTED FROM HIS OWN GASTRIC FLUIDS BECOMING CORROSIVE BECAUSE OF LITTLE BLUE MUSHROOMS.
WHOA! WHERE CAN YOU FIND THE MUSHROOMS?
BETWEEN GOBLIN TOES, BUT THEY'D KILL A MAMMAL LIKE YOU.
NAH, I'M INVINCIBLE. THAT WOULDN'T KILL ME.
HERE THEN, I'VE STILL GOT A FEW LEFT. EAT ONE AND SEE.
YOU DID RIGHT BY NOT EATING IT. YOU'D REALLY BE DEAD.
GROUMCH!
RHAAA!
PRAISE BE TO MARVIN THE FIRST. I'M LIKE HIM, AND I'LL BECOME A MASTER OF THE TONG DEUM.
I'LL SPIT FLAMES ON MY ENEMIES.
HKKHK!
KKH!
IT DOESN'T WORK.

YOU SEEM LIKE YOU'RE PRETTY TOUGH, RABBIT. THE MUSHROOM DIDN'T EVEN GIVE YOU DIARRHEA.

I'D EVEN HAVE PREFERRED GETTING FLAMING DIARRHEA THAN HAVING NOTHING AT ALL.

STOP IDENTIFYING YOURSELF WITH MARVIN, RABBIT. TWO BEINGS CAN NEVER BE ALIKE.

I DIDN'T CHOOSE MY DESTINY, OLD MAN.

I AM MARVIN.

AH! THERE WE GO! THAT'S ORLANDOH'S HOUSE, ISN'T IT?

NO. ORLANDOH LIVES IN A CRYPT LIKE ME.

THAT'S THE HUT OF SPIRITS. HE SPENDS ALL HIS TIME THERE.

WHAT'S HE DO THERE?

HE GUIDES DRAGONS LIKE ME WHO SENSE IT'S TIME TO DIE.

IS HE...IS HE SOME SORT OF MAGICIAN?

YES, A DRAGON SHAMAN.

AH ...

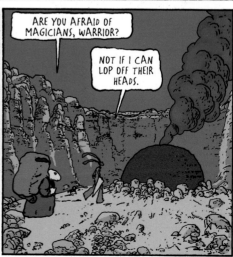

ARE YOU AFRAID OF MAGICIANS, WARRIOR?

NOT IF I CAN LOP OFF THEIR HEADS.

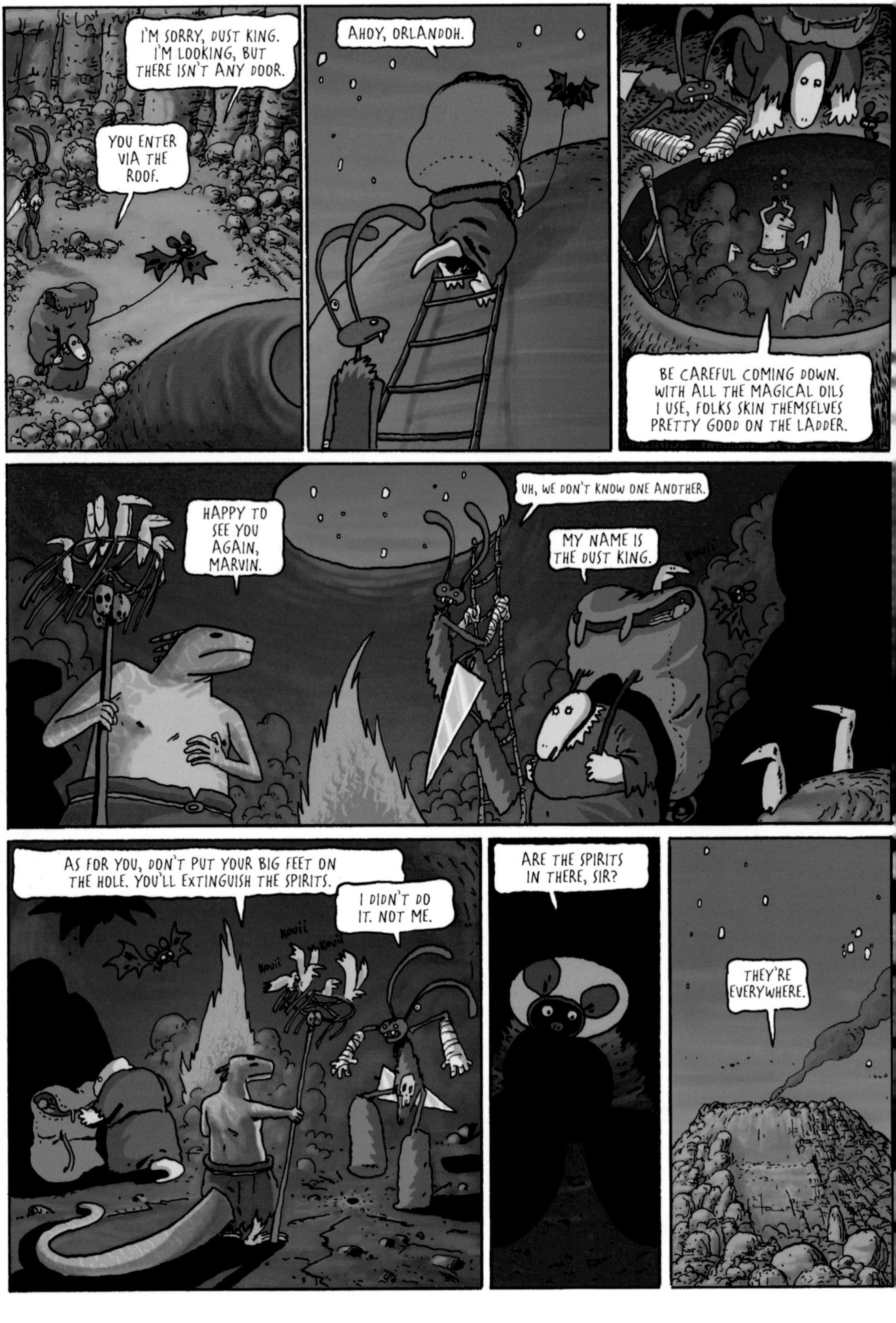
I'M SORRY, DUST KING. I'M LOOKING, BUT THERE ISN'T ANY DOOR.
YOU ENTER VIA THE ROOF.
AHOY, ORLANDOH.
BE CAREFUL COMING DOWN. WITH ALL THE MAGICAL OILS I USE, FOLKS SKIN THEMSELVES PRETTY GOOD ON THE LADDER.
HAPPY TO SEE YOU AGAIN, MARVIN.
UH, WE DON'T KNOW ONE ANOTHER.
MY NAME IS THE DUST KING.
AS FOR YOU, DON'T PUT YOUR BIG FEET ON THE HOLE. YOU'LL EXTINGUISH THE SPIRITS.
I DIDN'T DO IT. NOT ME.
ARE THE SPIRITS IN THERE, SIR?
THEY'RE EVERYWHERE.

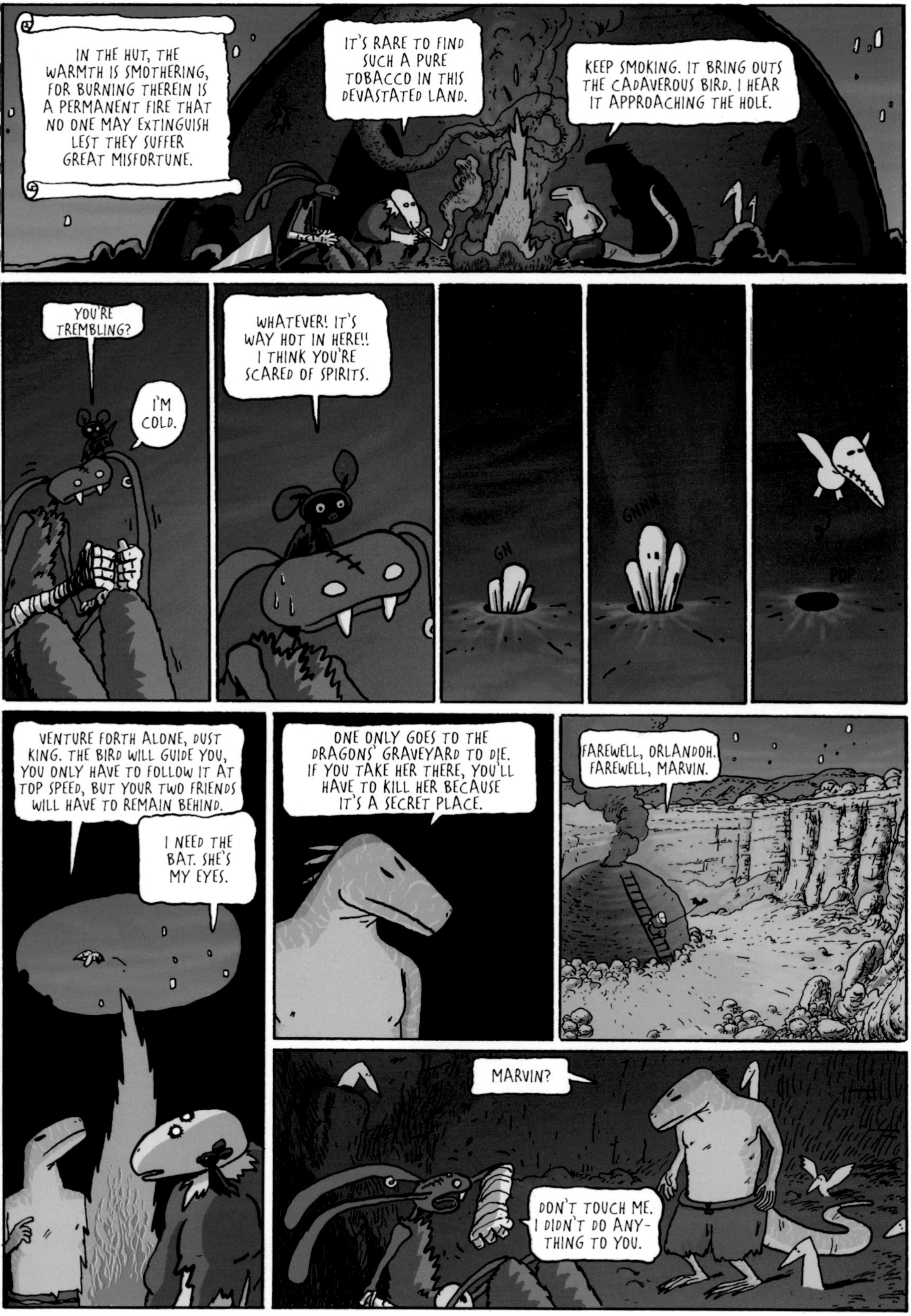

IN THE HUT, THE WARMTH IS SMOTHERING, FOR BURNING THEREIN IS A PERMANENT FIRE THAT NO ONE MAY EXTINGUISH LEST THEY SUFFER GREAT MISFORTUNE.
IT'S RARE TO FIND SUCH A PURE TOBACCO IN THIS DEVASTATED LAND.
KEEP SMOKING. IT BRING OUTS THE CADAVEROUS BIRD. I HEAR IT APPROACHING THE HOLE.
YOU'RE TREMBLING?
I'M COLD.
WHATEVER! IT'S WAY HOT IN HERE!! I THINK YOU'RE SCARED OF SPIRITS.
GN
GNNN
POP
VENTURE FORTH ALONE, DUST KING. THE BIRD WILL GUIDE YOU, YOU ONLY HAVE TO FOLLOW IT AT TOP SPEED, BUT YOUR TWO FRIENDS WILL HAVE TO REMAIN BEHIND.
I NEED THE BAT. SHE'S MY EYES.
ONE ONLY GOES TO THE DRAGONS' GRAVEYARD TO DIE. IF YOU TAKE HER THERE, YOU'LL HAVE TO KILL HER BECAUSE IT'S A SECRET PLACE.
FAREWELL, ORLANDOH. FAREWELL, MARVIN.
MARVIN?
DON'T TOUCH ME. I DIDN'T DO ANYTHING TO YOU.

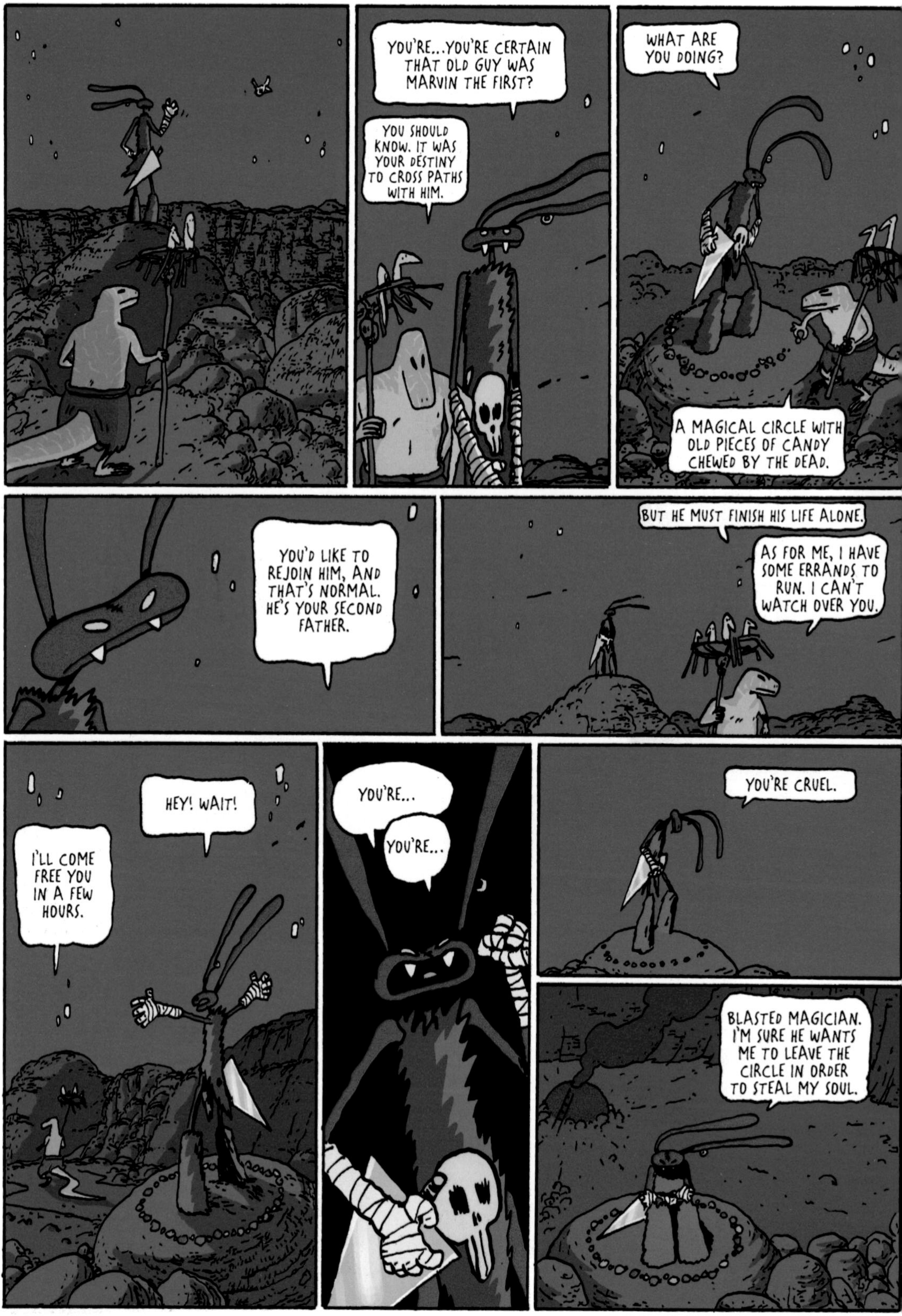
YOU'RE...YOU'RE CERTAIN THAT OLD GUY WAS MARVIN THE FIRST?
YOU SHOULD KNOW. IT WAS YOUR DESTINY TO CROSS PATHS WITH HIM.
WHAT ARE YOU DOING?
A MAGICAL CIRCLE WITH OLD PIECES OF CANDY CHEWED BY THE DEAD.
YOU'D LIKE TO REJOIN HIM, AND THAT'S NORMAL. HE'S YOUR SECOND FATHER.
BUT HE MUST FINISH HIS LIFE ALONE.
AS FOR ME, I HAVE SOME ERRANDS TO RUN. I CAN'T WATCH OVER YOU.
HEY! WAIT!
I'LL COME FREE YOU IN A FEW HOURS.
YOU'RE...
YOU'RE...
YOU'RE CRUEL.
BLASTED MAGICIAN. I'M SURE HE WANTS ME TO LEAVE THE CIRCLE IN ORDER TO STEAL MY SOUL.

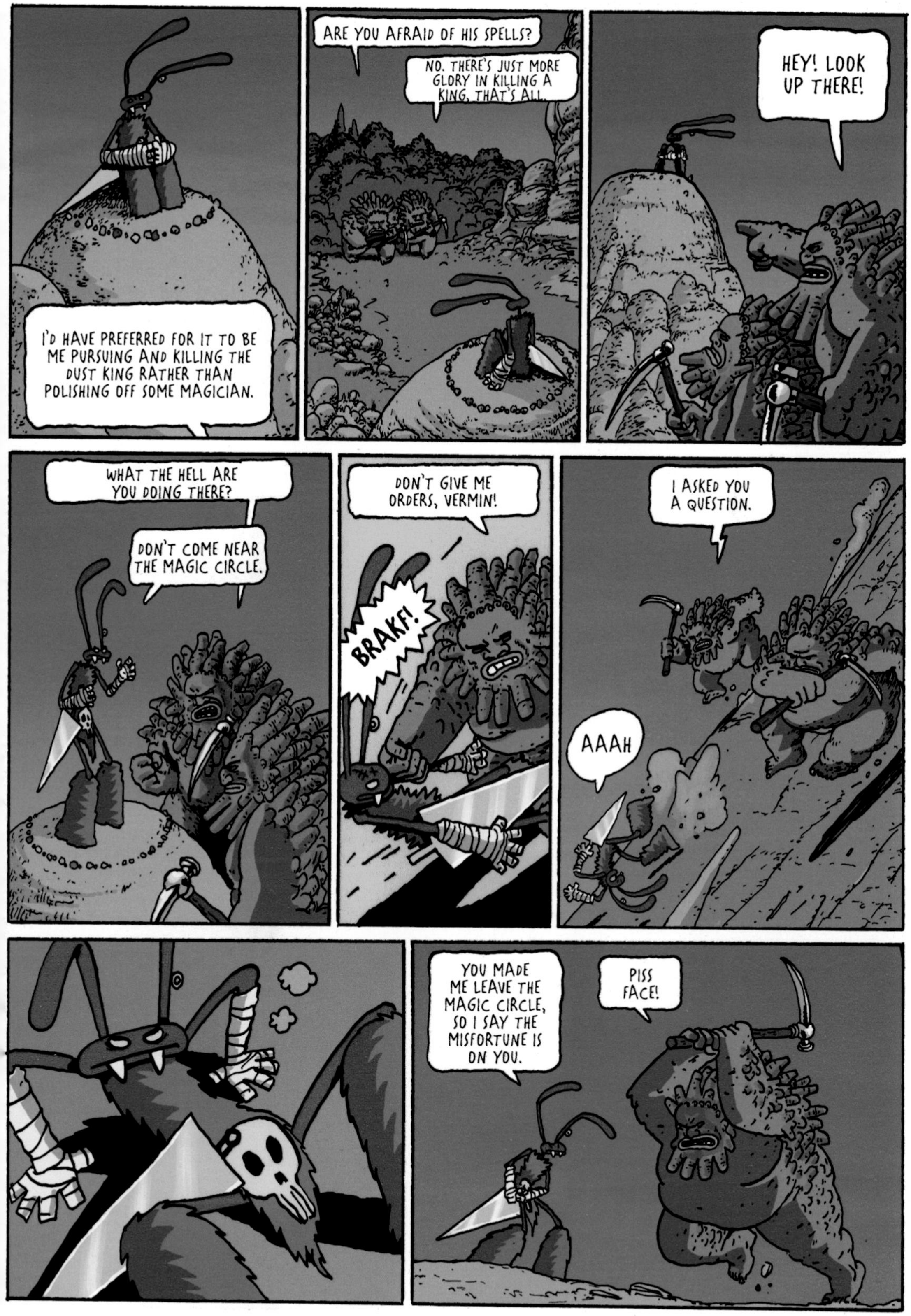
I'D HAVE PREFERRED FOR IT TO BE ME PURSUING AND KILLING THE DUST KING RATHER THAN POLISHING OFF SOME MAGICIAN.
ARE YOU AFRAID OF HIS SPELLS?
NO. THERE'S JUST MORE GLORY IN KILLING A KING, THAT'S ALL.
HEY! LOOK UP THERE!
WHAT THE HELL ARE YOU DOING THERE?
DON'T COME NEAR THE MAGIC CIRCLE.
DON'T GIVE ME ORDERS, VERMIN!
BRAKF!
I ASKED YOU A QUESTION.
AAAH
YOU MADE ME LEAVE THE MAGIC CIRCLE, SO I SAY THE MISFORTUNE IS ON YOU.
PISS FACE!

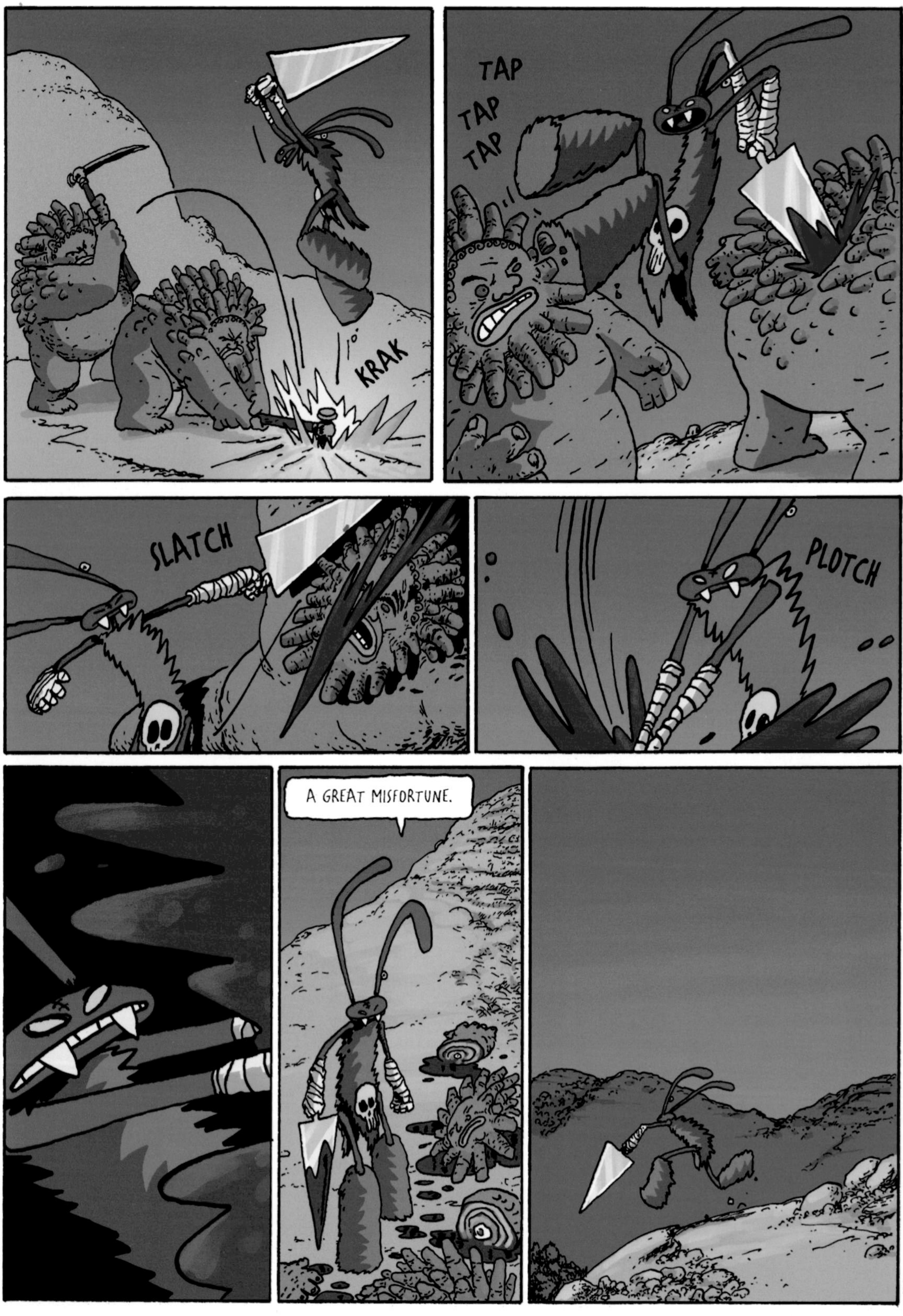
KRAK
TAP
TAP
TAP
SLATCH
PLOTCH
A GREAT MISFORTUNE.

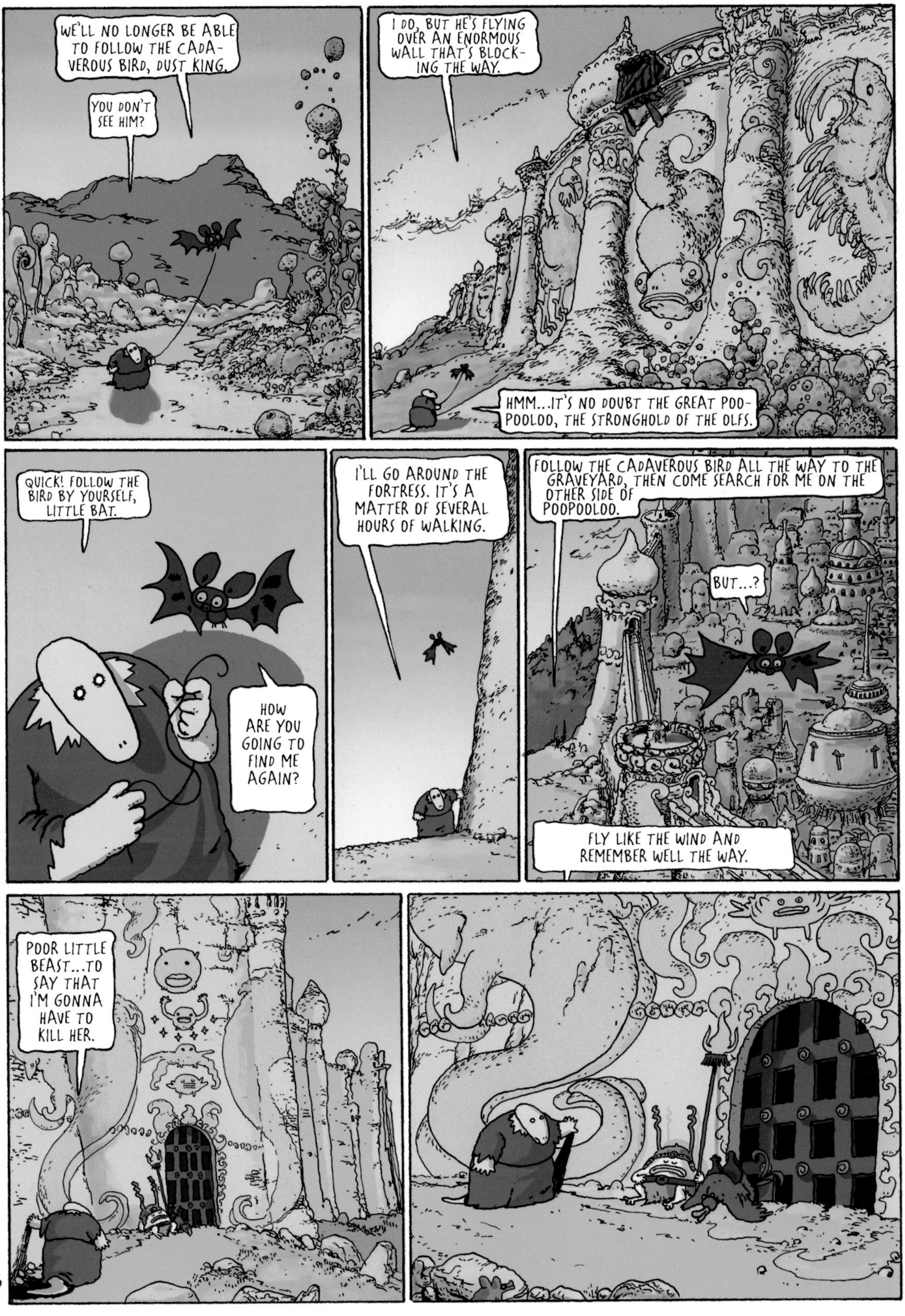
WE'LL NO LONGER BE ABLE TO FOLLOW THE CADAVEROUS BIRD, DUST KING.
YOU DON'T SEE HIM?
I DO, BUT HE'S FLYING OVER AN ENORMOUS WALL THAT'S BLOCKING THE WAY.
HMM...IT'S NO DOUBT THE GREAT POOPOOLOO, THE STRONGHOLD OF THE OLFS.
QUICK! FOLLOW THE BIRD BY YOURSELF, LITTLE BAT.
HOW ARE YOU GOING TO FIND ME AGAIN?
I'LL GO AROUND THE FORTRESS. IT'S A MATTER OF SEVERAL HOURS OF WALKING.
FOLLOW THE CADAVEROUS BIRD ALL THE WAY TO THE GRAVEYARD, THEN COME SEARCH FOR ME ON THE OTHER SIDE OF POOPOOLOO.
BUT...?
FLY LIKE THE WIND AND REMEMBER WELL THE WAY.
POOR LITTLE BEAST...TO SAY THAT I'M GONNA HAVE TO KILL HER.

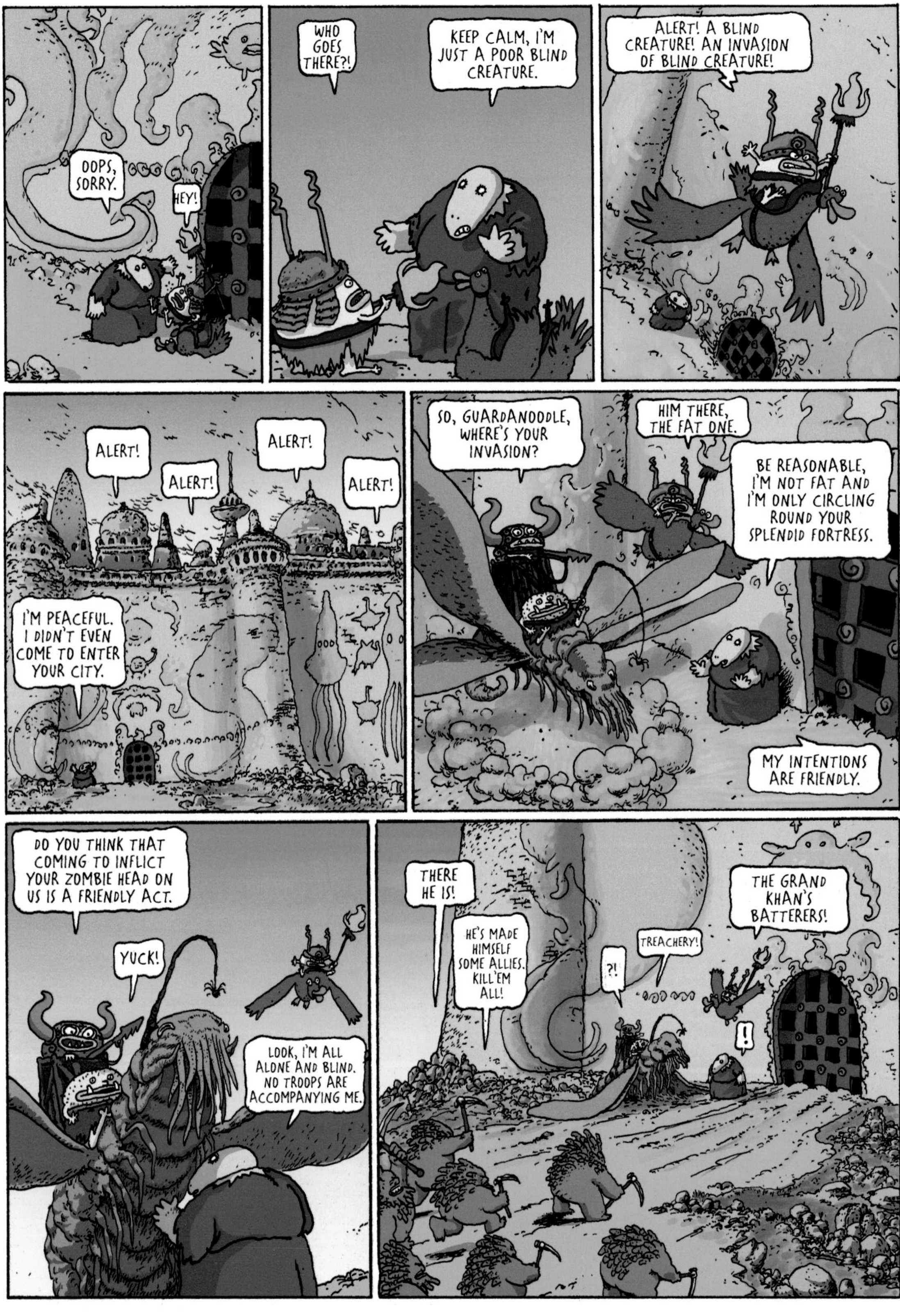
OOPS, SORRY.
HEY!
WHO GOES THERE?!
KEEP CALM, I'M JUST A POOR BLIND CREATURE.
ALERT! A BLIND CREATURE! AN INVASION OF BLIND CREATURE!
ALERT!
ALERT!
ALERT!
ALERT!
I'M PEACEFUL. I DIDN'T EVEN COME TO ENTER YOUR CITY.
SO, GUARDANODDLE, WHERE'S YOUR INVASION?
HIM THERE, THE FAT ONE.
BE REASONABLE, I'M NOT FAT AND I'M ONLY CIRCLING ROUND YOUR SPLENDID FORTRESS.
MY INTENTIONS ARE FRIENDLY.
DO YOU THINK THAT COMING TO INFLICT YOUR ZOMBIE HEAD ON US IS A FRIENDLY ACT.
YUCK!
LOOK, I'M ALL ALONE AND BLIND. NO TROOPS ARE ACCOMPANYING ME.
THERE HE IS!
HE'S MADE HIMSELF SOME ALLIES. KILL'EM ALL!
?!
TREACHERY!
THE GRAND KHAN'S BATTERERS!
!

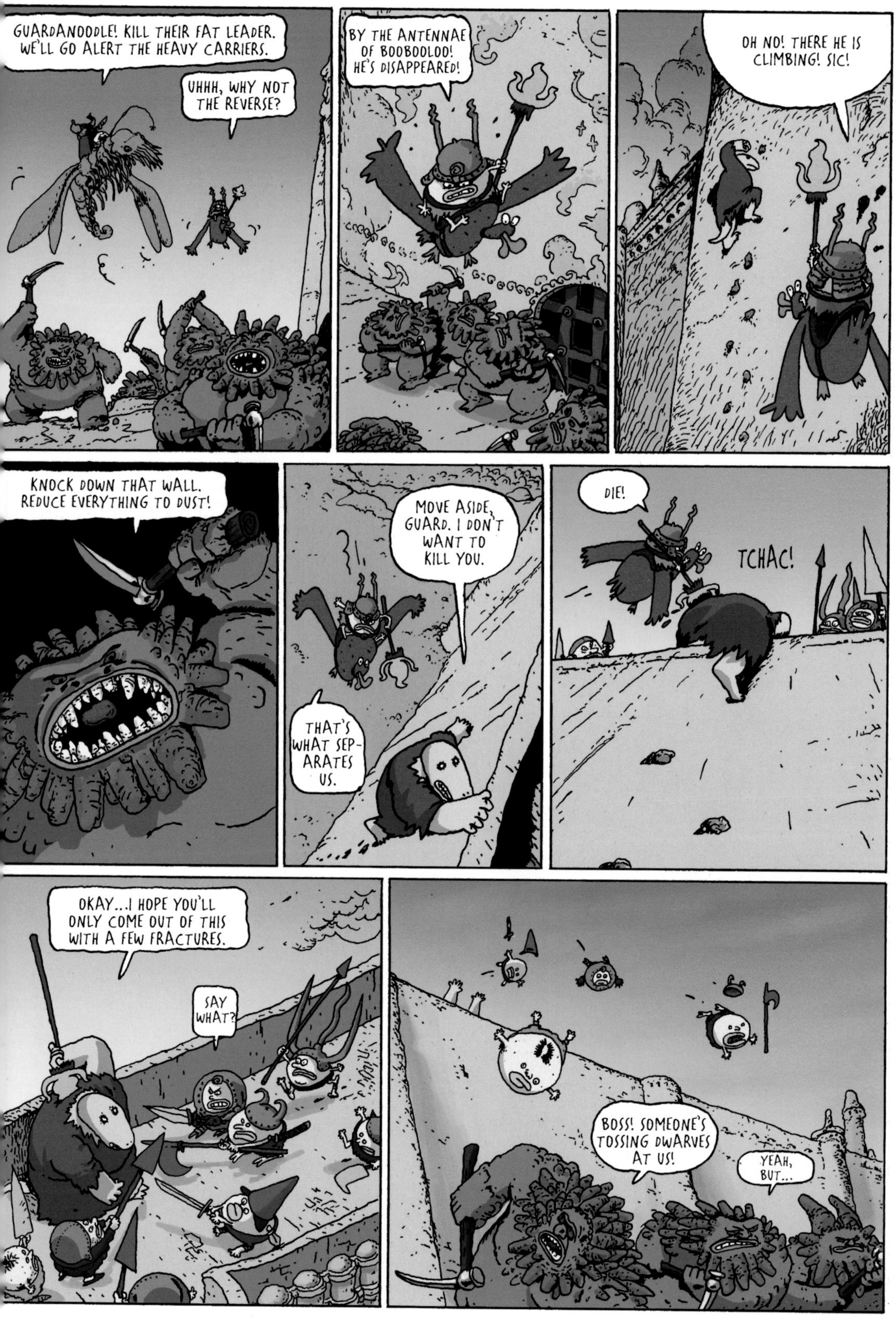
GUARDANOODLE! KILL THEIR FAT LEADER. WE'LL GO ALERT THE HEAVY CARRIERS.
UHHH, WHY NOT THE REVERSE?
BY THE ANTENNAE OF BOOBOOLOO! HE'S DISAPPEARED!
OH NO! THERE HE IS CLIMBING! SIC!
KNOCK DOWN THAT WALL. REDUCE EVERYTHING TO DUST!
MOVE ASIDE, GUARD. I DON'T WANT TO KILL YOU.
THAT'S WHAT SEP-ARATES US.
DIE!
TCHAC!
OKAY...I HOPE YOU'LL ONLY COME OUT OF THIS WITH A FEW FRACTURES.
SAY WHAT?
BOSS! SOMEONE'S TOSSING DWARVES AT US!
YEAH, BUT...

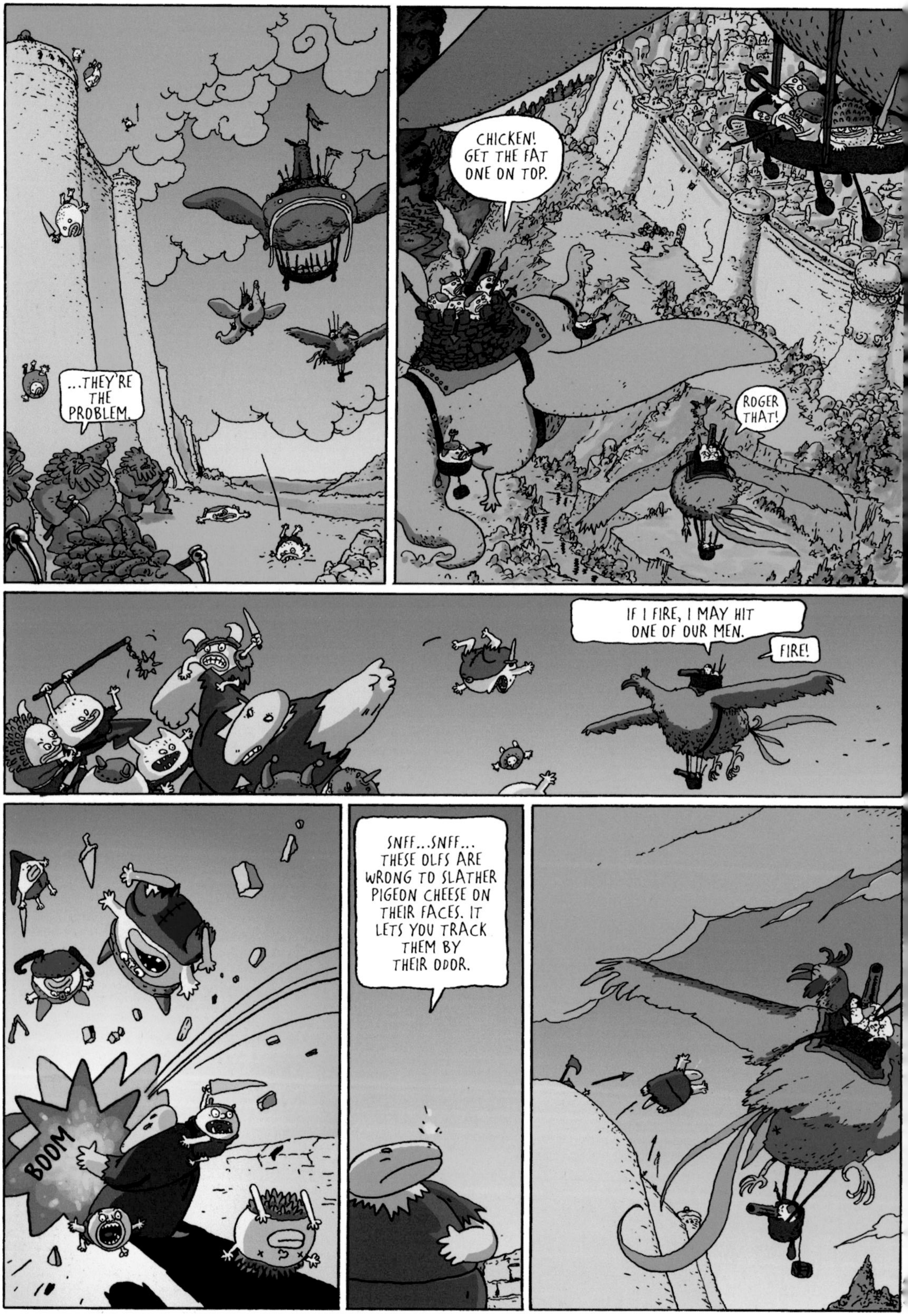
...THEY'RE THE PROBLEM.
CHICKEN! GET THE FAT ONE ON TOP.
ROGER THAT!
IF I FIRE, I MAY HIT ONE OF OUR MEN.
FIRE!
BOOM
SNFF...SNFF... THESE OLFS ARE WRONG TO SLATHER PIGEON CHEESE ON THEIR FACES. IT LETS YOU TRACK THEM BY THEIR ODOR.

OFF!

TCHAK!

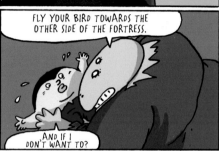

FLY YOUR BIRD TOWARDS THE OTHER SIDE OF THE FORTRESS.

AND IF I DON'T WANT TO?

THEN I'LL TWIST YOUR FINGERS.

YOWIE! OK! I'LL DO IT!

BOOM

WHAT HAPPENED? THE FLIGHT IS ERRATIC.

A SMALL PROBLEM.

PLOM

A CANNON SHOT HAS DECAPITATED OUR CHICKEN.

FLY ABOVE HIM. WE'LL JUMP DOWN AND FINISH HIM OFF WITH A PICKAX!

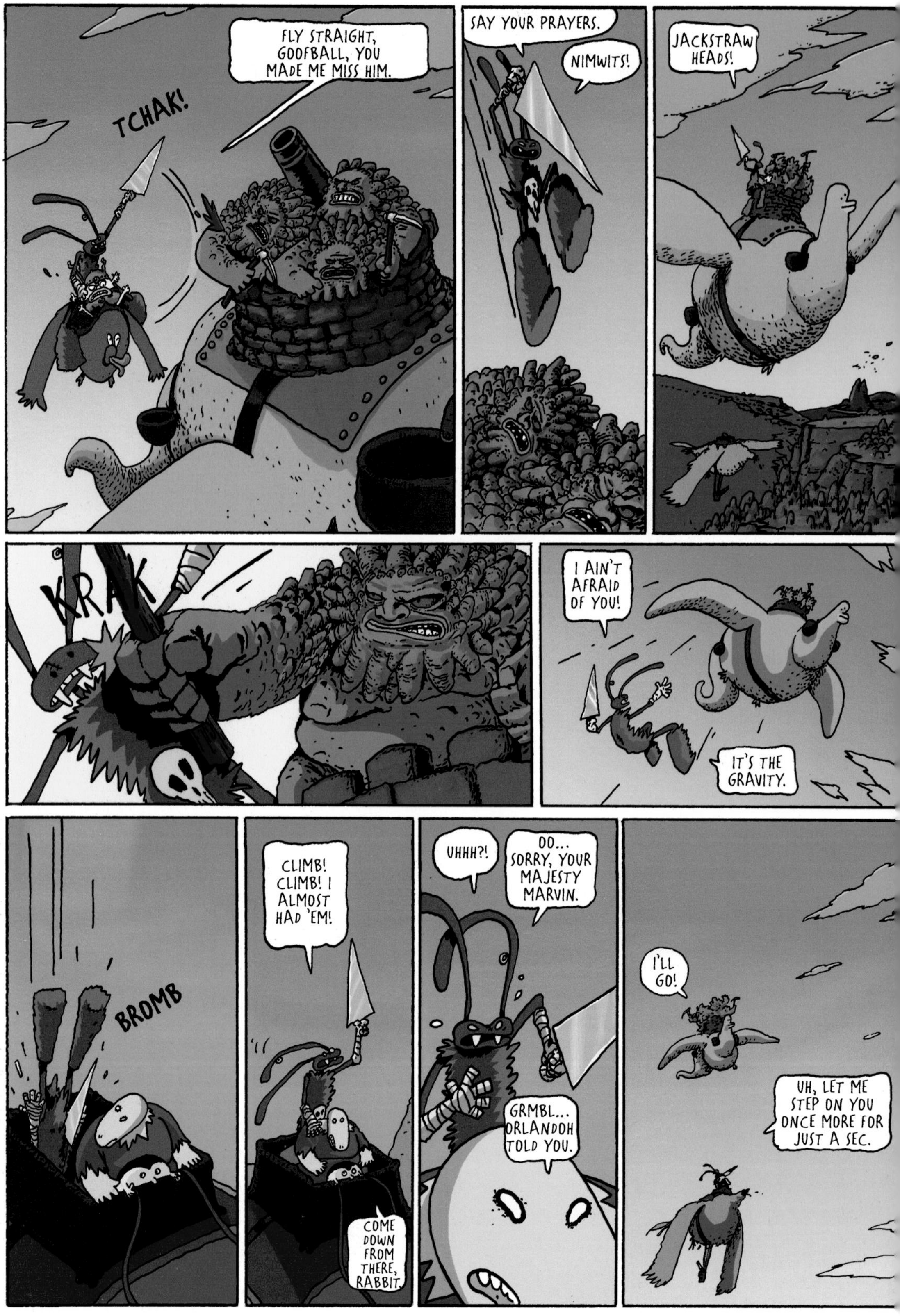

FLY STRAIGHT, GOOFBALL, YOU MADE ME MISS HIM.
TCHAK!
SAY YOUR PRAYERS.
NIMWITS!
JACKSTRAW HEADS!
KRAK
I AIN'T AFRAID OF YOU!
IT'S THE GRAVITY.
BROMB
CLIMB! CLIMB! I ALMOST HAD 'EM!
COME DOWN FROM THERE, RABBIT.
UHHH?!
OO... SORRY, YOUR MAJESTY MARVIN.
GRMBL... ORLANDOH TOLD YOU.
I'LL GO!
UH, LET ME STEP ON YOU ONCE MORE FOR JUST A SEC.

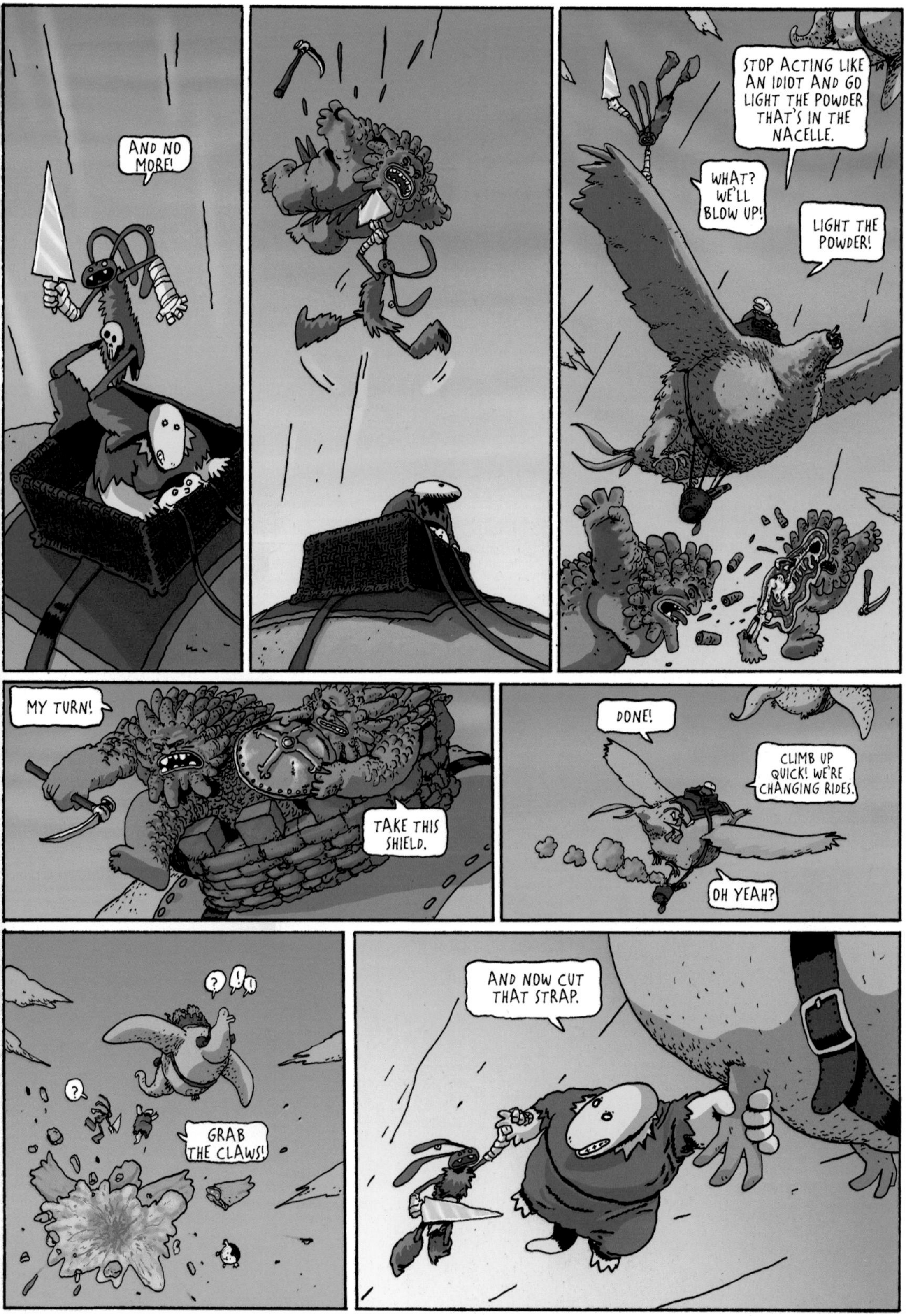
AND NO MORE!
STOP ACTING LIKE AN IDIOT AND GO LIGHT THE POWDER THAT'S IN THE NACELLE.
WHAT? WE'LL BLOW UP!
LIGHT THE POWDER!
MY TURN!
TAKE THIS SHIELD.
DONE!
CLIMB UP QUICK! WE'RE CHANGING RIDES.
OH YEAH?
?!!
?
GRAB THE CLAWS!
AND NOW CUT THAT STRAP.

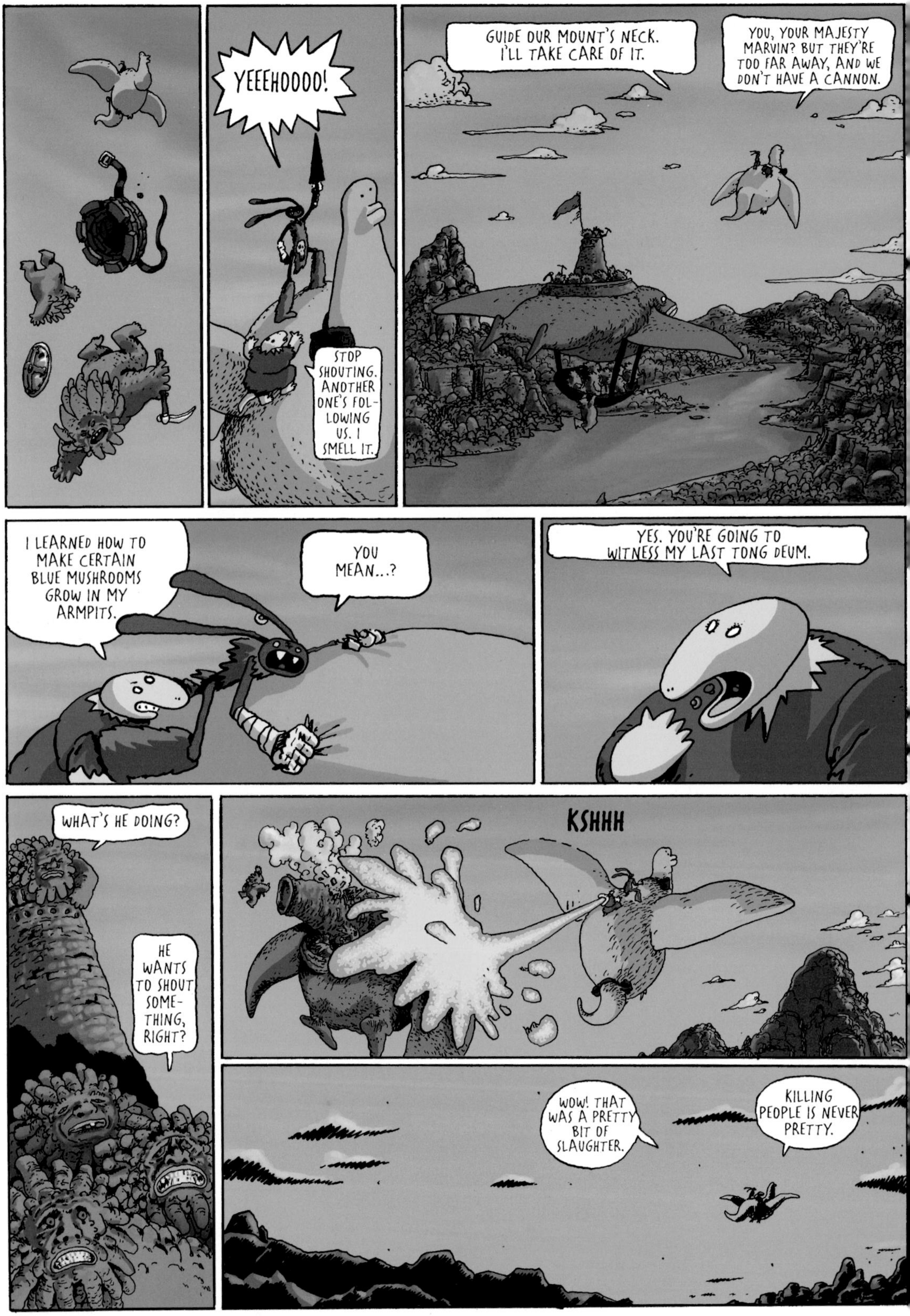
YEEEHOOOO!
STOP SHOUTING. ANOTHER ONE'S FOL-LOWING US. I SMELL IT.
GUIDE OUR MOUNT'S NECK. I'LL TAKE CARE OF IT.
YOU, YOUR MAJESTY MARVIN? BUT THEY'RE TOO FAR AWAY, AND WE DON'T HAVE A CANNON.
I LEARNED HOW TO MAKE CERTAIN BLUE MUSHROOMS GROW IN MY ARMPITS.
YOU MEAN...?
YES. YOU'RE GOING TO WITNESS MY LAST TONG DEUM.
WHAT'S HE DOING?
HE WANTS TO SHOUT SOME-THING, RIGHT?
KSHHH
WOW! THAT WAS A PRETTY BIT OF SLAUGHTER.
KILLING PEOPLE IS NEVER PRETTY.

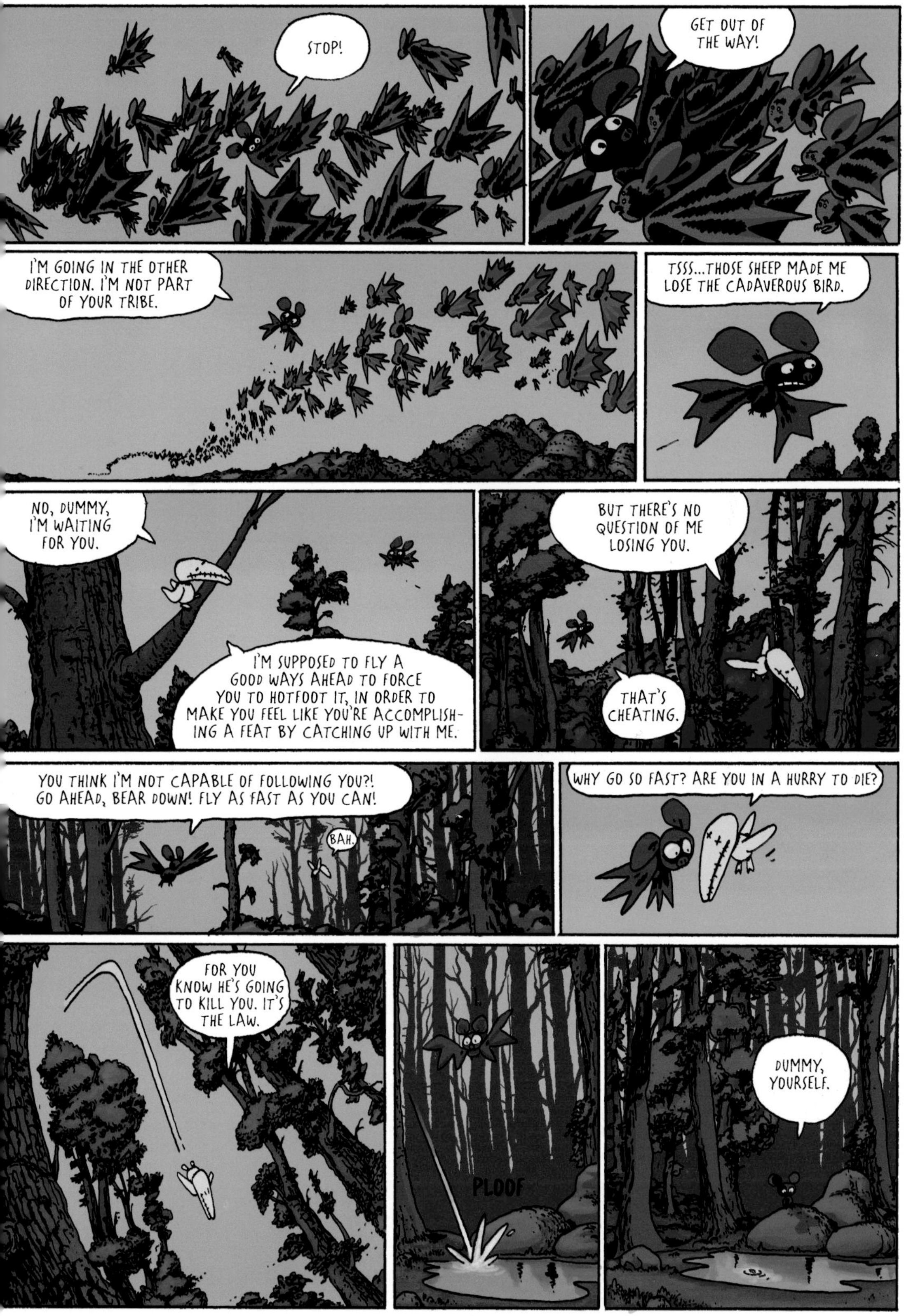
STOP!
GET OUT OF THE WAY!
I'M GOING IN THE OTHER DIRECTION. I'M NOT PART OF YOUR TRIBE.
TSSS...THOSE SHEEP MADE ME LOSE THE CADAVEROUS BIRD.
NO, DUMMY, I'M WAITING FOR YOU.
I'M SUPPOSED TO FLY A GOOD WAYS AHEAD TO FORCE YOU TO HOTFOOT IT, IN ORDER TO MAKE YOU FEEL LIKE YOU'RE ACCOMPLISHING A FEAT BY CATCHING UP WITH ME.
BUT THERE'S NO QUESTION OF ME LOSING YOU.
THAT'S CHEATING.
YOU THINK I'M NOT CAPABLE OF FOLLOWING YOU?! GO AHEAD, BEAR DOWN! FLY AS FAST AS YOU CAN!
BAH.
WHY GO SO FAST? ARE YOU IN A HURRY TO DIE?
FOR YOU KNOW HE'S GOING TO KILL YOU. IT'S THE LAW.
PLOOF
DUMMY, YOURSELF.

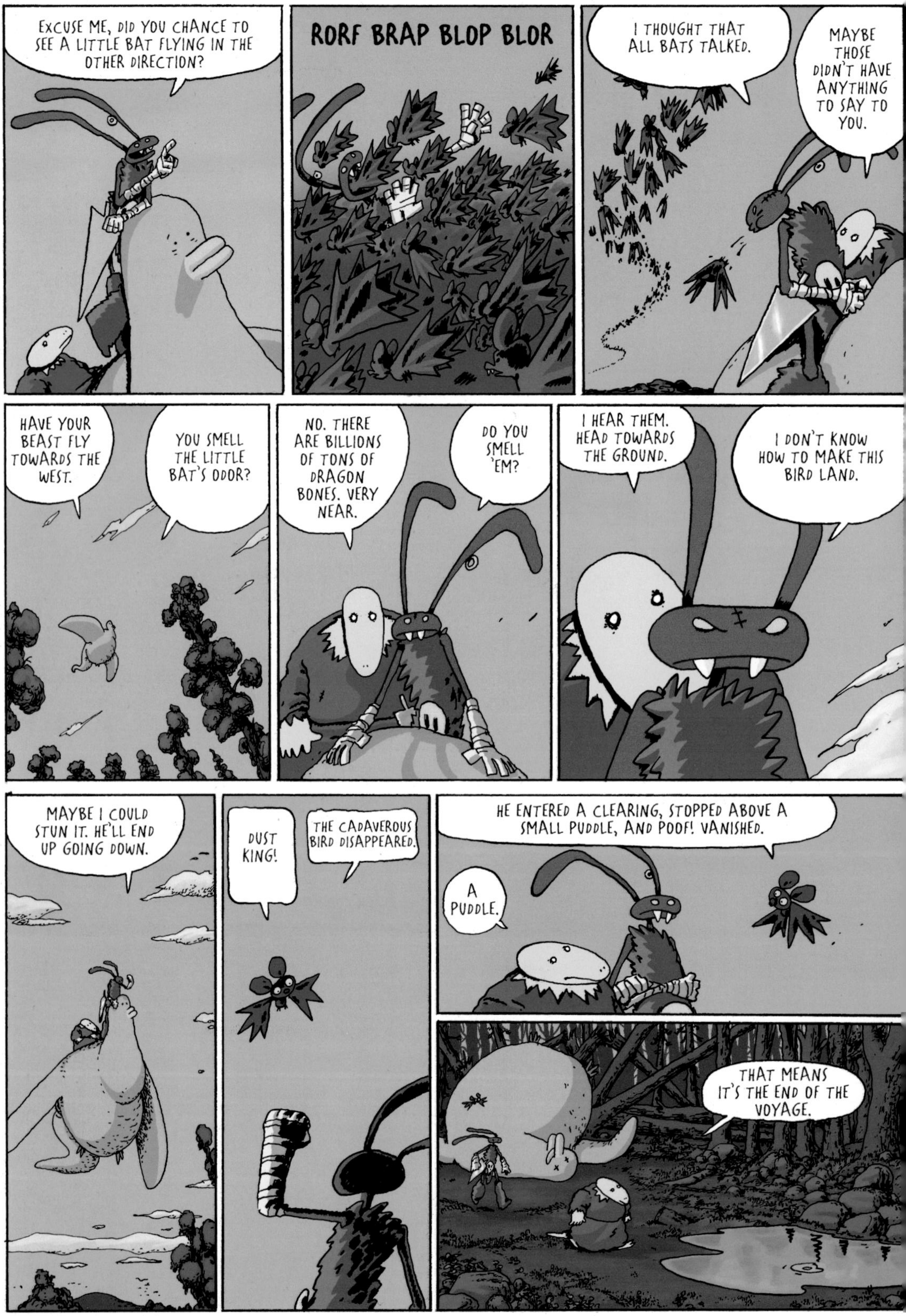
EXCUSE ME, DID YOU CHANCE TO SEE A LITTLE BAT FLYING IN THE OTHER DIRECTION?
RORF BRAP BLOP BLOR
I THOUGHT THAT ALL BATS TALKED.
MAYBE THOSE DIDN'T HAVE ANYTHING TO SAY TO YOU.
HAVE YOUR BEAST FLY TOWARDS THE WEST.
YOU SMELL THE LITTLE BAT'S ODOR?
NO. THERE ARE BILLIONS OF TONS OF DRAGON BONES. VERY NEAR.
DO YOU SMELL 'EM?
I HEAR THEM. HEAD TOWARDS THE GROUND.
I DON'T KNOW HOW TO MAKE THIS BIRD LAND.
MAYBE I COULD STUN IT. HE'LL END UP GOING DOWN.
DUST KING!
THE CADAVEROUS BIRD DISAPPEARED.
HE ENTERED A CLEARING, STOPPED ABOVE A SMALL PUDDLE, AND POOF! VANISHED.
A PUDDLE.
THAT MEANS IT'S THE END OF THE VOYAGE.

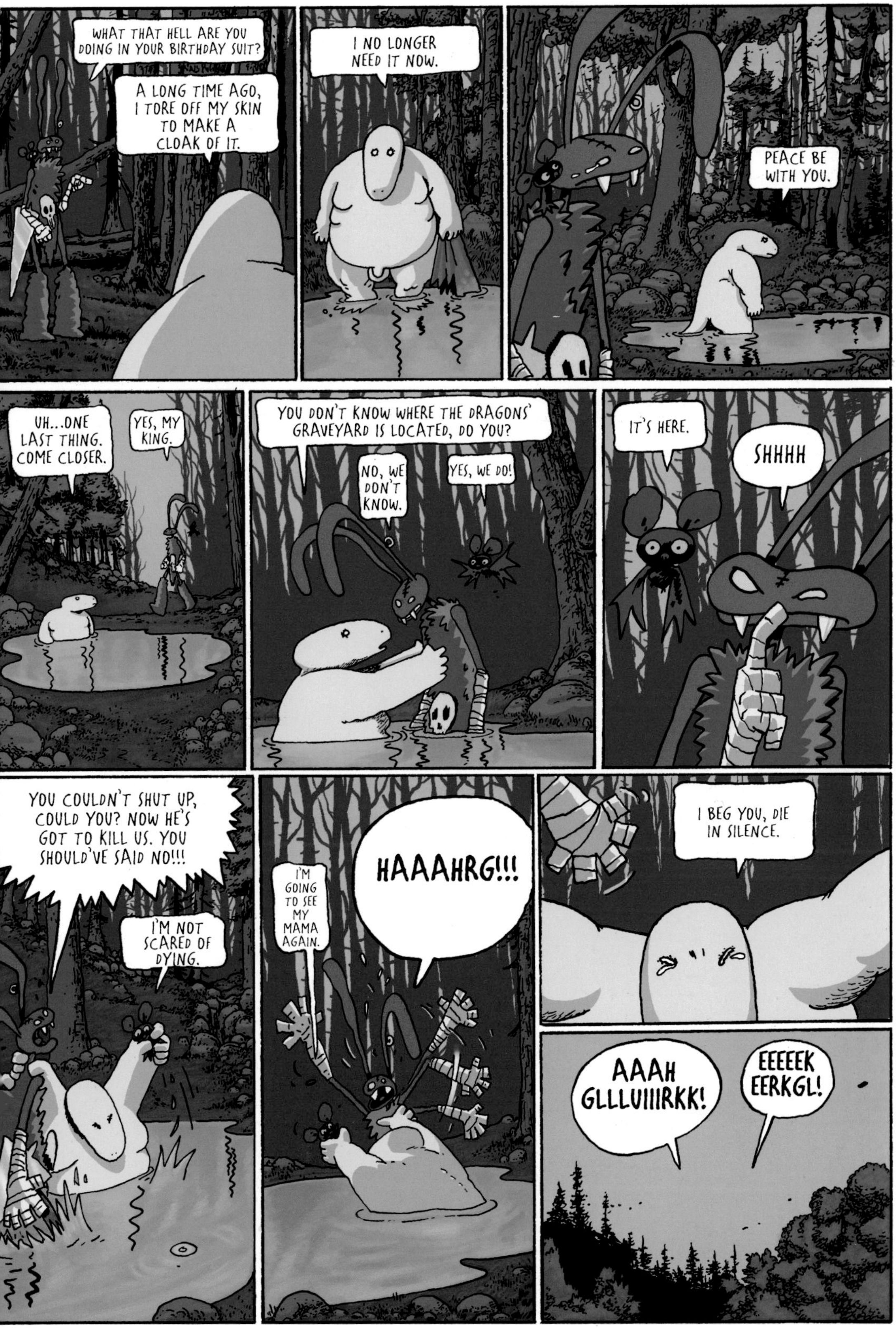
WHAT THAT HELL ARE YOU DOING IN YOUR BIRTHDAY SUIT?
A LONG TIME AGO, I TORE OFF MY SKIN TO MAKE A CLOAK OF IT.
I NO LONGER NEED IT NOW.
PEACE BE WITH YOU.
UH...ONE LAST THING. COME CLOSER.
YES, MY KING.
YOU DON'T KNOW WHERE THE DRAGONS' GRAVEYARD IS LOCATED, DO YOU?
NO, WE DON'T KNOW.
YES, WE DO!
IT'S HERE.
SHHHH
YOU COULDN'T SHUT UP, COULD YOU? NOW HE'S GOT TO KILL US. YOU SHOULD'VE SAID NO!!!
I'M NOT SCARED OF DYING.
I'M GOING TO SEE MY MAMA AGAIN.
HAAAHRG!!!
I BEG YOU, DIE IN SILENCE.
AAAH GLLLUIIIRKK!
EEEEEK EERKGL!

SORRY, MY LITTLE FRIENDS, I CAN'T STEEL MYSELF TO STRANGLING YOU.

TH...THAT'S NICE.

SO I'M GOING TO DROWN YOU.

I'M TOO OLD. I NO LONGER HAVE THE STRENGTH TO TAKE LIFE.

HHH

HHHH

GO BACK TO THE SURFACE AND EAT THE LITTLE RED BERRIES THAT ARE IN MY POCKET.

THEY'RE POISON.

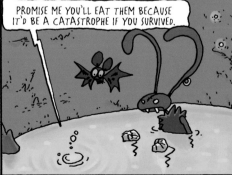

PROMISE ME YOU'LL EAT THEM BECAUSE IT'D BE A CATASTROPHE IF YOU SURVIVED.

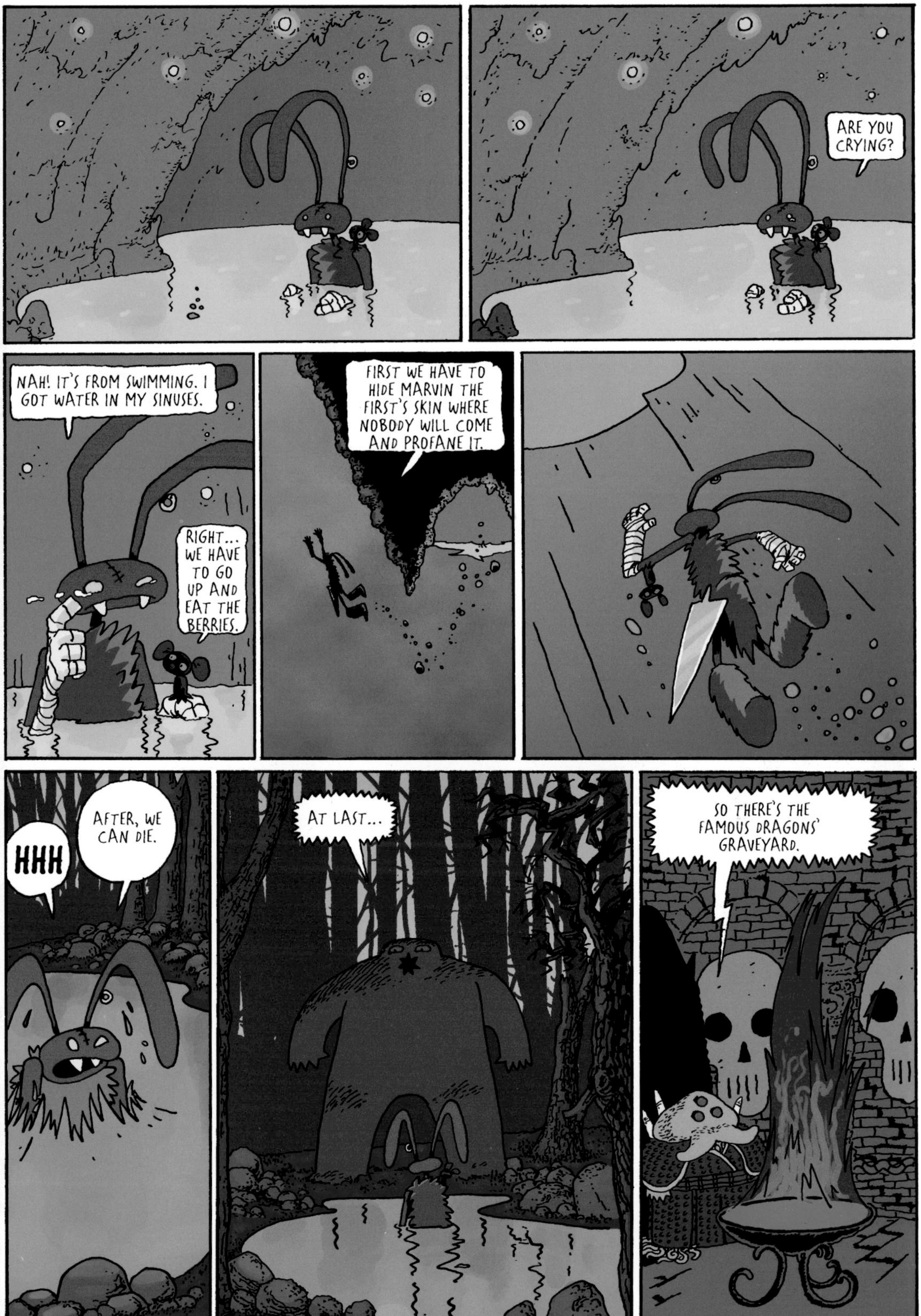
ARE YOU CRYING?
NAH! IT'S FROM SWIMMING. I GOT WATER IN MY SINUSES.
RIGHT... WE HAVE TO GO UP AND EAT THE BERRIES.
FIRST WE HAVE TO HIDE MARVIN THE FIRST'S SKIN WHERE NOBODY WILL COME AND PROFANE IT.
HHH
AFTER, WE CAN DIE.
AT LAST...
SO THERE'S THE FAMOUS DRAGONS' GRAVEYARD.

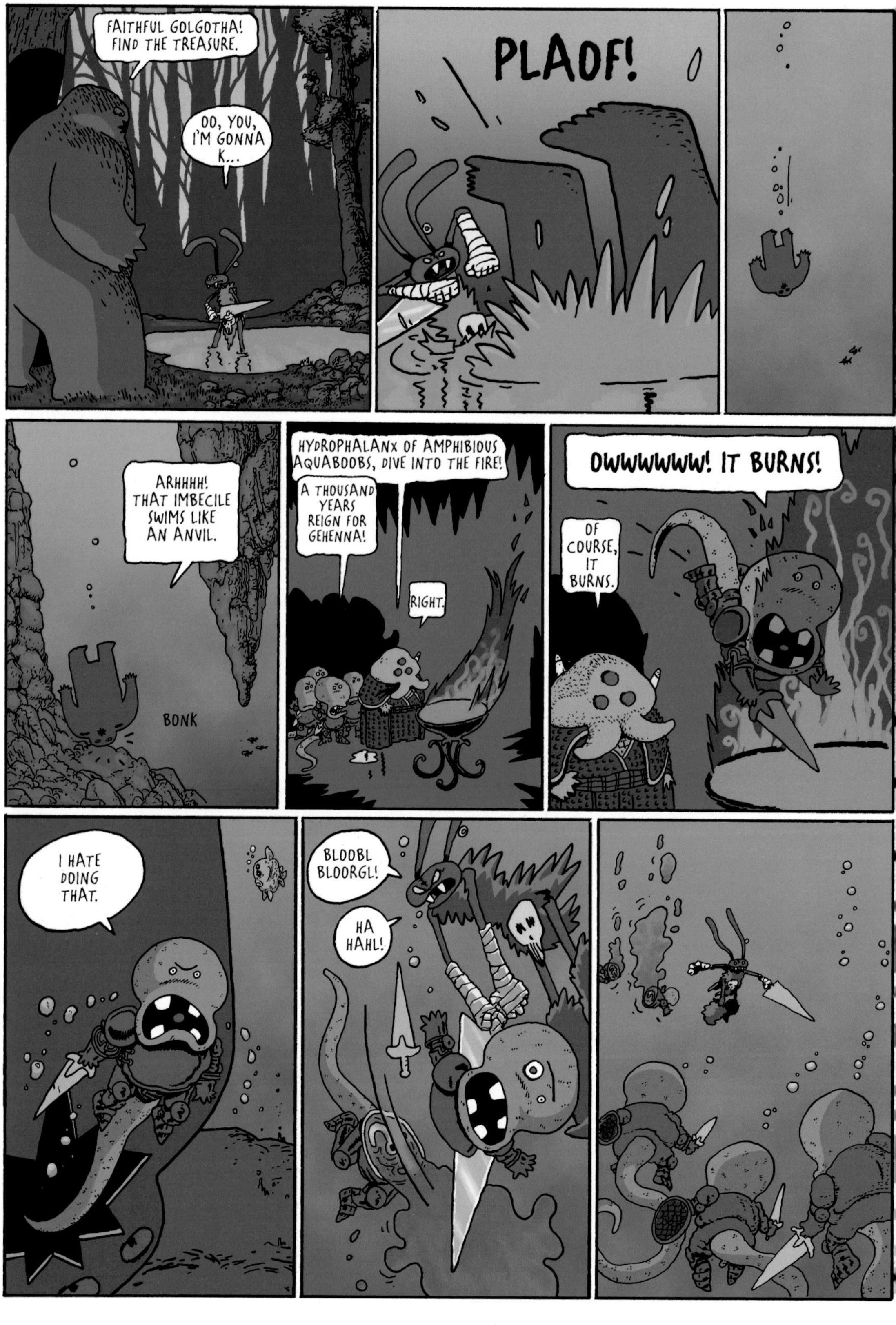
FAITHFUL GOLGOTHA! FIND THE TREASURE.
OO, YOU, I'M GONNA K...
PLAOF!
ARHHHH! THAT IMBECILE SWIMS LIKE AN ANVIL.
BONK
HYDROPHALANX OF AMPHIBIOUS AQUABOOBS, DIVE INTO THE FIRE!
A THOUSAND YEARS REIGN FOR GEHENNA!
RIGHT.
OWWWWWW! IT BURNS!
OF COURSE, IT BURNS.
I HATE DOING THAT.
BLOOBL BLOORGL!
HA HAHL!

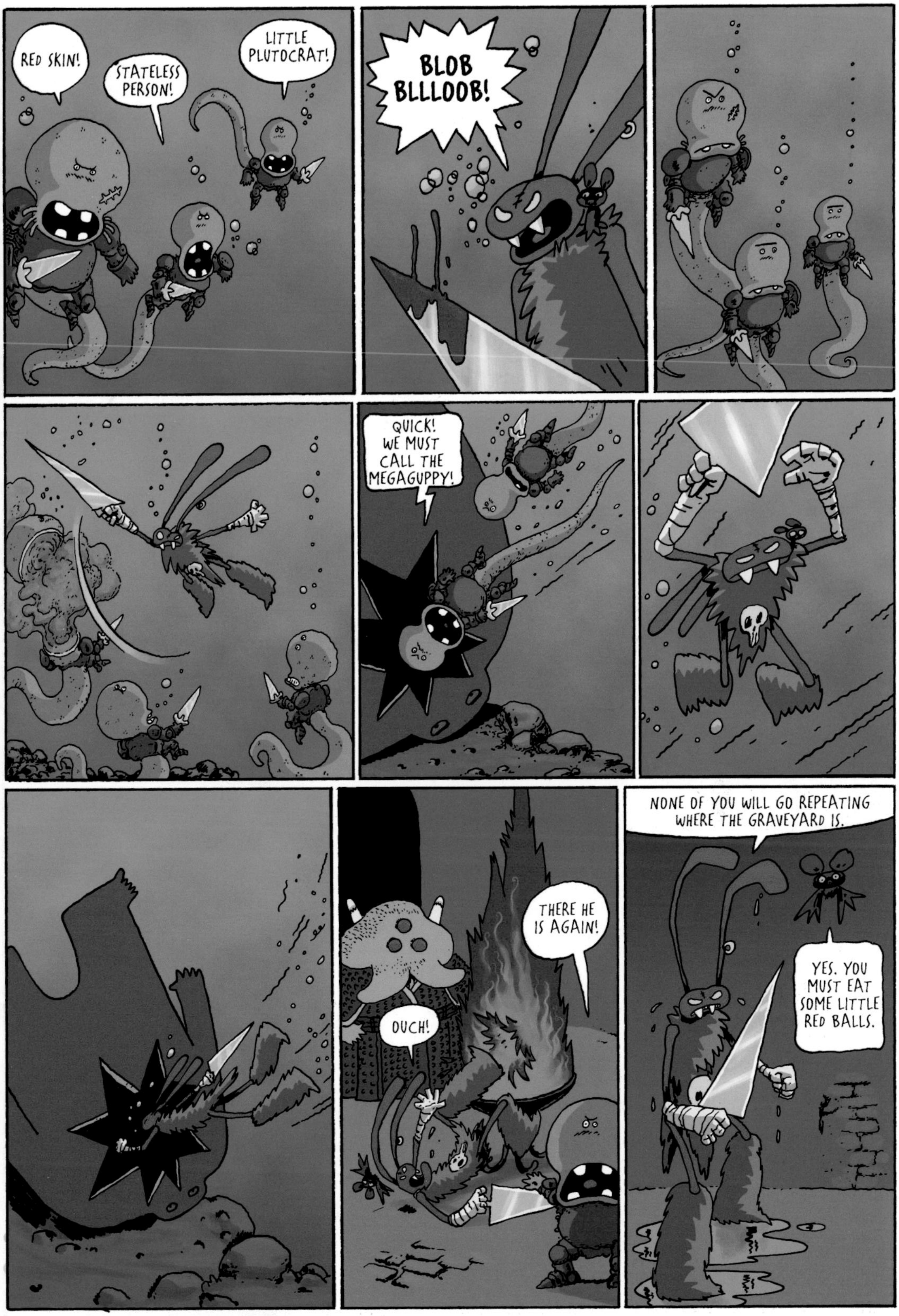
RED SKIN!
STATELESS PERSON!
LITTLE PLUTOCRAT!
BLOB BLLLOOB!
QUICK! WE MUST CALL THE MEGAGUPPY!
THERE HE IS AGAIN!
OUCH!
NONE OF YOU WILL GO REPEATING WHERE THE GRAVEYARD IS.
YES. YOU MUST EAT SOME LITTLE RED BALLS.

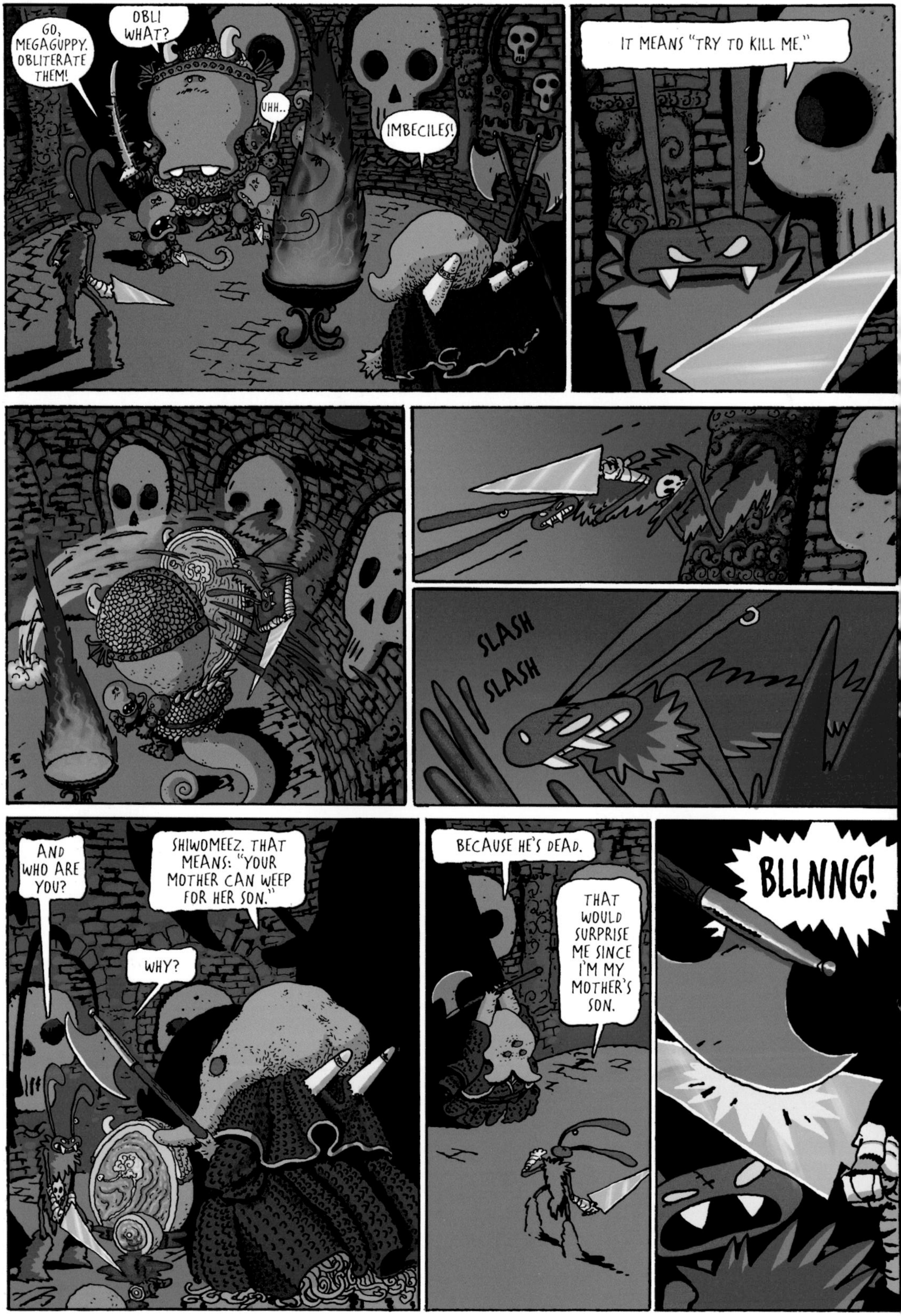
GO, MEGAGUPPY. OBLITERATE THEM!
OBLI WHAT?
UHH..
IMBECILES!
IT MEANS "TRY TO KILL ME."
SLASH
SLASH
AND WHO ARE YOU?
SHIWOMEEZ. THAT MEANS: "YOUR MOTHER CAN WEEP FOR HER SON."
WHY?
BECAUSE HE'S DEAD.
THAT WOULD SURPRISE ME SINCE I'M MY MOTHER'S SON.
BLLNNG!

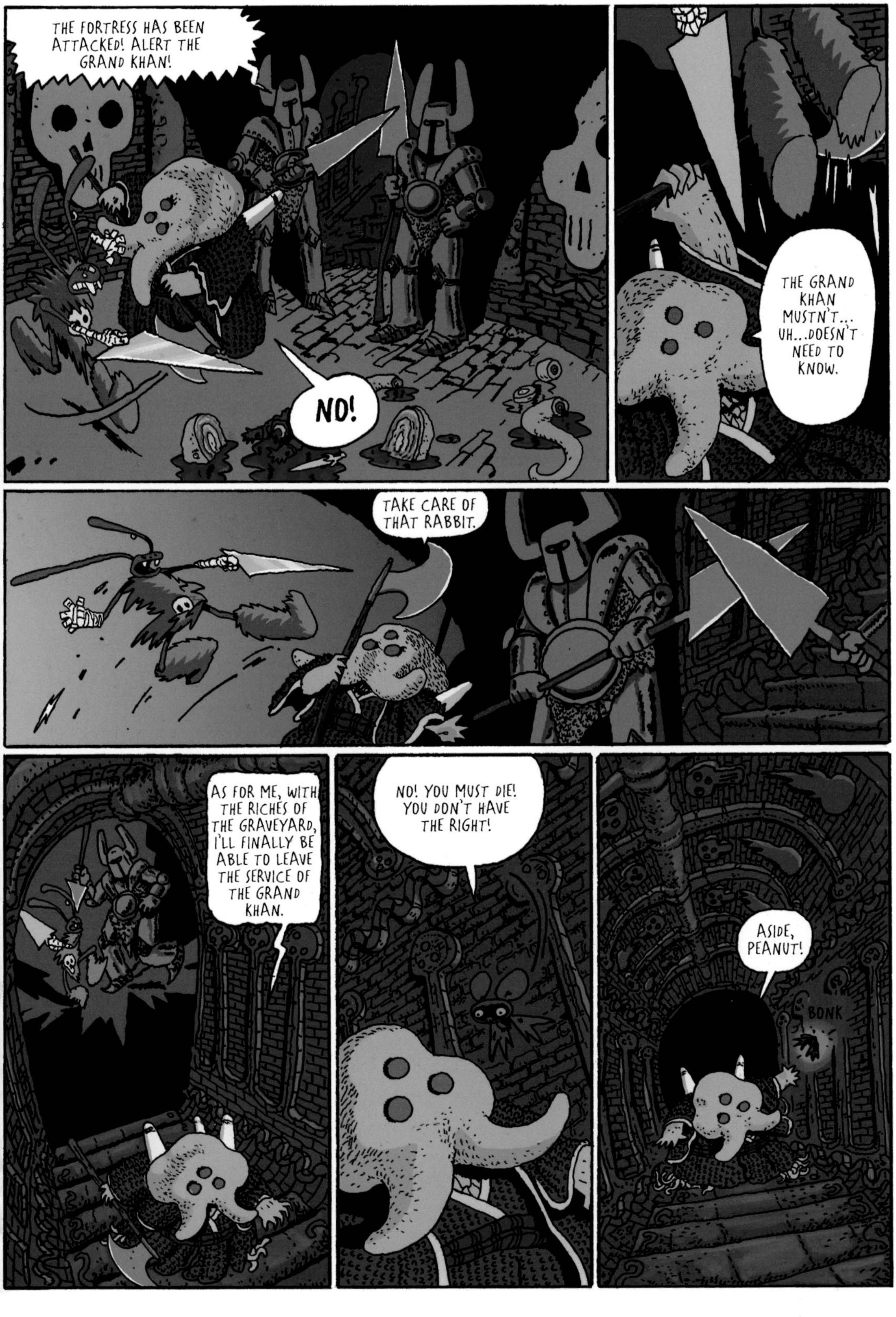
THE FORTRESS HAS BEEN ATTACKED! ALERT THE GRAND KHAN!
NO!
THE GRAND KHAN MUSTN'T... UH...DOESN'T NEED TO KNOW.
TAKE CARE OF THAT RABBIT.
AS FOR ME, WITH THE RICHES OF THE GRAVEYARD, I'LL FINALLY BE ABLE TO LEAVE THE SERVICE OF THE GRAND KHAN.
NO! YOU MUST DIE! YOU DON'T HAVE THE RIGHT!
ASIDE, PEANUT!
BONK

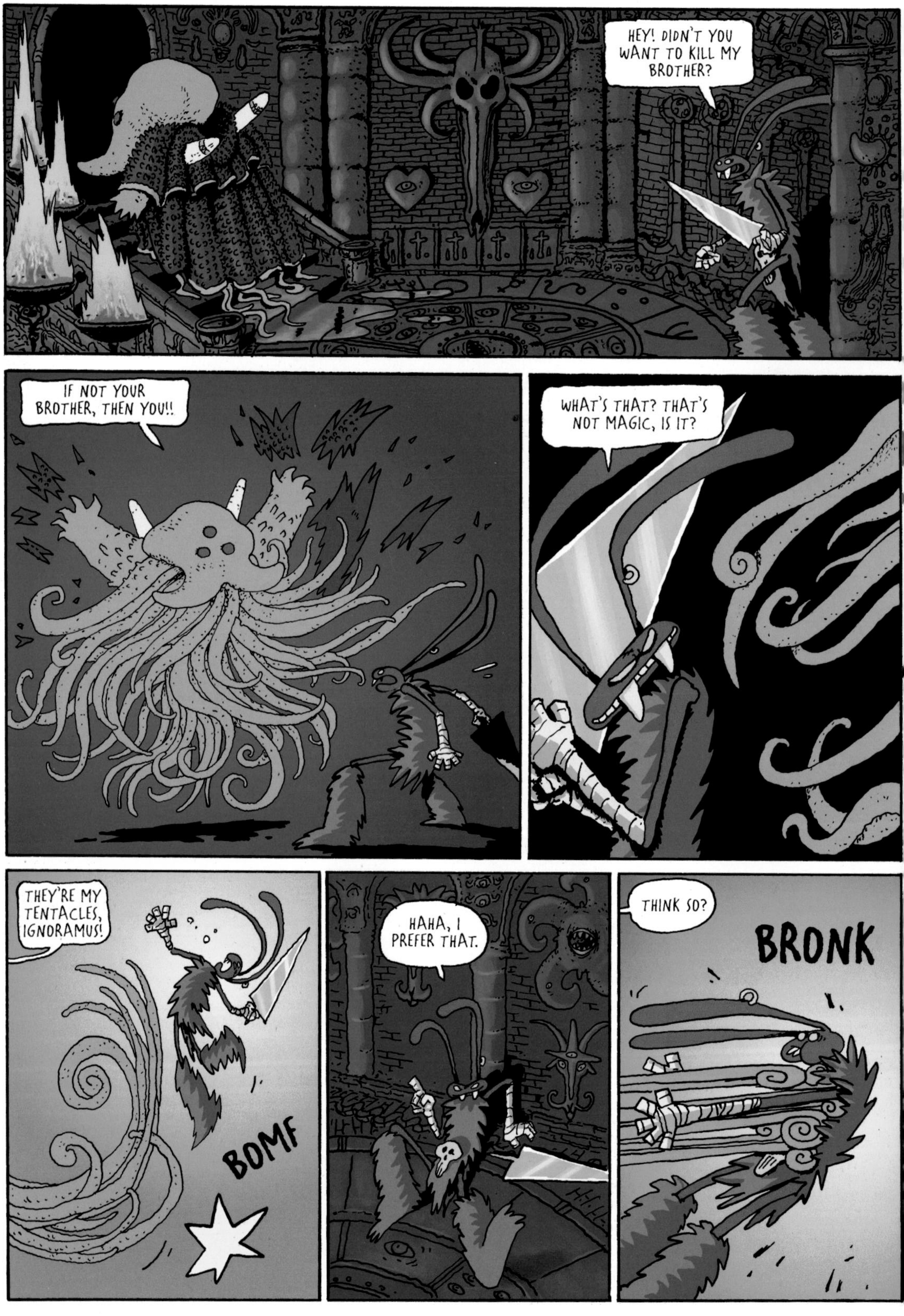
HEY! DIDN'T YOU WANT TO KILL MY BROTHER?
IF NOT YOUR BROTHER, THEN YOU!!
WHAT'S THAT? THAT'S NOT MAGIC, IS IT?
THEY'RE MY TENTACLES, IGNORAMUS!
BOMF
HAHA, I PREFER THAT.
THINK SO?
BRONK

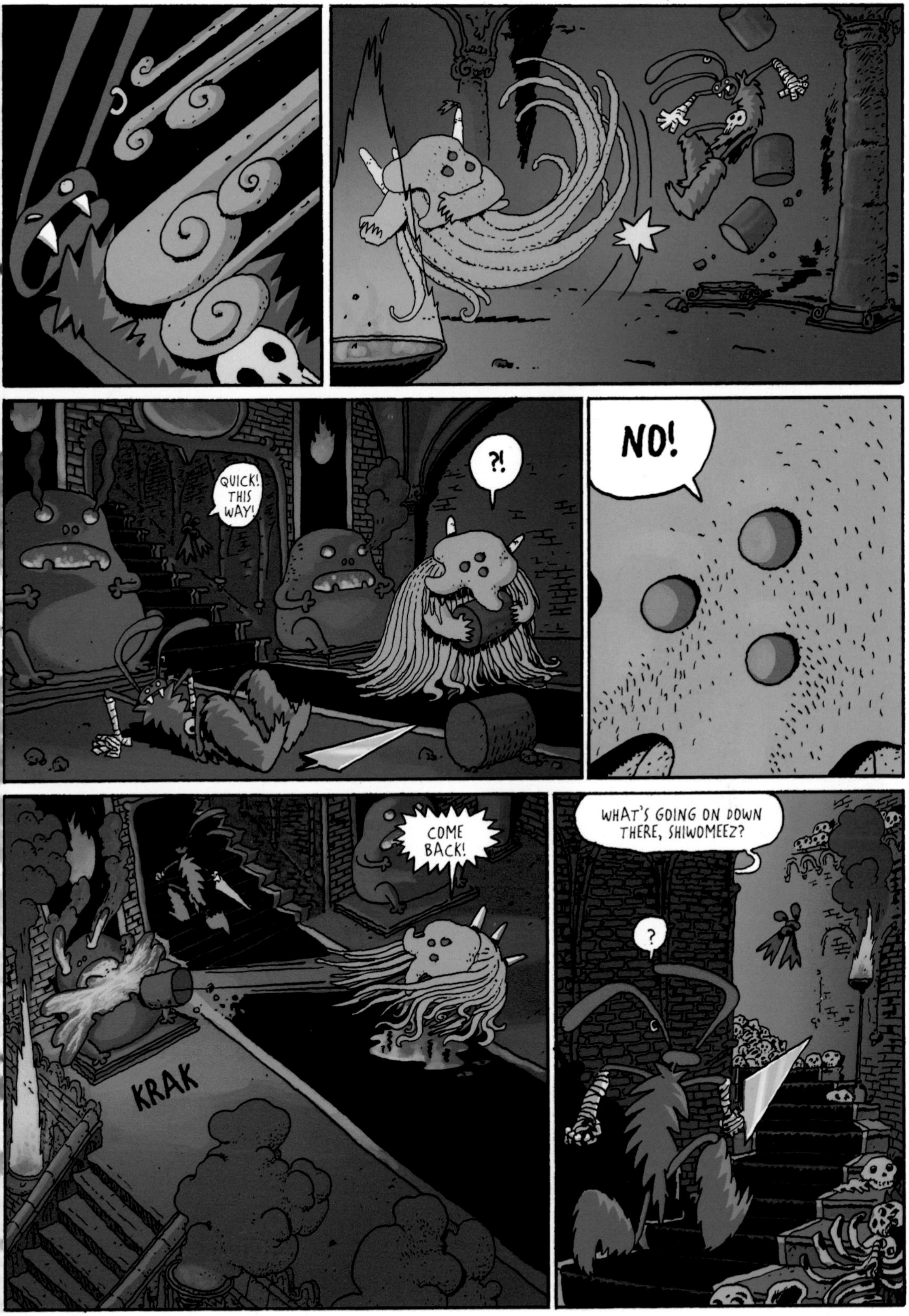
QUICK! THIS WAY!
?!
NO!
COME BACK!
KRAK
WHAT'S GOING ON DOWN THERE, SHIWOMEEZ?
?

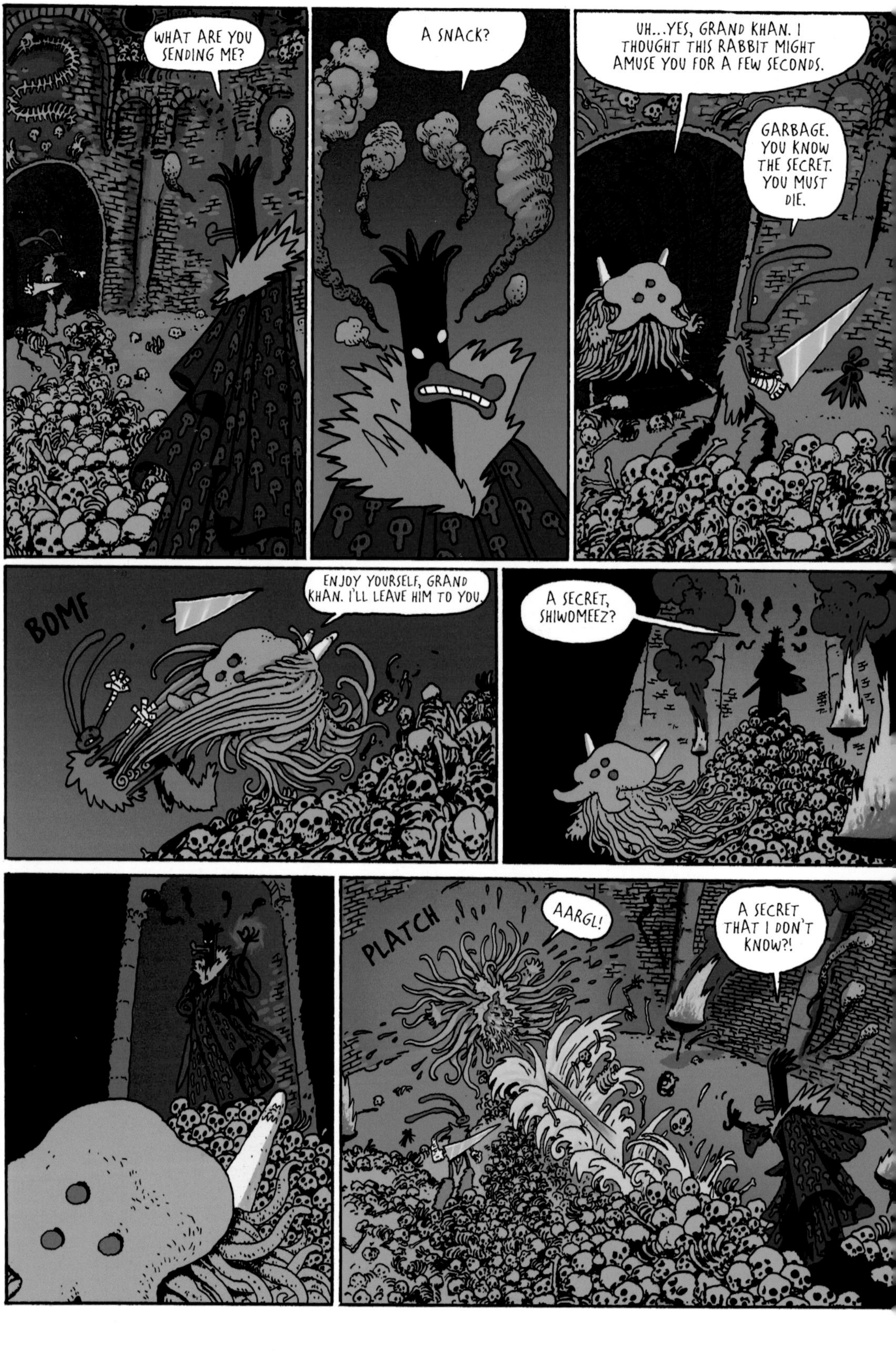
WHAT ARE YOU SENDING ME?
A SNACK?
UH...YES, GRAND KHAN. I THOUGHT THIS RABBIT MIGHT AMUSE YOU FOR A FEW SECONDS.
GARBAGE. YOU KNOW THE SECRET. YOU MUST DIE.
BOMF
ENJOY YOURSELF, GRAND KHAN. I'LL LEAVE HIM TO YOU.
A SECRET, SHIWOMEEZ?
PLATCH
AARGL!
A SECRET THAT I DON'T KNOW?!

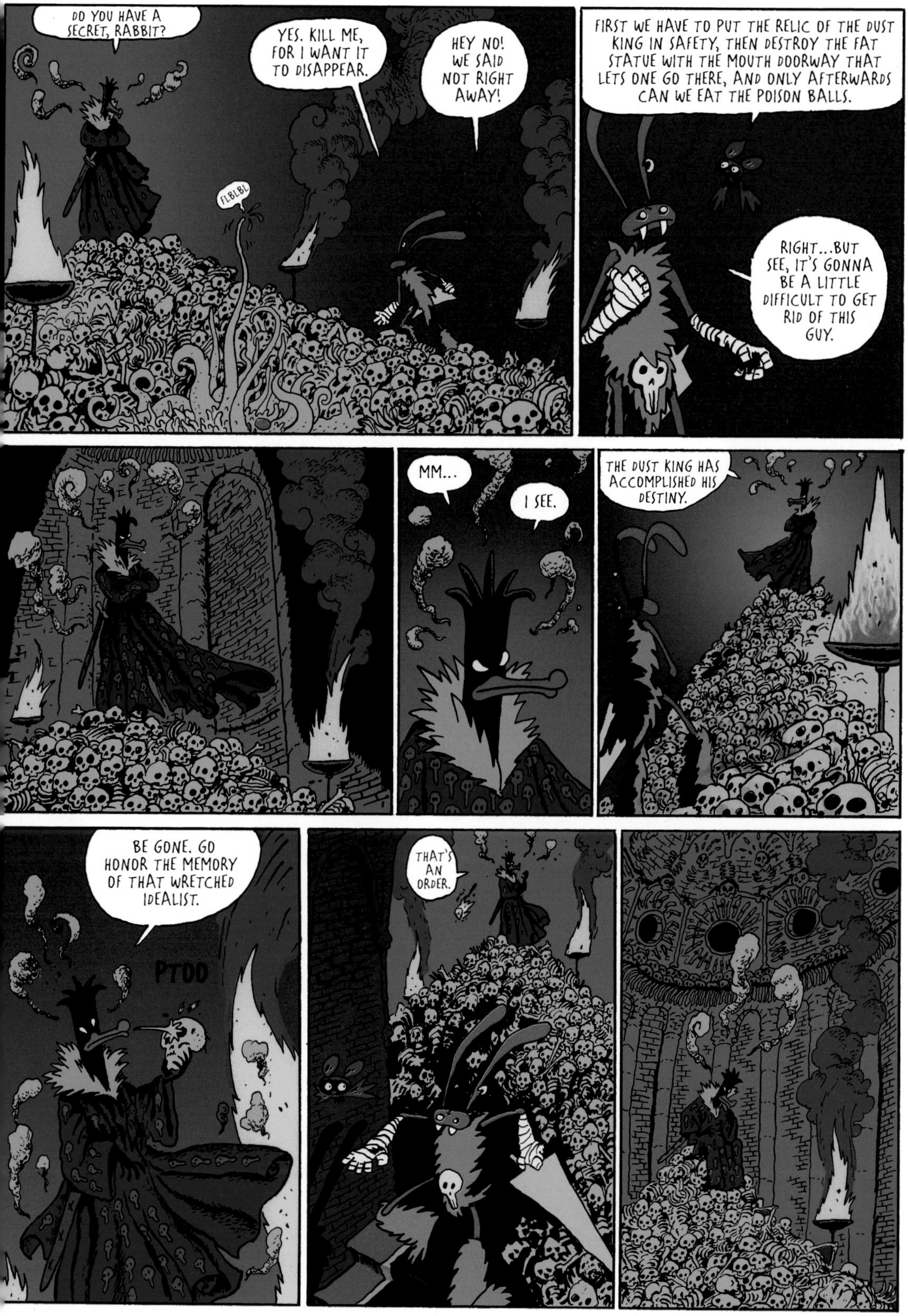
DO YOU HAVE A SECRET, RABBIT?
YES. KILL ME, FOR I WANT IT TO DISAPPEAR.
FLBLBL
HEY NO! WE SAID NOT RIGHT AWAY!
FIRST WE HAVE TO PUT THE RELIC OF THE DUST KING IN SAFETY, THEN DESTROY THE FAT STATUE WITH THE MOUTH DOORWAY THAT LETS ONE GO THERE, AND ONLY AFTERWARDS CAN WE EAT THE POISON BALLS.
RIGHT...BUT SEE, IT'S GONNA BE A LITTLE DIFFICULT TO GET RID OF THIS GUY.
MM...
I SEE.
THE DUST KING HAS ACCOMPLISHED HIS DESTINY.
BE GONE. GO HONOR THE MEMORY OF THAT WRETCHED IDEALIST.
PTOO
THAT'S AN ORDER.

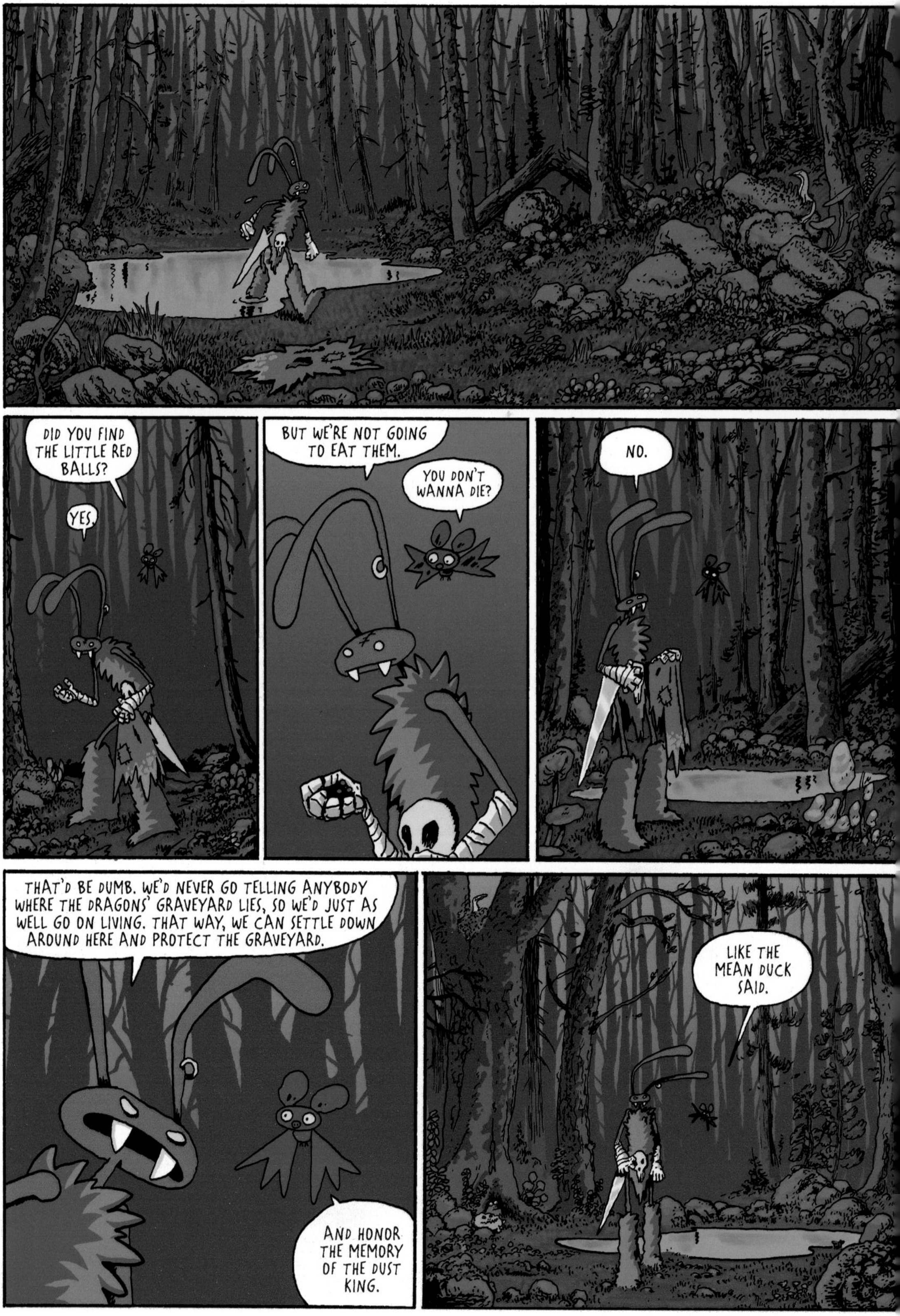
DID YOU FIND THE LITTLE RED BALLS?
YES.
BUT WE'RE NOT GOING TO EAT THEM.
YOU DON'T WANNA DIE?
NO.
THAT'D BE DUMB. WE'D NEVER GO TELLING ANYBODY WHERE THE DRAGONS' GRAVEYARD LIES, SO WE'D JUST AS WELL GO ON LIVING. THAT WAY, WE CAN SETTLE DOWN AROUND HERE AND PROTECT THE GRAVEYARD.
AND HONOR THE MEMORY OF THE DUST KING.
LIKE THE MEAN DUCK SAID.

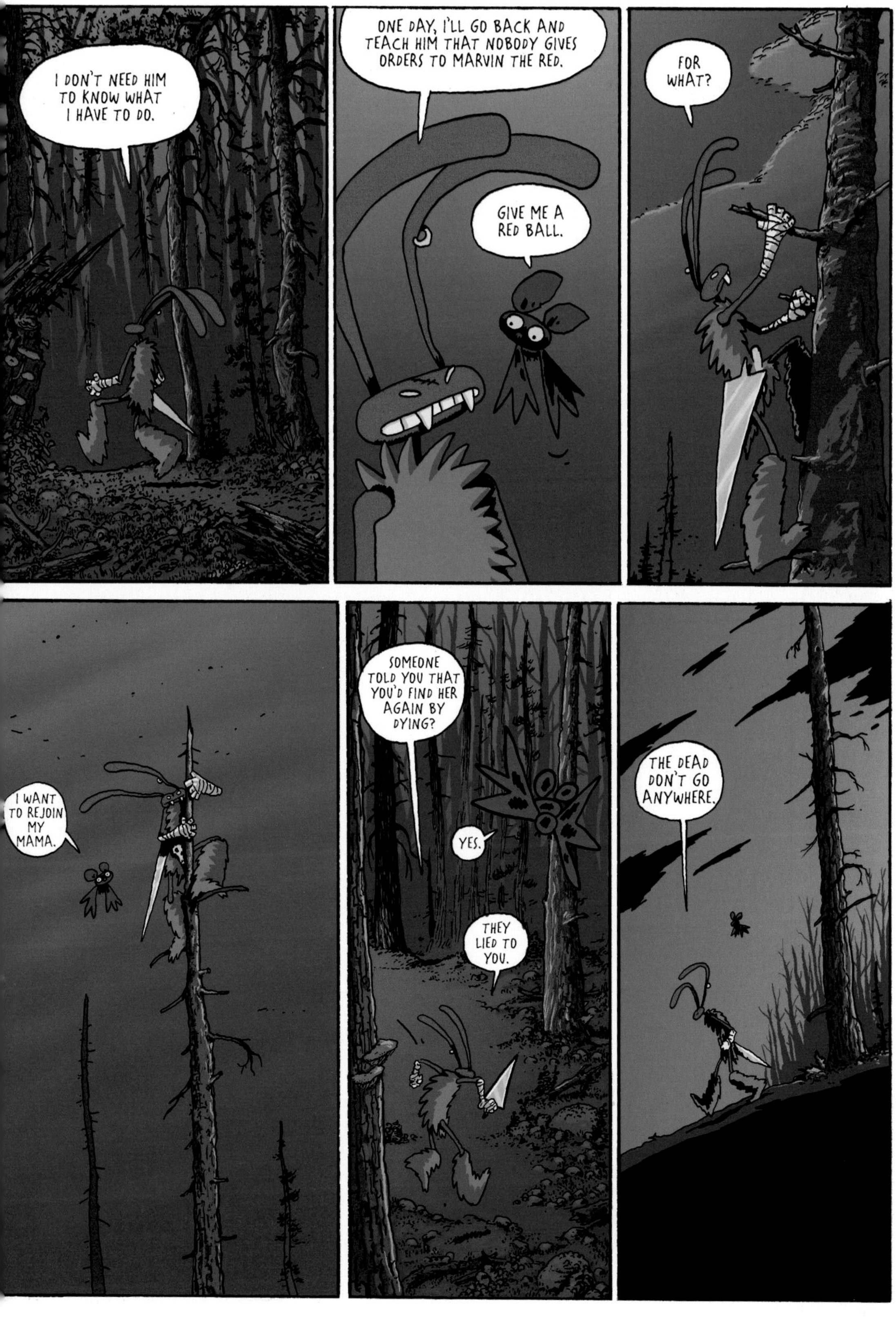
I DON'T NEED HIM TO KNOW WHAT I HAVE TO DO.
ONE DAY, I'LL GO BACK AND TEACH HIM THAT NOBODY GIVES ORDERS TO MARVIN THE RED.
GIVE ME A RED BALL.
FOR WHAT?
I WANT TO REJOIN MY MAMA.
SOMEONE TOLD YOU THAT YOU'D FIND HER AGAIN BY DYING?
YES.
THEY LIED TO YOU.
THE DEAD DON'T GO ANYWHERE.

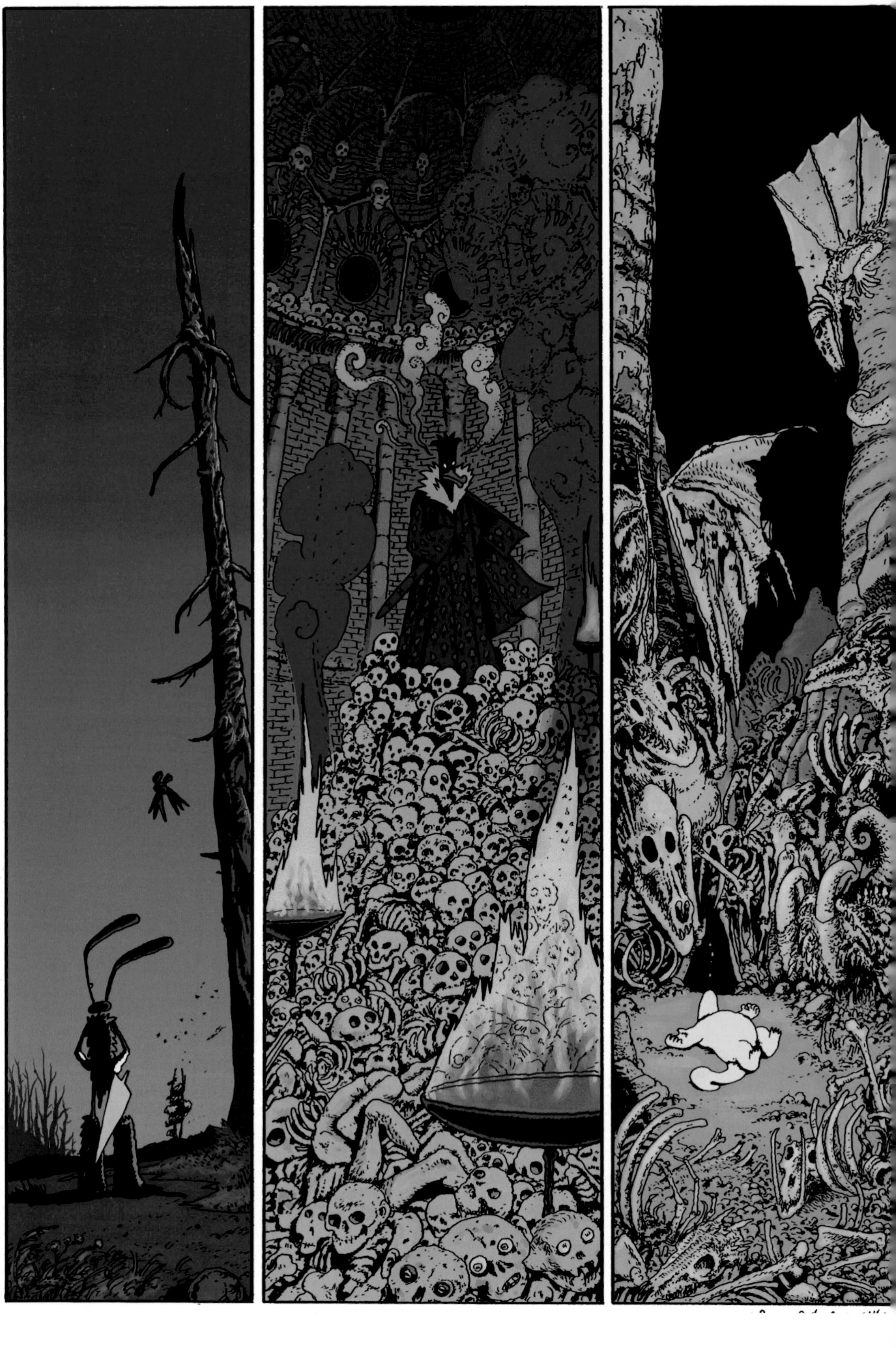

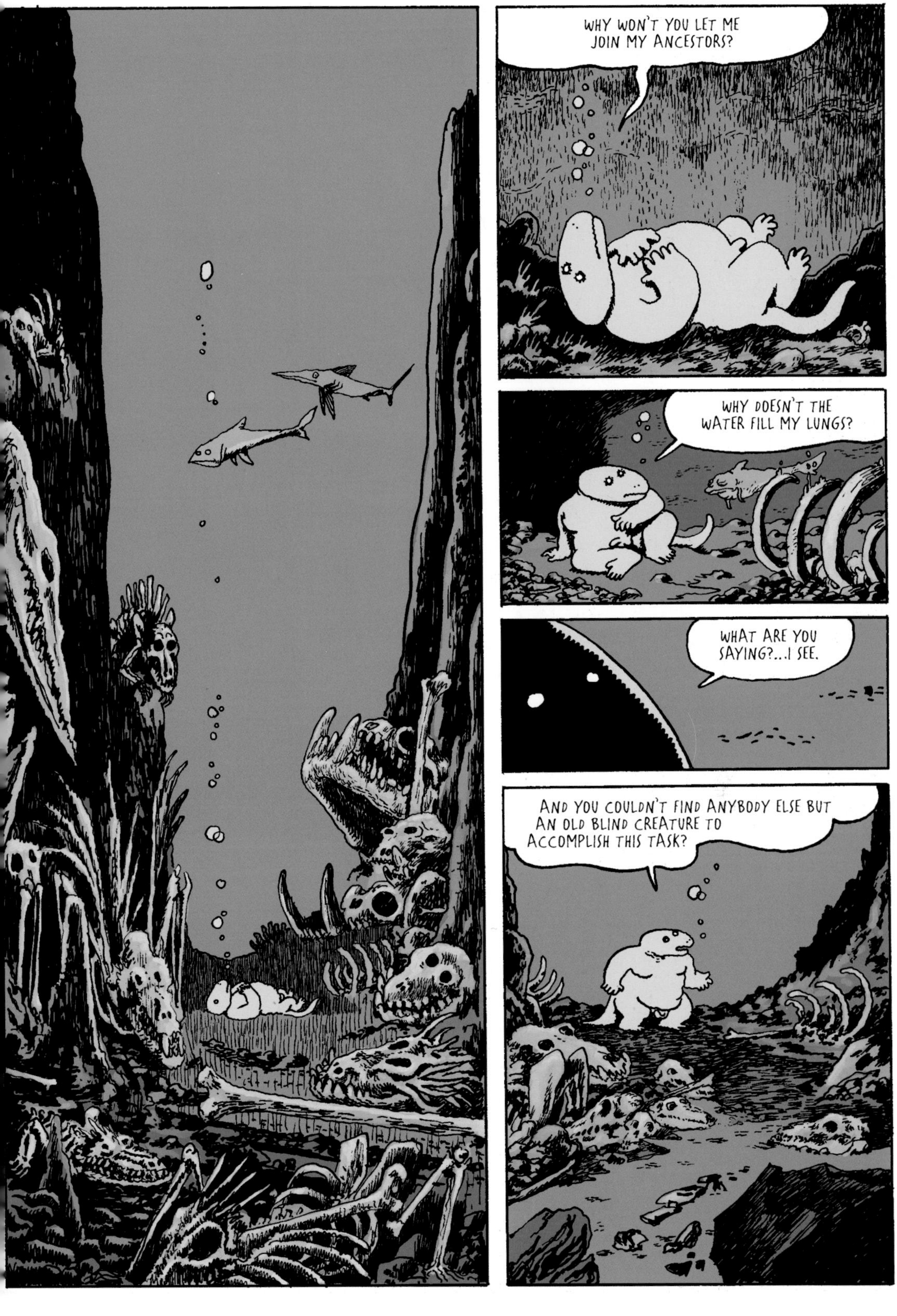
WHY WON'T YOU LET ME JOIN MY ANCESTORS?
WHY DOESN'T THE WATER FILL MY LUNGS?
WHAT ARE YOU SAYING?...I SEE.
AND YOU COULDN'T FIND ANYBODY ELSE BUT AN OLD BLIND CREATURE TO ACCOMPLISH THIS TASK?

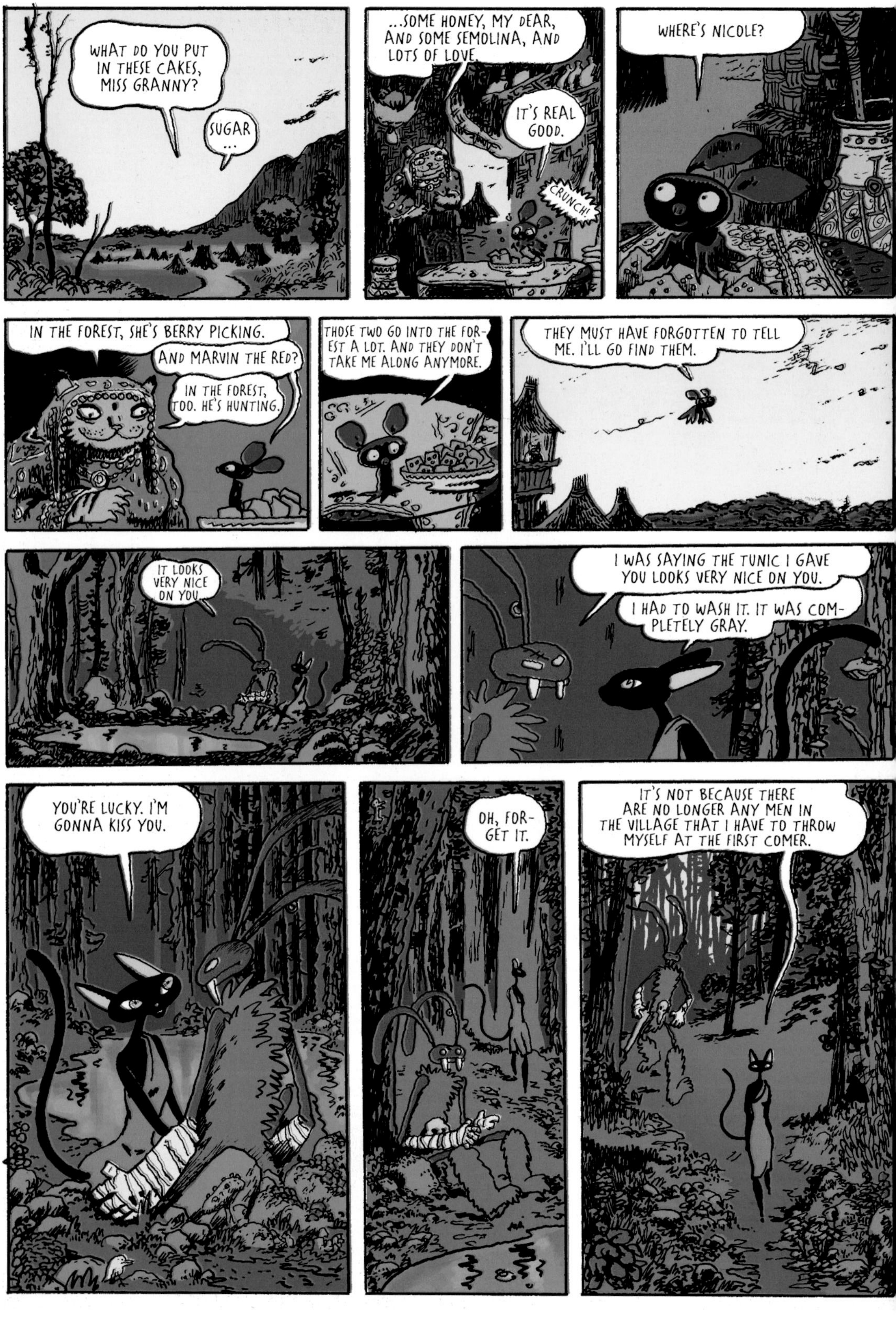
WHAT DO YOU PUT IN THESE CAKES, MISS GRANNY?
SUGAR ...
...SOME HONEY, MY DEAR, AND SOME SEMOLINA, AND LOTS OF LOVE.
IT'S REAL GOOD.
CRUNCH!
WHERE'S NICOLE?
IN THE FOREST, SHE'S BERRY PICKING.
AND MARVIN THE RED?
IN THE FOREST, TOO. HE'S HUNTING.
THOSE TWO GO INTO THE FOREST A LOT. AND THEY DON'T TAKE ME ALONG ANYMORE.
THEY MUST HAVE FORGOTTEN TO TELL ME. I'LL GO FIND THEM.
IT LOOKS VERY NICE ON YOU.
I WAS SAYING THE TUNIC I GAVE YOU LOOKS VERY NICE ON YOU.
I HAD TO WASH IT. IT WAS COMPLETELY GRAY.
YOU'RE LUCKY. I'M GONNA KISS YOU.
OH, FORGET IT.
IT'S NOT BECAUSE THERE ARE NO LONGER ANY MEN IN THE VILLAGE THAT I HAVE TO THROW MYSELF AT THE FIRST COMER.

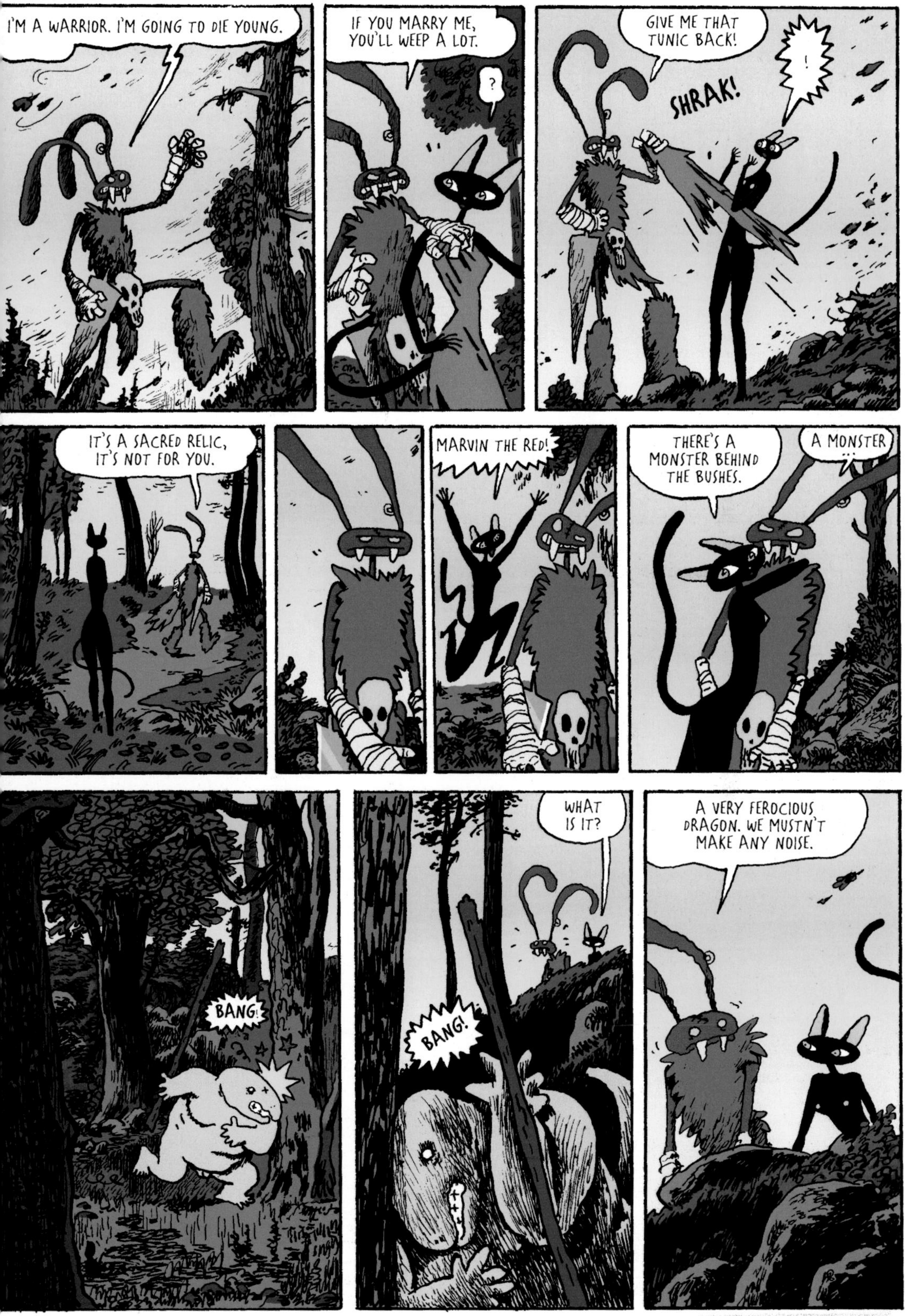

I'M A WARRIOR. I'M GOING TO DIE YOUNG.
IF YOU MARRY ME, YOU'LL WEEP A LOT.
?
GIVE ME THAT TUNIC BACK!
SHRAK!
!
IT'S A SACRED RELIC, IT'S NOT FOR YOU.
MARVIN THE RED!
THERE'S A MONSTER BEHIND THE BUSHES.
A MONSTER ...
BANG!
BANG!
WHAT IS IT?
A VERY FEROCIOUS DRAGON. WE MUSTN'T MAKE ANY NOISE.

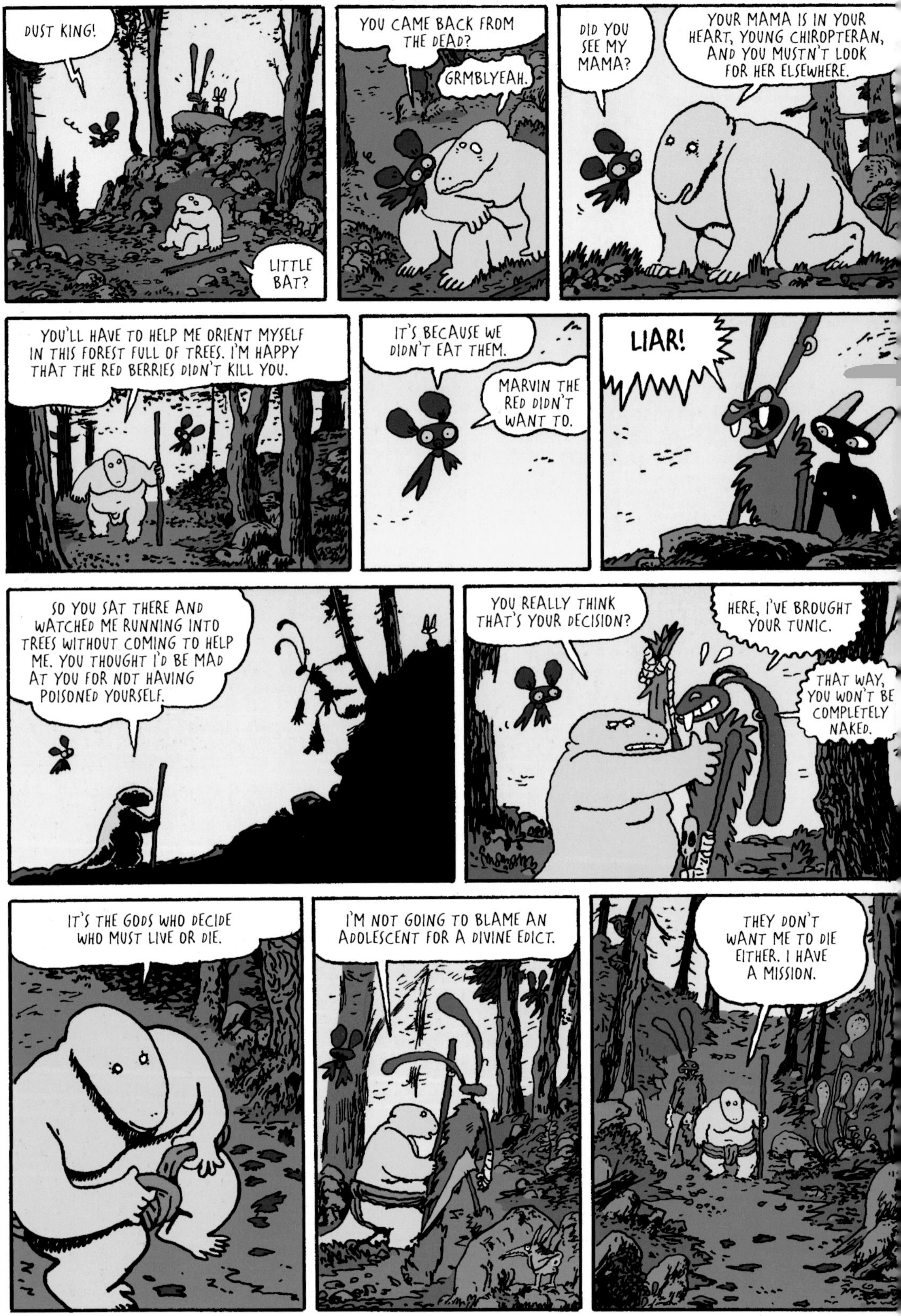
DUST KING!
LITTLE BAT?
YOU CAME BACK FROM THE DEAD?
GRMBLYEAH.
DID YOU SEE MY MAMA?
YOUR MAMA IS IN YOUR HEART, YOUNG CHIROPTERAN, AND YOU MUSTN'T LOOK FOR HER ELSEWHERE.
YOU'LL HAVE TO HELP ME ORIENT MYSELF IN THIS FOREST FULL OF TREES. I'M HAPPY THAT THE RED BERRIES DIDN'T KILL YOU.
IT'S BECAUSE WE DIDN'T EAT THEM.
MARVIN THE RED DIDN'T WANT TO.
LIAR!
SO YOU SAT THERE AND WATCHED ME RUNNING INTO TREES WITHOUT COMING TO HELP ME. YOU THOUGHT I'D BE MAD AT YOU FOR NOT HAVING POISONED YOURSELF.
YOU REALLY THINK THAT'S YOUR DECISION?
HERE, I'VE BROUGHT YOUR TUNIC.
THAT WAY, YOU WON'T BE COMPLETELY NAKED.
IT'S THE GODS WHO DECIDE WHO MUST LIVE OR DIE.
I'M NOT GOING TO BLAME AN ADOLESCENT FOR A DIVINE EDICT.
THEY DON'T WANT ME TO DIE EITHER. I HAVE A MISSION.

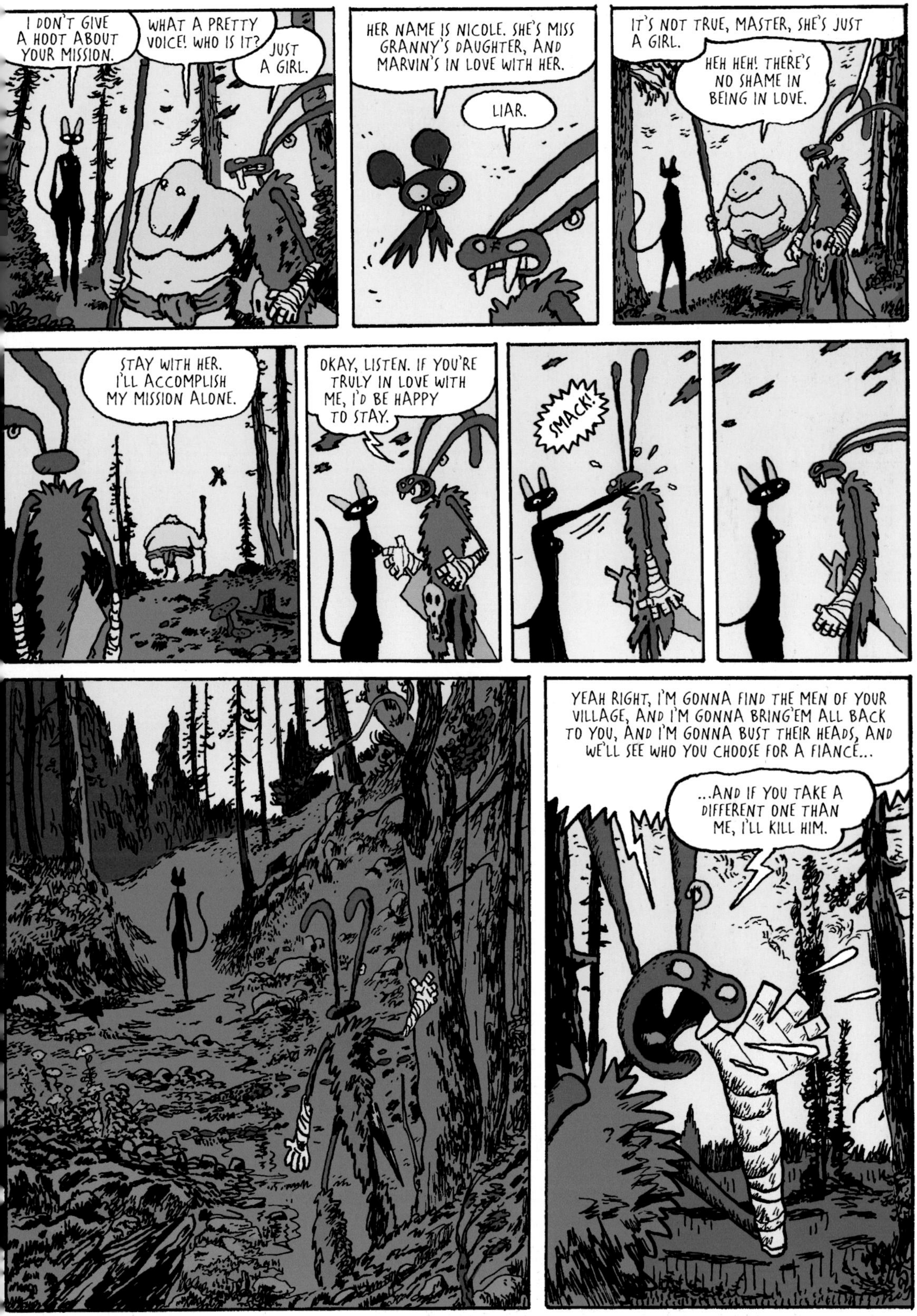
I DON'T GIVE A HOOT ABOUT YOUR MISSION.
WHAT A PRETTY VOICE! WHO IS IT?
JUST A GIRL.
HER NAME IS NICOLE. SHE'S MISS GRANNY'S DAUGHTER, AND MARVIN'S IN LOVE WITH HER.
LIAR.
IT'S NOT TRUE, MASTER, SHE'S JUST A GIRL.
HEH HEH! THERE'S NO SHAME IN BEING IN LOVE.
STAY WITH HER. I'LL ACCOMPLISH MY MISSION ALONE.
OKAY, LISTEN. IF YOU'RE TRULY IN LOVE WITH ME, I'D BE HAPPY TO STAY.
SMACK!
YEAH RIGHT, I'M GONNA FIND THE MEN OF YOUR VILLAGE, AND I'M GONNA BRING'EM ALL BACK TO YOU, AND I'M GONNA BUST THEIR HEADS, AND WE'LL SEE WHO YOU CHOOSE FOR A FIANCÉ...
...AND IF YOU TAKE A DIFFERENT ONE THAN ME, I'LL KILL HIM.

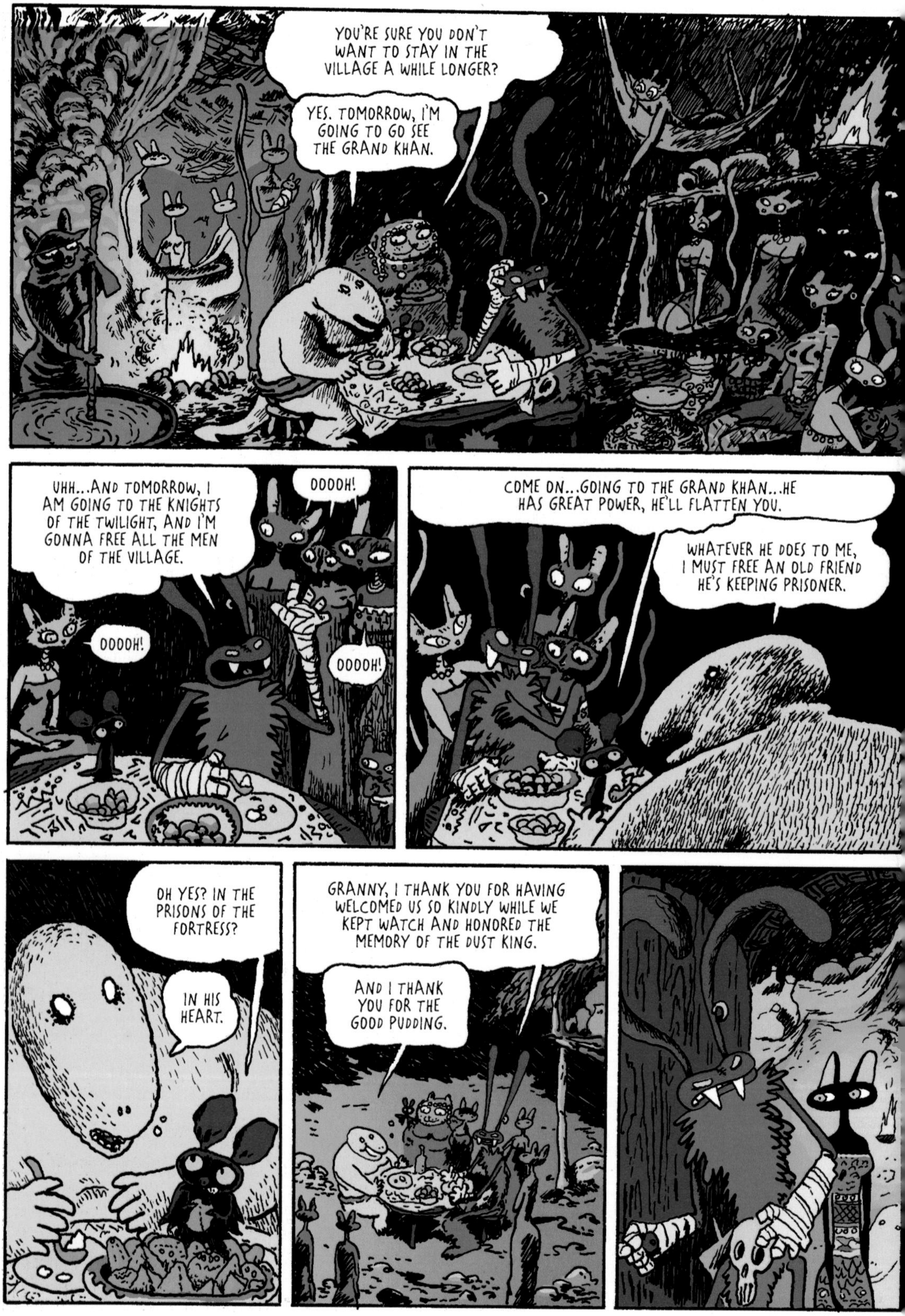
YOU'RE SURE YOU DON'T WANT TO STAY IN THE VILLAGE A WHILE LONGER?
YES. TOMORROW, I'M GOING TO GO SEE THE GRAND KHAN.
UHH...AND TOMORROW, I AM GOING TO THE KNIGHTS OF THE TWILIGHT, AND I'M GONNA FREE ALL THE MEN OF THE VILLAGE.
OOOOH!
OOOOH!
OOOOH!
COME ON...GOING TO THE GRAND KHAN...HE HAS GREAT POWER, HE'LL FLATTEN YOU.
WHATEVER HE DOES TO ME, I MUST FREE AN OLD FRIEND HE'S KEEPING PRISONER.
OH YES? IN THE PRISONS OF THE FORTRESS?
IN HIS HEART.
GRANNY, I THANK YOU FOR HAVING WELCOMED US SO KINDLY WHILE WE KEPT WATCH AND HONORED THE MEMORY OF THE DUST KING.
AND I THANK YOU FOR THE GOOD PUDDING.

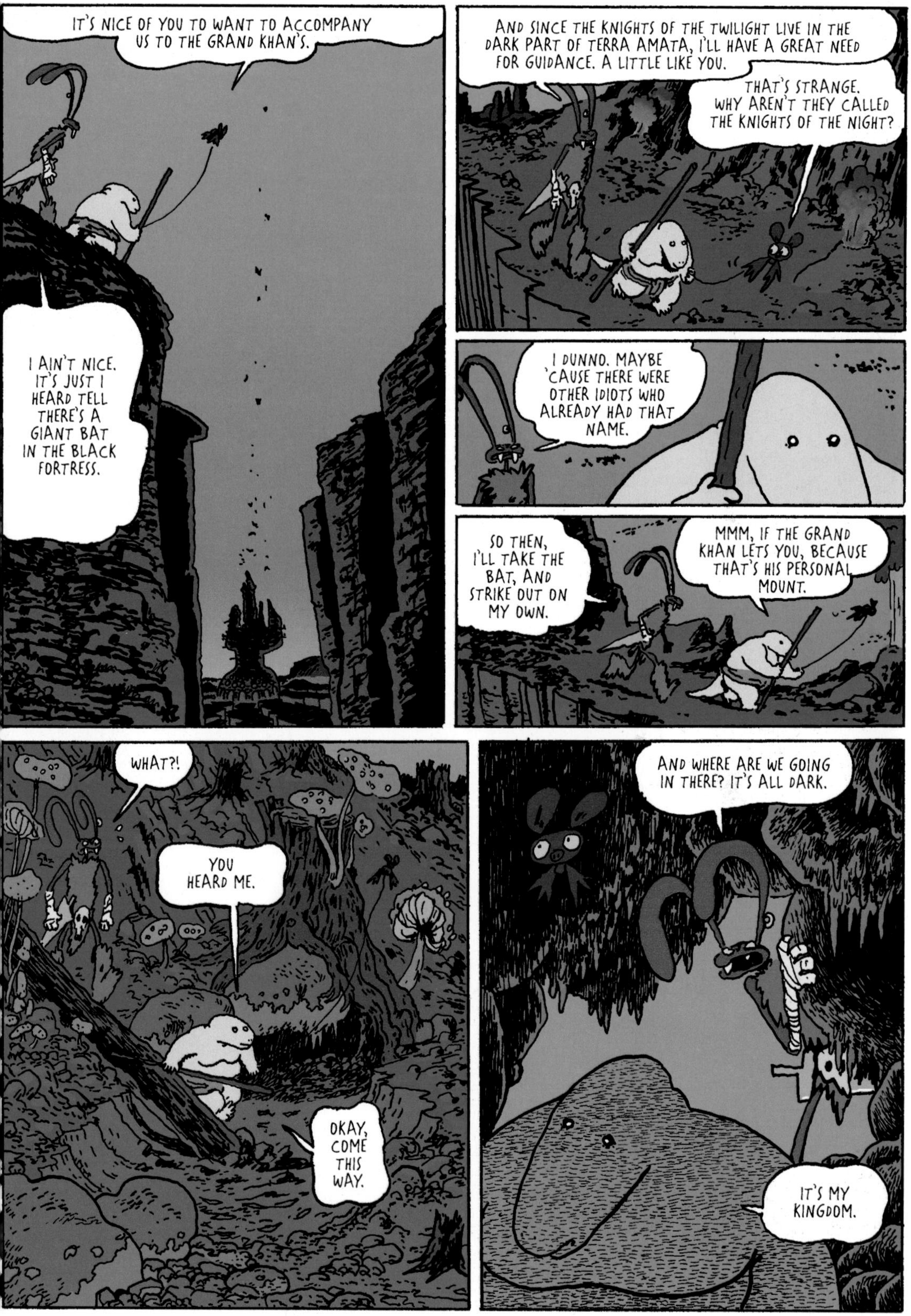
IT'S NICE OF YOU TO WANT TO ACCOMPANY US TO THE GRAND KHAN'S.
I AIN'T NICE. IT'S JUST I HEARD TELL THERE'S A GIANT BAT IN THE BLACK FORTRESS.
AND SINCE THE KNIGHTS OF THE TWILIGHT LIVE IN THE DARK PART OF TERRA AMATA, I'LL HAVE A GREAT NEED FOR GUIDANCE. A LITTLE LIKE YOU.
THAT'S STRANGE. WHY AREN'T THEY CALLED THE KNIGHTS OF THE NIGHT?
I DUNNO. MAYBE 'CAUSE THERE WERE OTHER IDIOTS WHO ALREADY HAD THAT NAME.
SO THEN, I'LL TAKE THE BAT, AND STRIKE OUT ON MY OWN.
MMM, IF THE GRAND KHAN LETS YOU, BECAUSE THAT'S HIS PERSONAL MOUNT.
WHAT?!
YOU HEARD ME.
OKAY, COME THIS WAY.
AND WHERE ARE WE GOING IN THERE? IT'S ALL DARK.
IT'S MY KINGDOM.

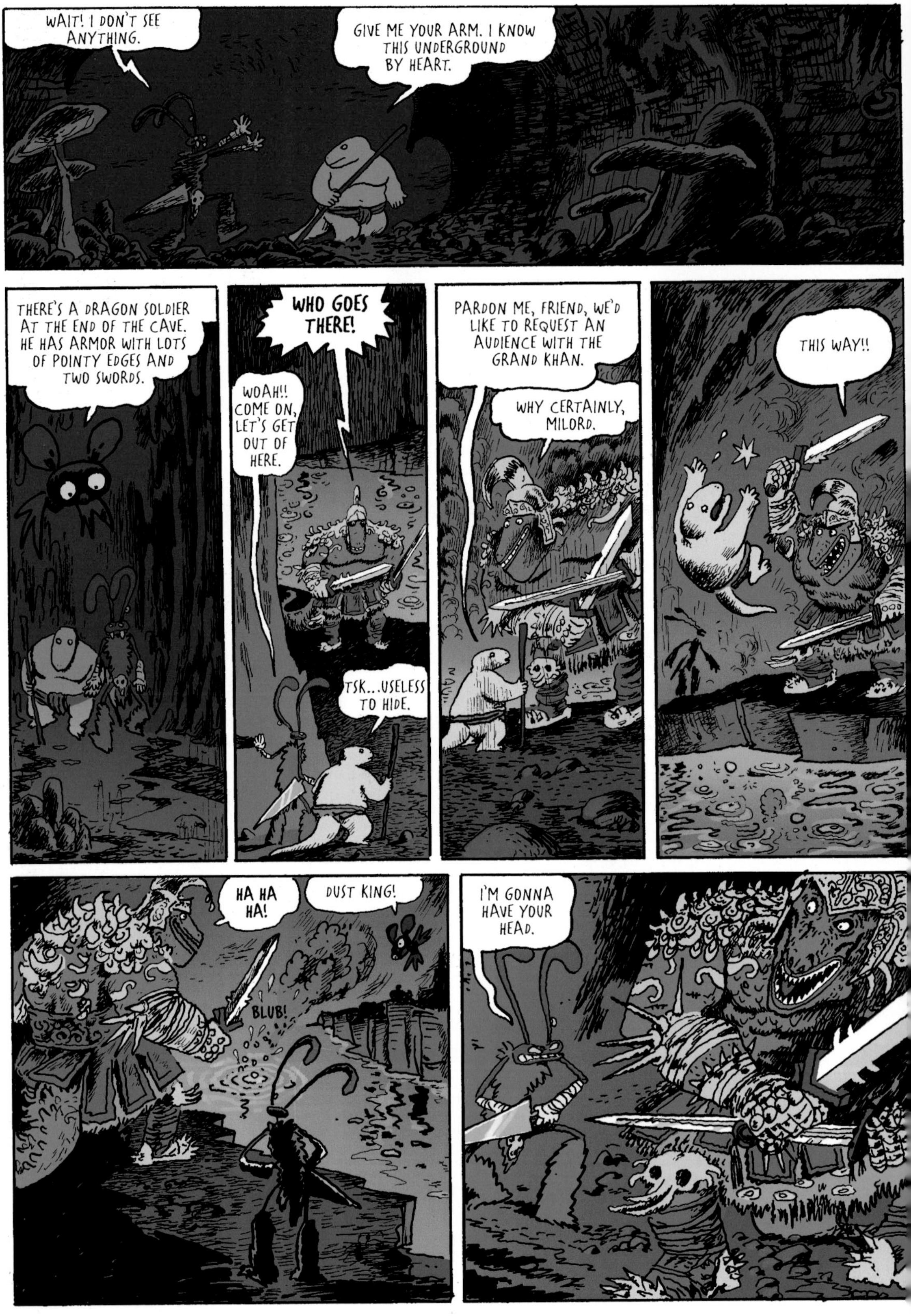
WAIT! I DON'T SEE ANYTHING.
GIVE ME YOUR ARM. I KNOW THIS UNDERGROUND BY HEART.
THERE'S A DRAGON SOLDIER AT THE END OF THE CAVE. HE HAS ARMOR WITH LOTS OF POINTY EDGES AND TWO SWORDS.
WHO GOES THERE!
WOAH!! COME ON, LET'S GET OUT OF HERE.
TSK...USELESS TO HIDE.
PARDON ME, FRIEND, WE'D LIKE TO REQUEST AN AUDIENCE WITH THE GRAND KHAN.
WHY CERTAINLY, MILORD.
THIS WAY!!
HA HA HA!
DUST KING!
BLUB!
I'M GONNA HAVE YOUR HEAD.

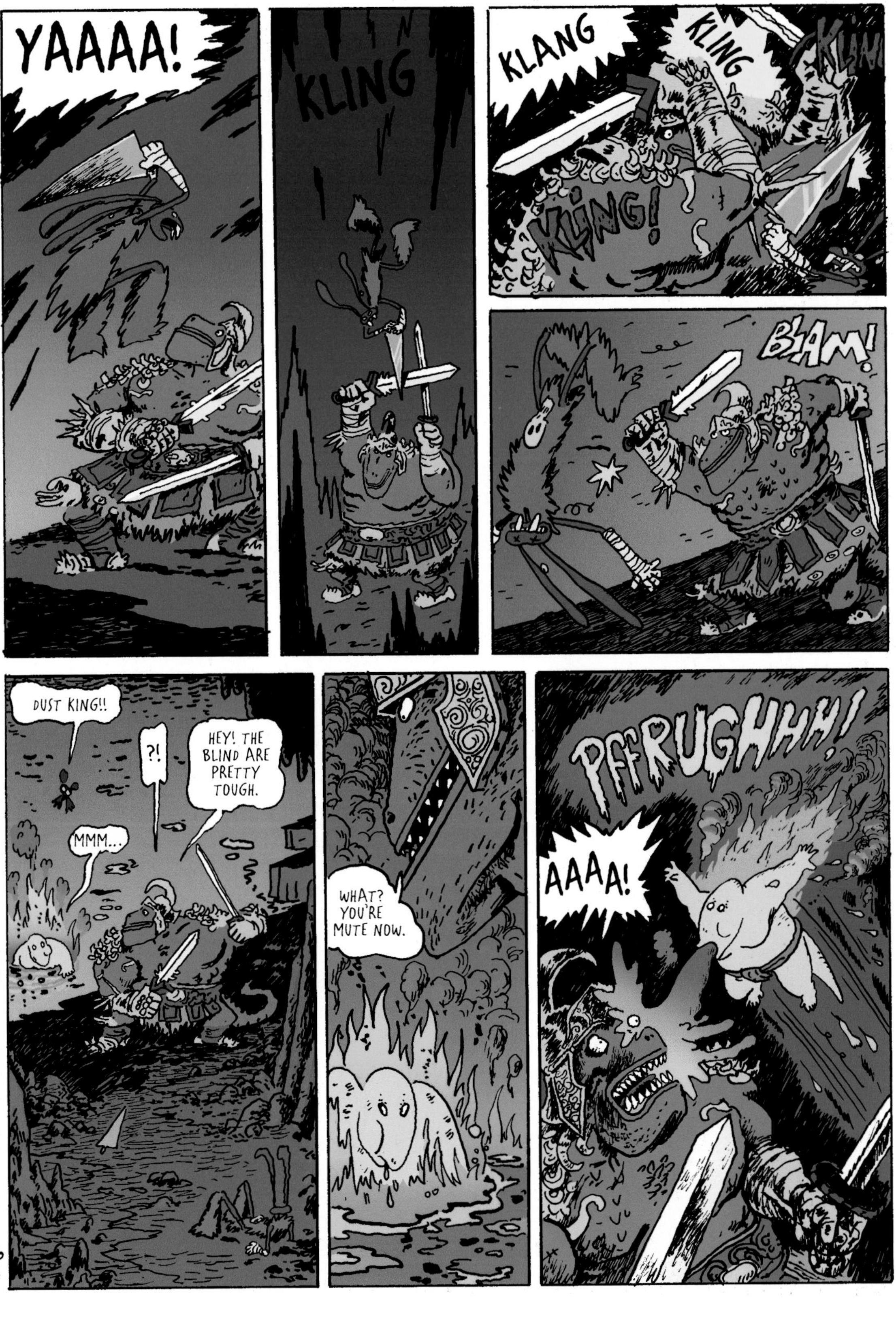
YAAAA!
KLING
KLANG
KLING
KLING!
BLAM!
DUST KING!!
?!
HEY! THE BLIND ARE PRETTY TOUGH.
MMM...
WHAT? YOU'RE MUTE NOW.
PFFRUGHHH!
AAAA!

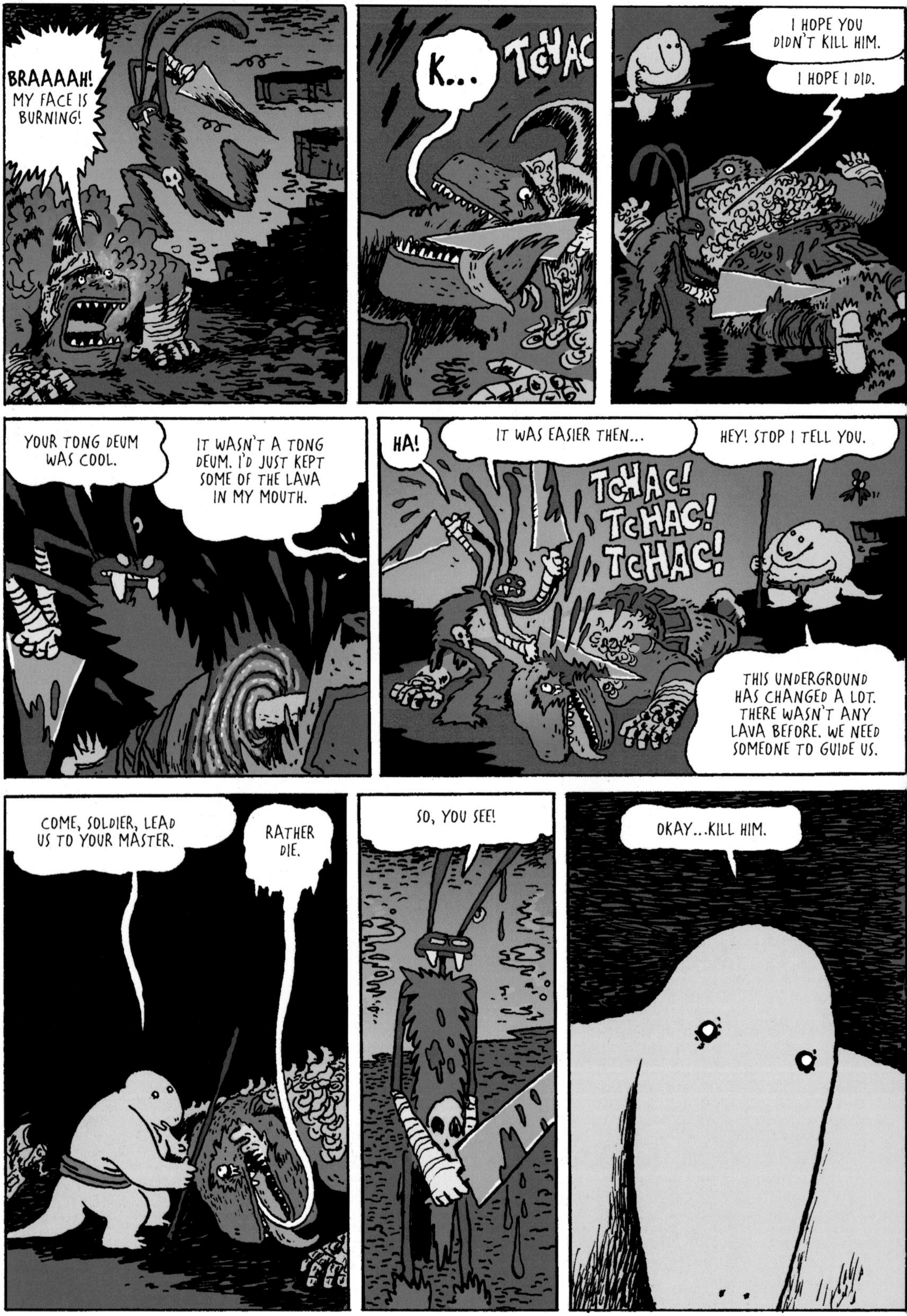
BRAAAAH! MY FACE IS BURNING!
K...
TCHAC
I HOPE YOU DIDN'T KILL HIM.
I HOPE I DID.
YOUR TONG DEUM WAS COOL.
IT WASN'T A TONG DEUM. I'D JUST KEPT SOME OF THE LAVA IN MY MOUTH.
HA!
IT WAS EASIER THEN...
HEY! STOP I TELL YOU.
TCHAC! TCHAC! TCHAC!
THIS UNDERGROUND HAS CHANGED A LOT. THERE WASN'T ANY LAVA BEFORE. WE NEED SOMEONE TO GUIDE US.
COME, SOLDIER, LEAD US TO YOUR MASTER.
RATHER DIE.
SO, YOU SEE!
OKAY...KILL HIM.

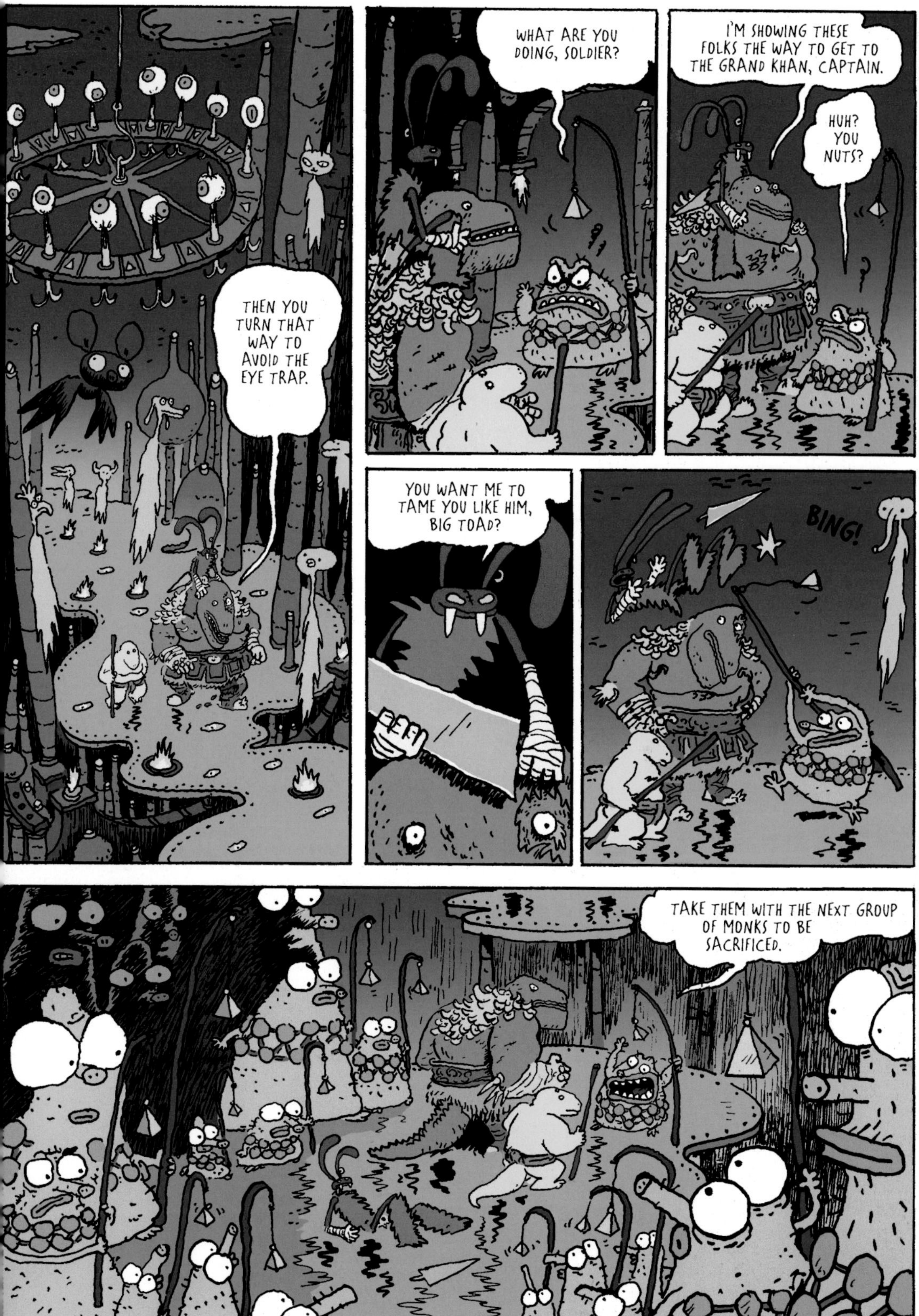
THEN YOU TURN THAT WAY TO AVOID THE EYE TRAP.
WHAT ARE YOU DOING, SOLDIER?
I'M SHOWING THESE FOLKS THE WAY TO GET TO THE GRAND KHAN, CAPTAIN.
HUH? YOU NUTS?
YOU WANT ME TO TAME YOU LIKE HIM, BIG TOAD?
BING!
TAKE THEM WITH THE NEXT GROUP OF MONKS TO BE SACRIFICED.

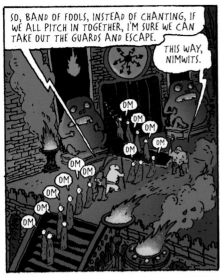

SO, BAND OF FOOLS, INSTEAD OF CHANTING, IF WE ALL PITCH IN TOGETHER, I'M SURE WE CAN TAKE OUT THE GUARDS AND ESCAPE.

THIS WAY, NIMWITS.

OM OM OM OM OM OM OM OM OM OM OM OM OM

DROP IT. THESE MONKS ARE VOLUNTEERS TO GET THEMSELVES KILLED. INDEED, IT'S THE ONLY THING OF INTEREST TO THEM.

FOR HIS DARK DESIGNS, THE GRAND KHAN NEEDS THE ENERGY FROM THE PEOPLE HE KILLS.

THAT'S WHY HE CREATED THIS RELIGION THAT SUPPLIES HIM WITH VOLUNTEERS TO SACRIFICE. A GLIMMER OF HUMANITY MAKES HIM RARELY USE FOLKS AGAINST THEIR WILL.

WHO CARES. HOW DO WE GET OUT OF HERE?

I'M GONNA TALK TO HIM. I HOPE HE'LL LISTEN TO ME.

YOU HOPE?

WELCOME TO YOUR DIVINE SACRIFICE.

LINE YOURSELVES UP AND I WON'T MAKE YOU SUFFER.

SO ARE YOU TALKING TO HIM OR WHAT?

WHEN IT'S MY TURN.

YOU ARE THE WISE AMONGST THE WISE. THE KINGDOM OF THE HEAVENS IS YOURS.

AMEN.

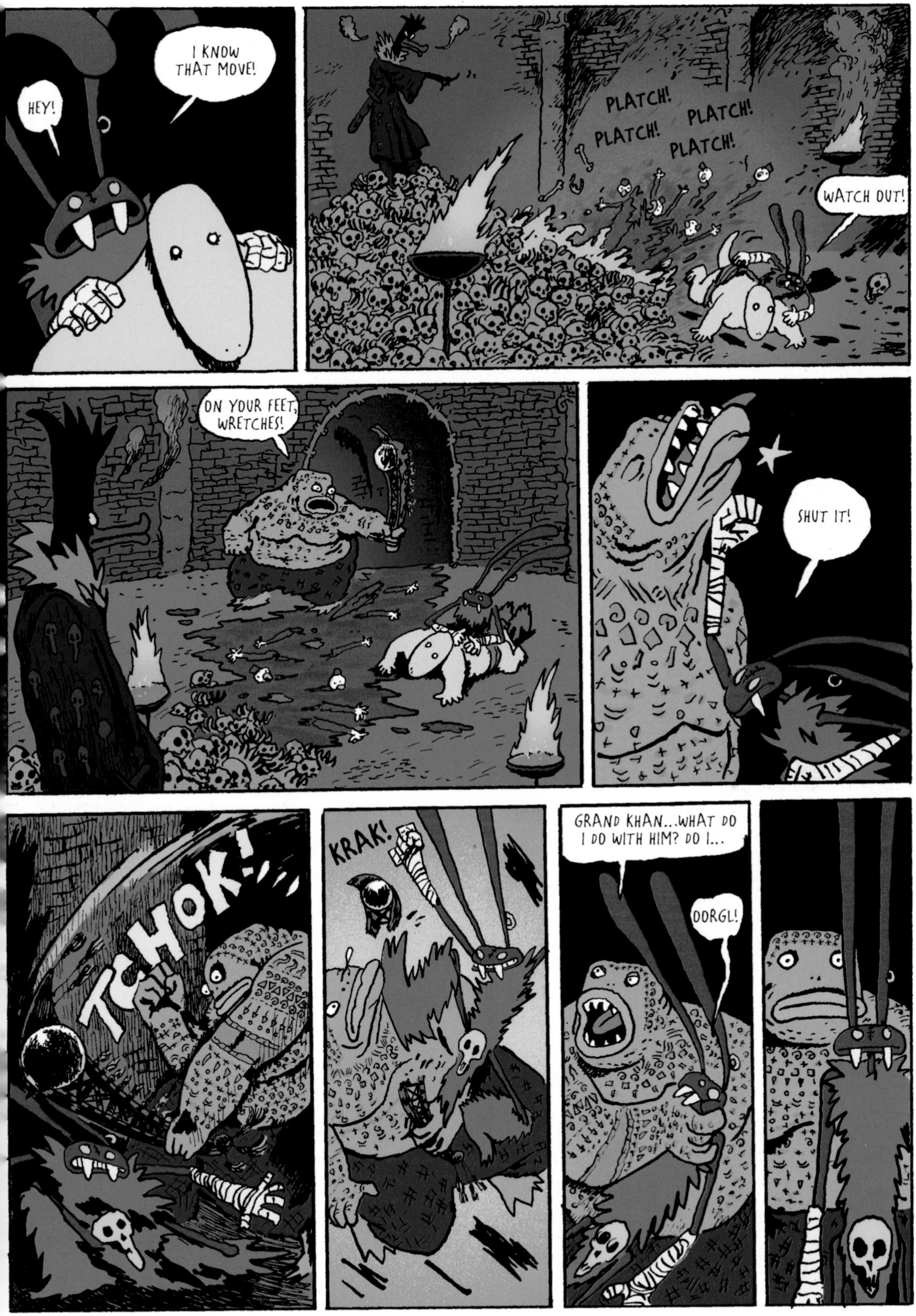
HEY!
I KNOW THAT MOVE!
PLATCH! PLATCH! PLATCH! PLATCH!
WATCH OUT!
ON YOUR FEET, WRETCHES!
SHUT IT!
TCHOK!
KRAK!
GRAND KHAN...WHAT DO I DO WITH HIM? DO I...
OORGL!

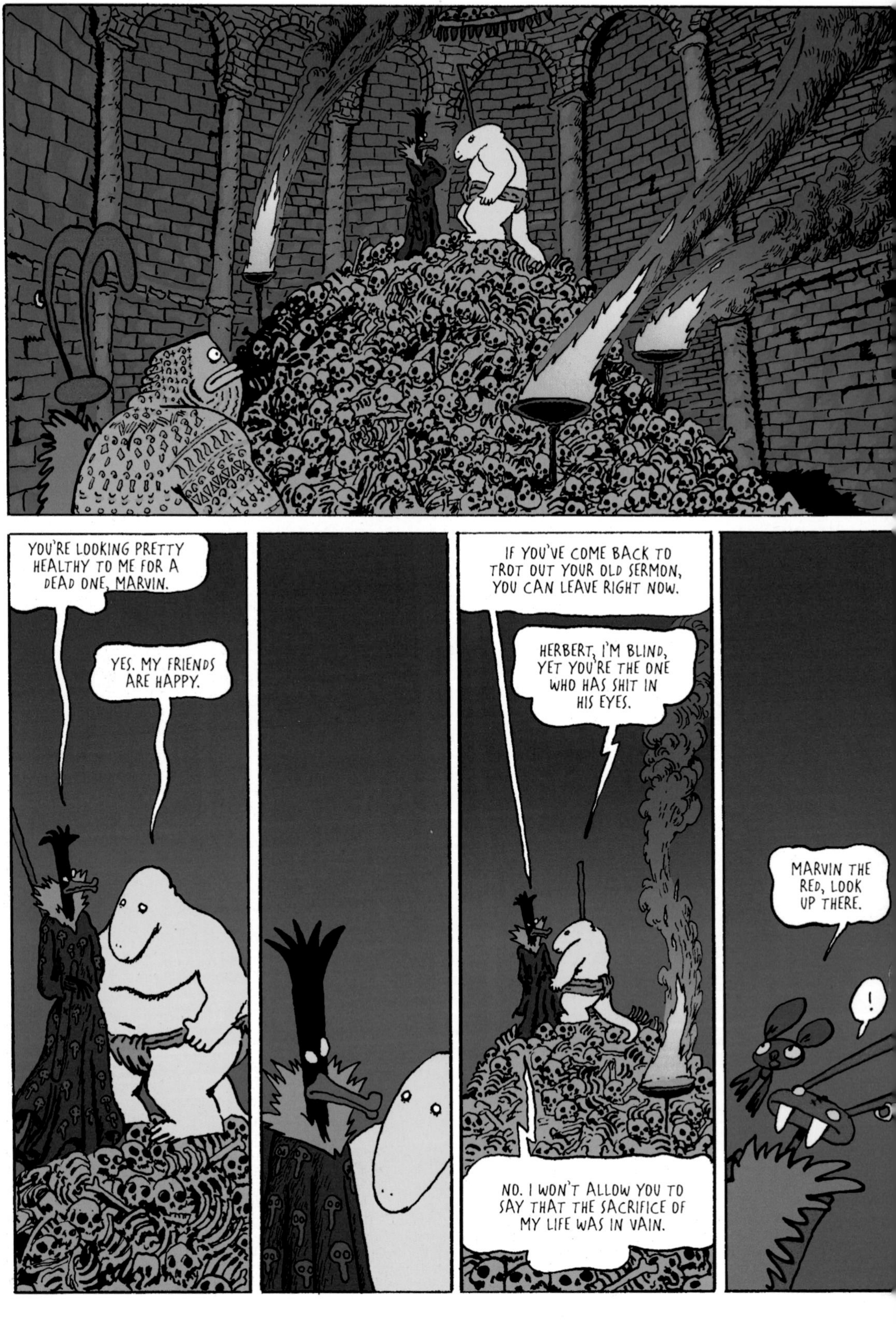
YOU'RE LOOKING PRETTY HEALTHY TO ME FOR A DEAD ONE, MARVIN.
YES. MY FRIENDS ARE HAPPY.
IF YOU'VE COME BACK TO TROT OUT YOUR OLD SERMON, YOU CAN LEAVE RIGHT NOW.
HERBERT, I'M BLIND, YET YOU'RE THE ONE WHO HAS SHIT IN HIS EYES.
NO. I WON'T ALLOW YOU TO SAY THAT THE SACRIFICE OF MY LIFE WAS IN VAIN.
MARVIN THE RED, LOOK UP THERE.
!

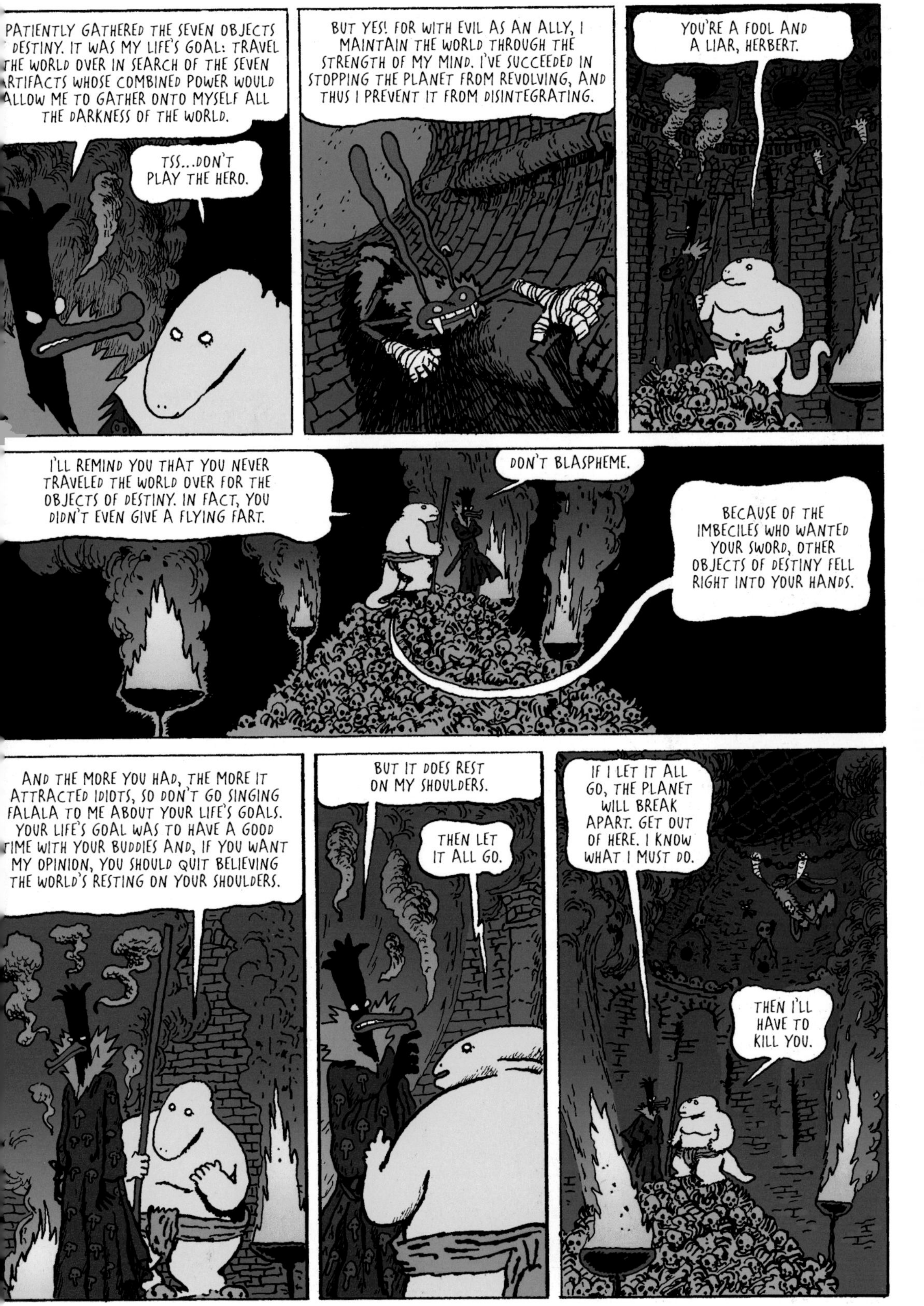
PATIENTLY GATHERED THE SEVEN OBJECTS DESTINY. IT WAS MY LIFE'S GOAL: TRAVEL THE WORLD OVER IN SEARCH OF THE SEVEN RTIFACTS WHOSE COMBINED POWER WOULD ALLOW ME TO GATHER ONTO MYSELF ALL THE DARKNESS OF THE WORLD.
TSS...DON'T PLAY THE HERO.
BUT YES! FOR WITH EVIL AS AN ALLY, I MAINTAIN THE WORLD THROUGH THE STRENGTH OF MY MIND. I'VE SUCCEEDED IN STOPPING THE PLANET FROM REVOLVING, AND THUS I PREVENT IT FROM DISINTEGRATING.
YOU'RE A FOOL AND A LIAR, HERBERT.
I'LL REMIND YOU THAT YOU NEVER TRAVELED THE WORLD OVER FOR THE OBJECTS OF DESTINY. IN FACT, YOU DIDN'T EVEN GIVE A FLYING FART.
DON'T BLASPHEME.
BECAUSE OF THE IMBECILES WHO WANTED YOUR SWORD, OTHER OBJECTS OF DESTINY FELL RIGHT INTO YOUR HANDS.
AND THE MORE YOU HAD, THE MORE IT ATTRACTED IDIOTS, SO DON'T GO SINGING FALALA TO ME ABOUT YOUR LIFE'S GOALS. YOUR LIFE'S GOAL WAS TO HAVE A GOOD TIME WITH YOUR BUDDIES AND, IF YOU WANT MY OPINION, YOU SHOULD QUIT BELIEVING THE WORLD'S RESTING ON YOUR SHOULDERS.
BUT IT DOES REST ON MY SHOULDERS.
THEN LET IT ALL GO.
IF I LET IT ALL GO, THE PLANET WILL BREAK APART. GET OUT OF HERE. I KNOW WHAT I MUST DO.
THEN I'LL HAVE TO KILL YOU.

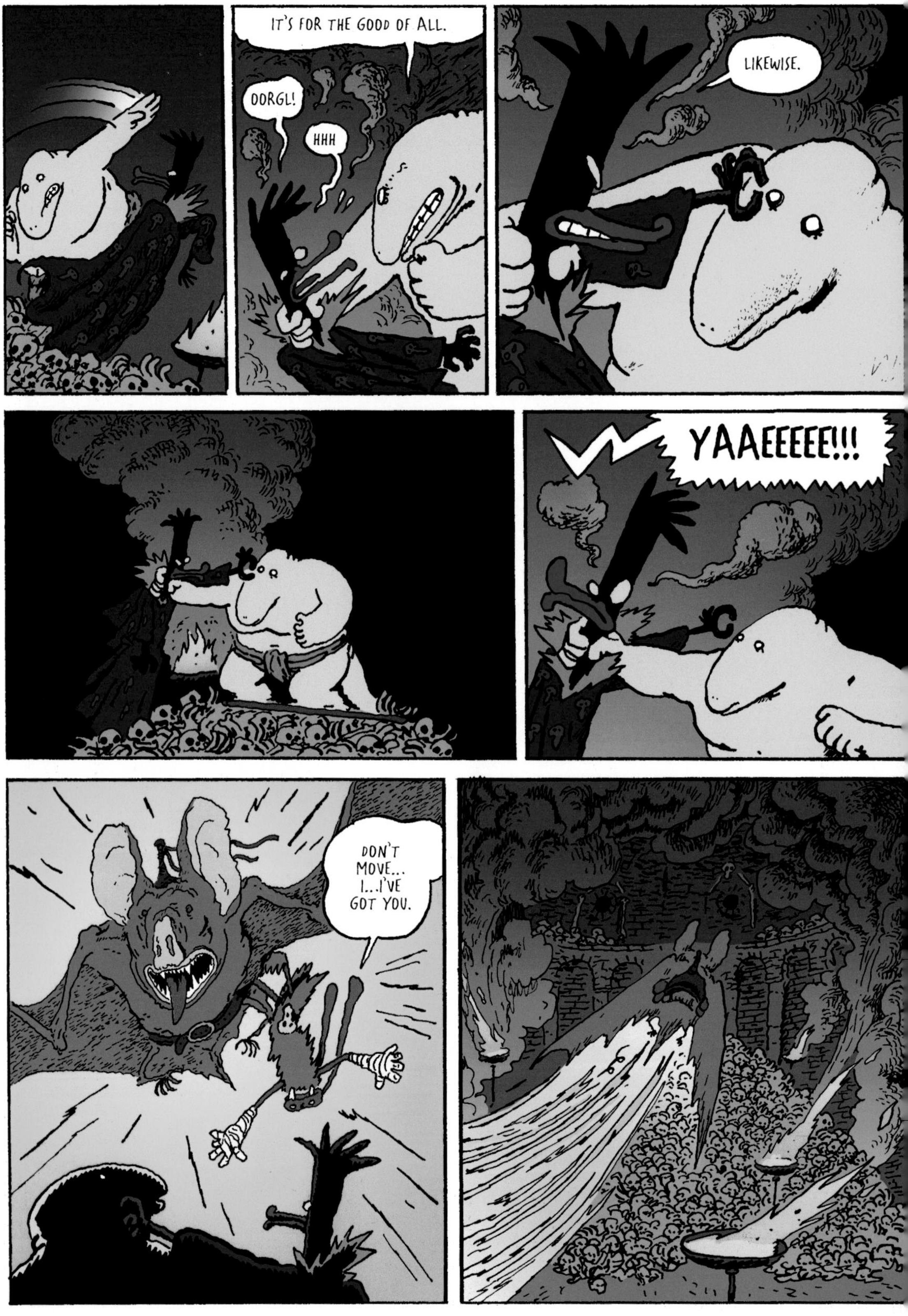
IT'S FOR THE GOOD OF ALL.
DORGL!
HHH
LIKEWISE.
YAAEEEEE!!!
DON'T MOVE... I...I'VE GOT YOU.

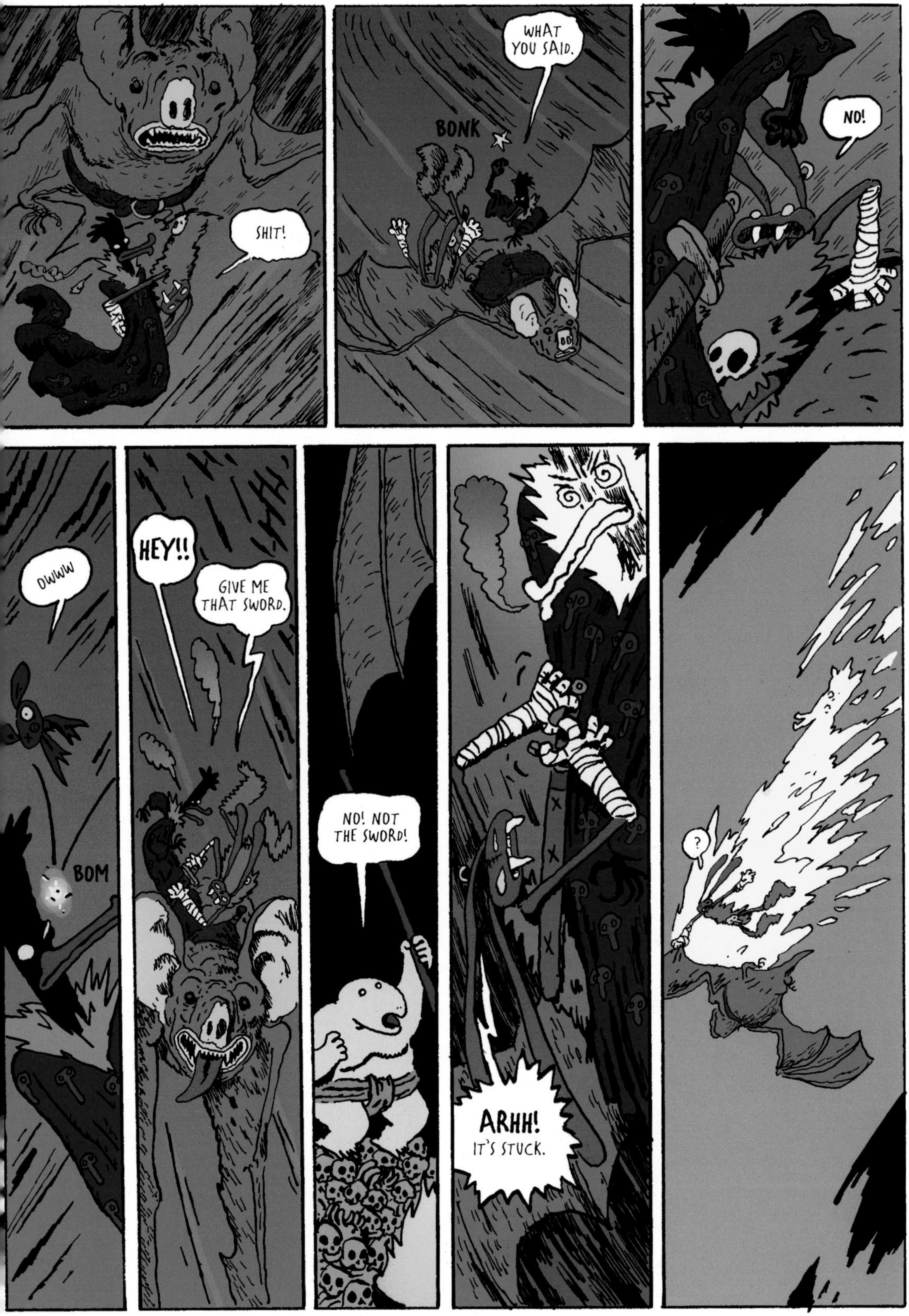
SHIT!
BONK
WHAT YOU SAID.
NO!
OWWW
BOM
HEY!!
GIVE ME THAT SWORD.
NO! NOT THE SWORD!
ARHH!
IT'S STUCK.
?

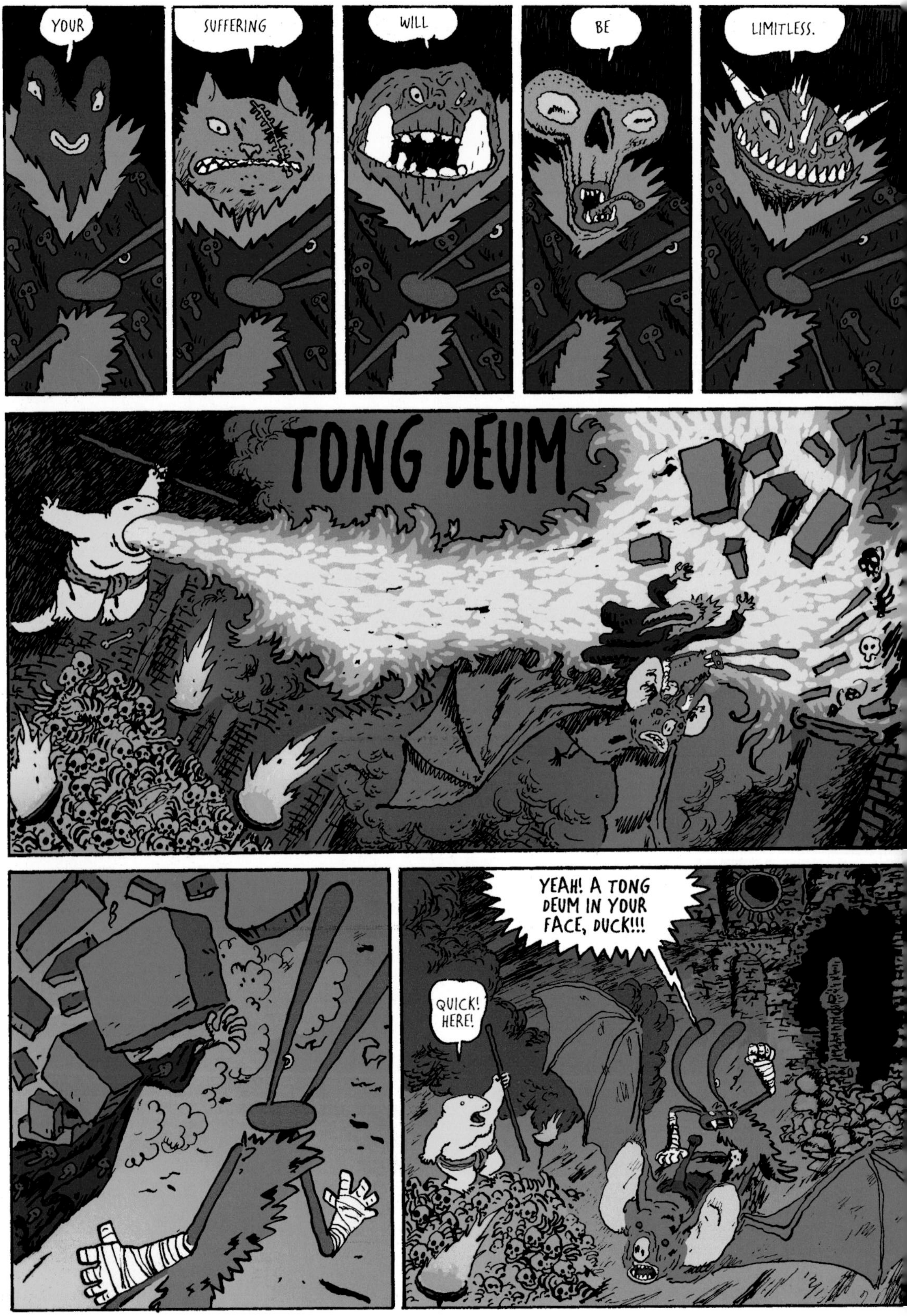
YOUR
SUFFERING
WILL
BE
LIMITLESS.
TONG DEUM
YEAH! A TONG DEUM IN YOUR FACE, DUCK!!!
QUICK! HERE!

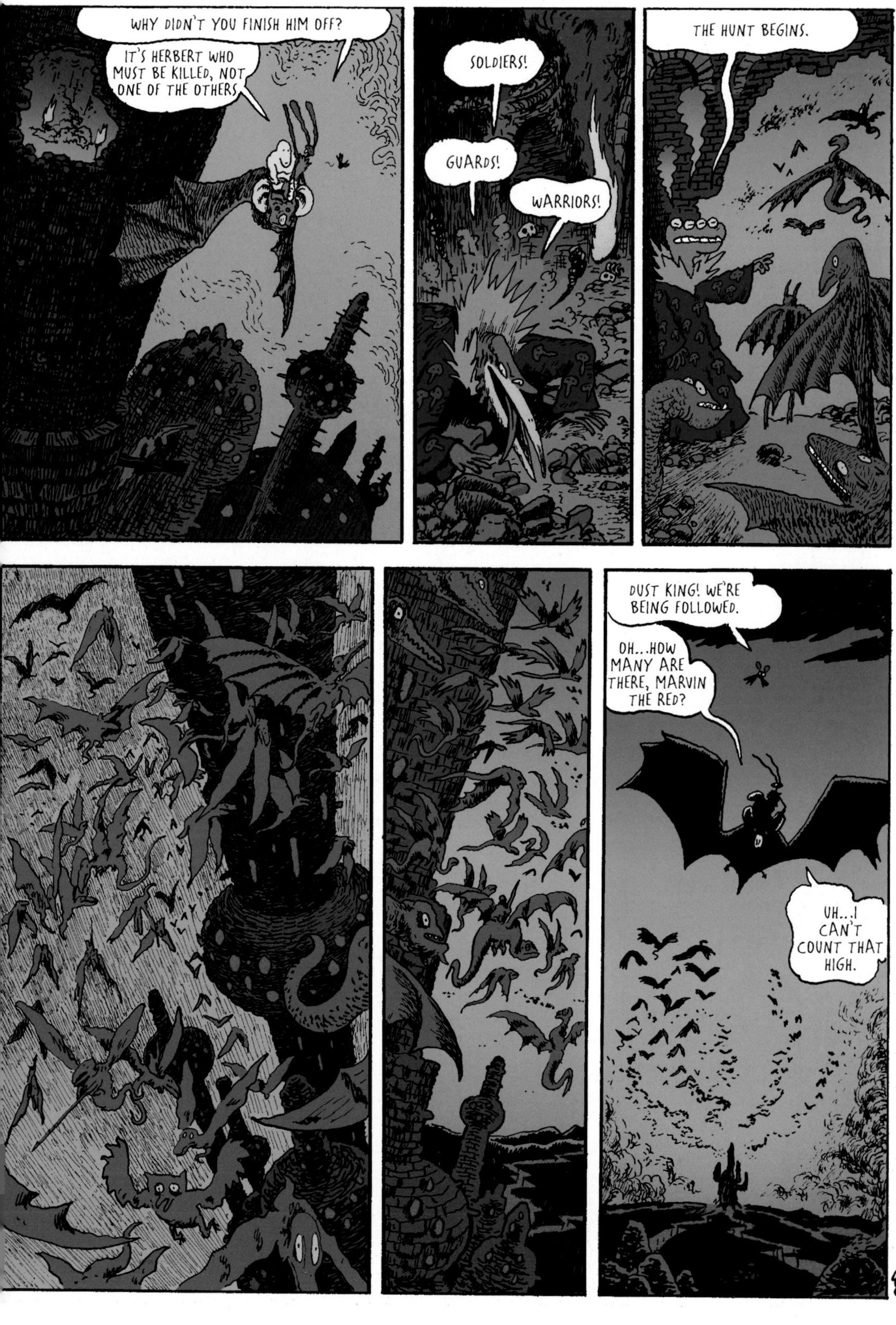
WHY DIDN'T YOU FINISH HIM OFF?
IT'S HERBERT WHO MUST BE KILLED, NOT ONE OF THE OTHERS.
SOLDIERS!
GUARDS!
WARRIORS!
THE HUNT BEGINS.
DUST KING! WE'RE BEING FOLLOWED.
OH...HOW MANY ARE THERE, MARVIN THE RED?
UH...I CAN'T COUNT THAT HIGH.

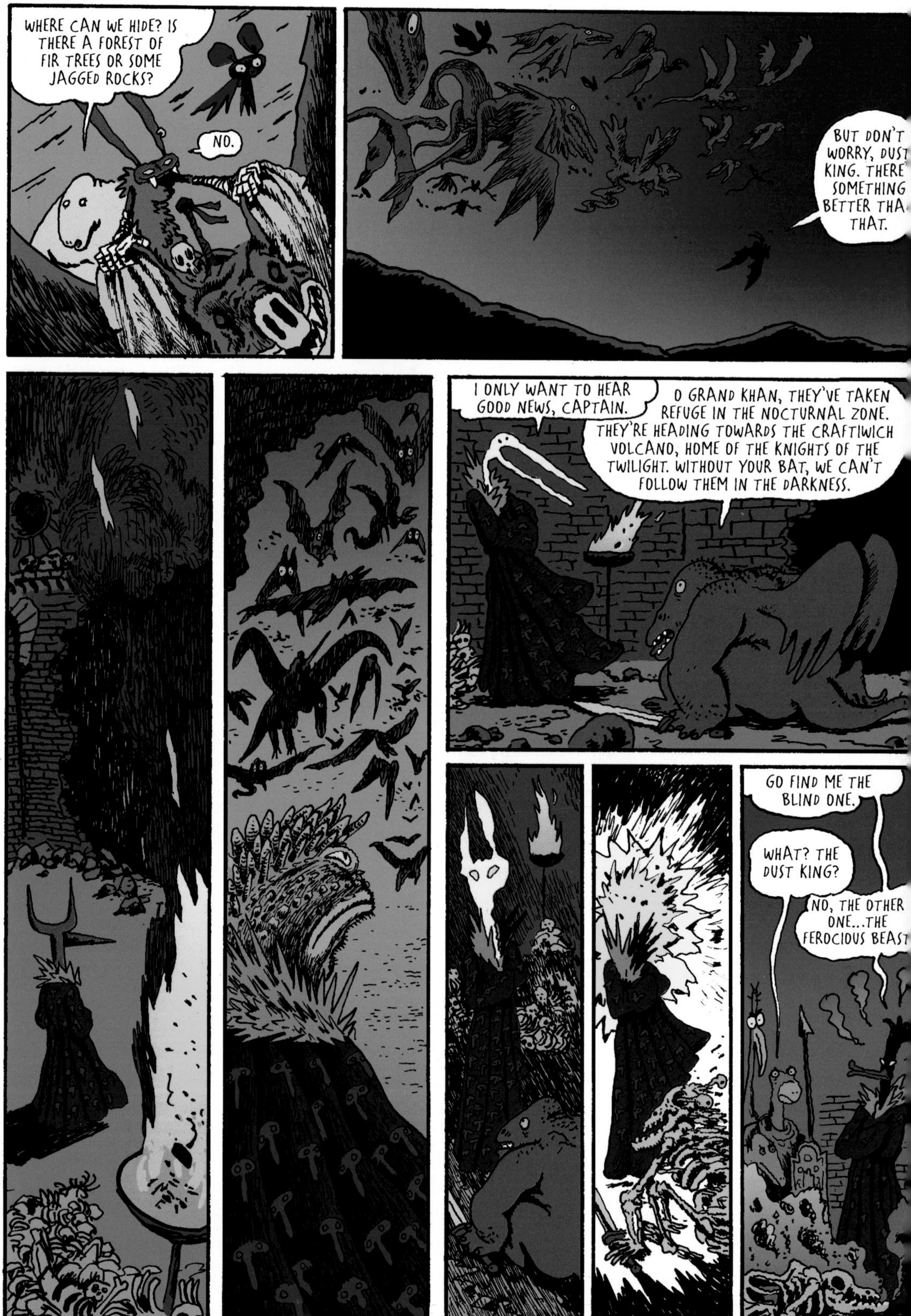
WHERE CAN WE HIDE? IS THERE A FOREST OF FIR TREES OR SOME JAGGED ROCKS?
NO.
BUT DON'T WORRY, DUST KING. THERE' SOMETHING BETTER THA THAT.
I ONLY WANT TO HEAR GOOD NEWS, CAPTAIN.
O GRAND KHAN, THEY'VE TAKEN REFUGE IN THE NOCTURNAL ZONE. THEY'RE HEADING TOWARDS THE CRAFTIWICH VOLCANO, HOME OF THE KNIGHTS OF THE TWILIGHT. WITHOUT YOUR BAT, WE CAN'T FOLLOW THEM IN THE DARKNESS.
GO FIND ME THE BLIND ONE.
WHAT? THE DUST KING?
NO, THE OTHER ONE...THE FEROCIOUS BEAST

THE ADJUSTMENTS WITH THE NITRO ARE MORE DELICATE THAN WITH DYNAMITE, GRAND DUKE.

I KNOW THEY'LL MANAGE. THEY HAVE NO CHOICE.

BOMBA!

BOMBA!

GRAND DUKE! THE GRAND KHAN'S MOUNT APPROACHES.

MMM...A SURPRISE VISIT... THAT'S JUST MY FATHER'S STYLE.

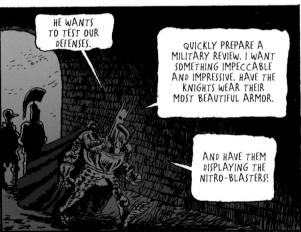

HE WANTS TO TEST OUR DEFENSES.

QUICKLY PREPARE A MILITARY REVIEW. I WANT SOMETHING IMPECCABLE AND IMPRESSIVE. HAVE THE KNIGHTS WEAR THEIR MOST BEAUTIFUL ARMOR.

AND HAVE THEM DISPLAYING THE NITRO-BLASTERS!

THE NITRO-BLASTERS STILL AREN'T READY TO FUNCTION CORRECTLY, GRAND DUKE.

DOESN'T MATTER. IT'S ENOUGH FOR MY FATHER TO BELIEVE THEY DO.

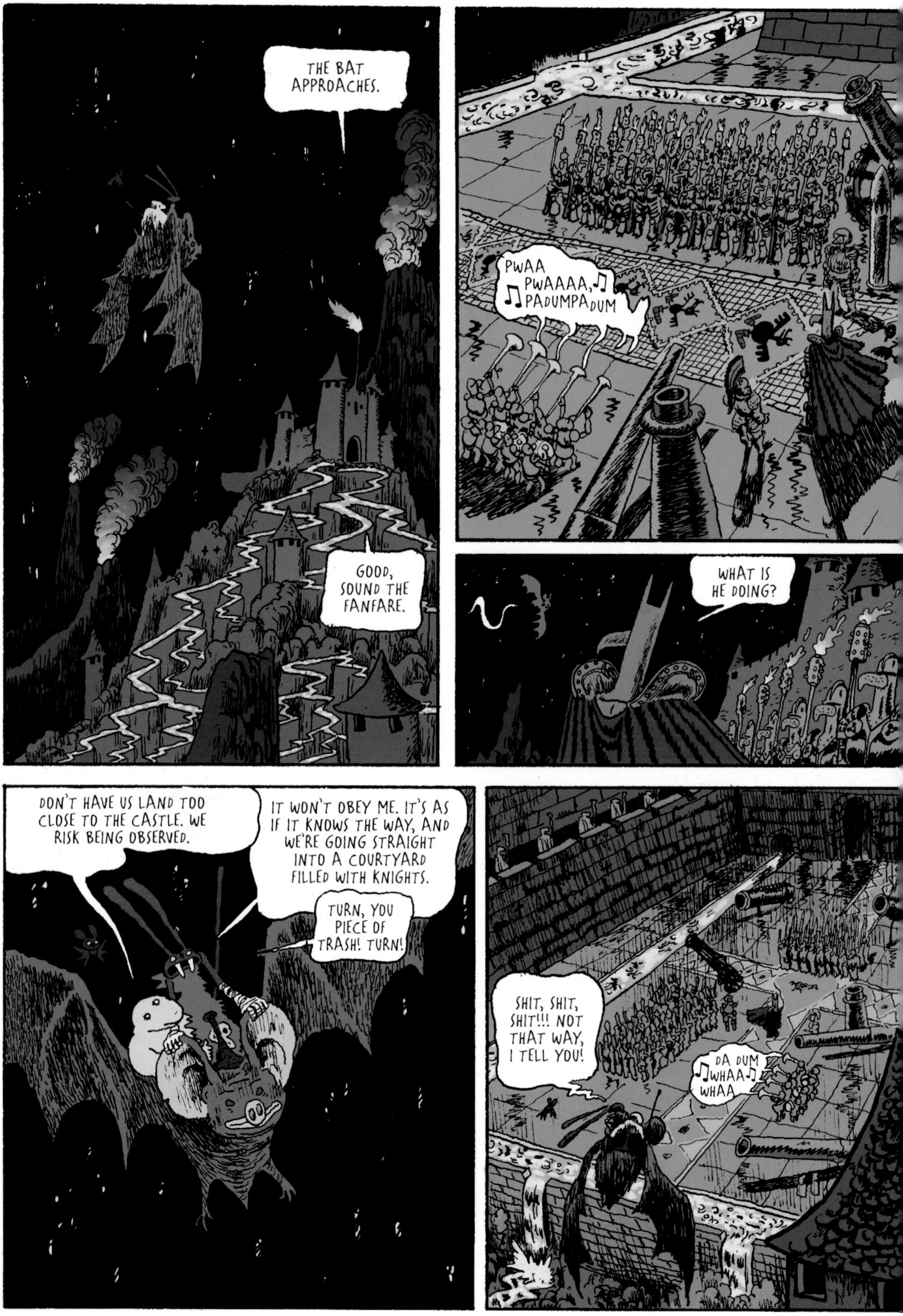
THE BAT APPROACHES.
GOOD, SOUND THE FANFARE.
PWAA PWAAAA, ♫ ♫ PADUMPA DUM
WHAT IS HE DOING?
DON'T HAVE US LAND TOO CLOSE TO THE CASTLE. WE RISK BEING OBSERVED.
IT WON'T OBEY ME. IT'S AS IF IT KNOWS THE WAY, AND WE'RE GOING STRAIGHT INTO A COURTYARD FILLED WITH KNIGHTS.
TURN, YOU PIECE OF TRASH! TURN!
SHIT, SHIT, SHIT!!! NOT THAT WAY, I TELL YOU!
DA DUM ♫ WHAA ♫ WHAA

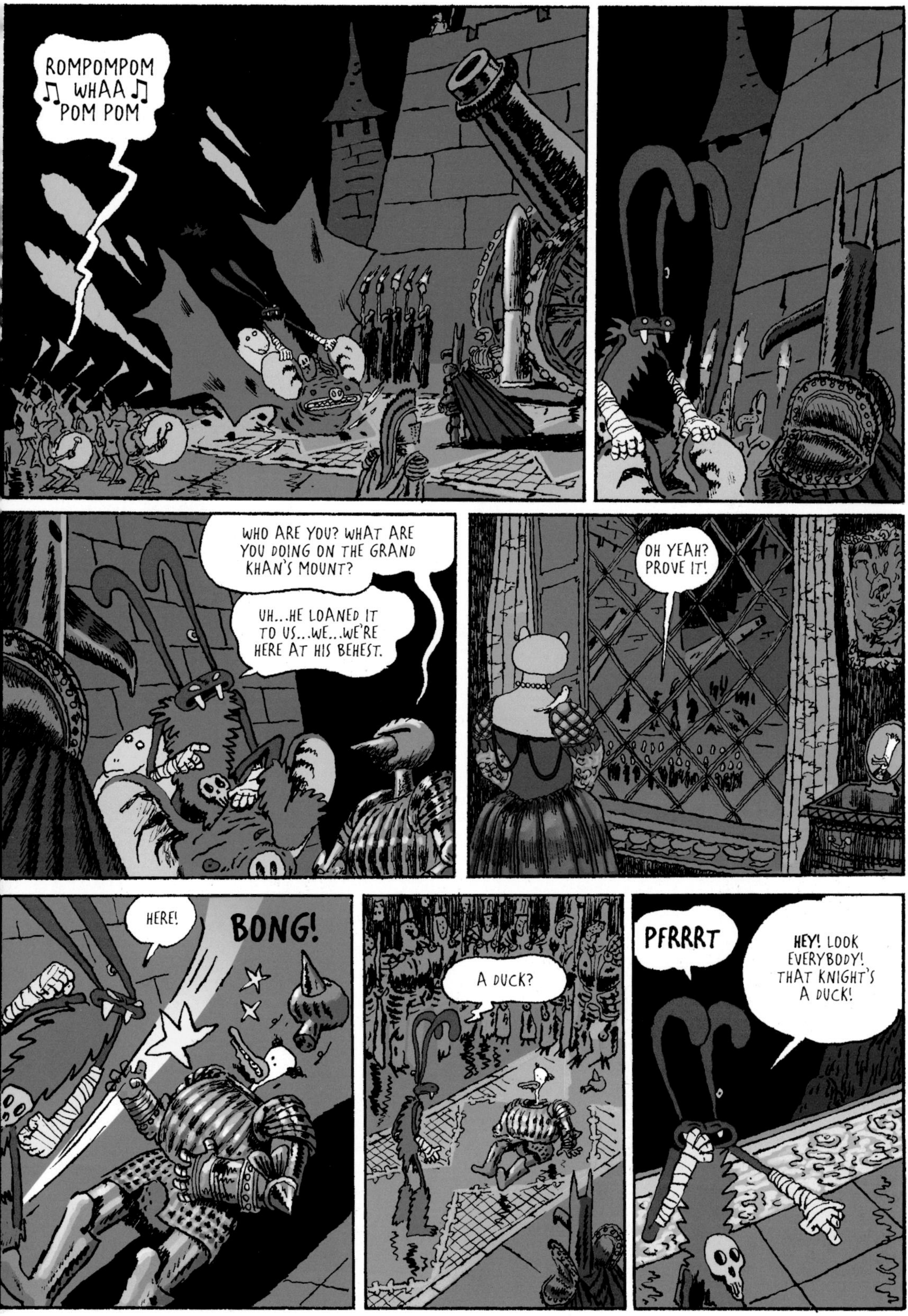
ROMPOMPOM ♫ WHAA ♫ POM POM
WHO ARE YOU? WHAT ARE YOU DOING ON THE GRAND KHAN'S MOUNT?
UH...HE LOANED IT TO US...WE...WE'RE HERE AT HIS BEHEST.
OH YEAH? PROVE IT!
HERE!
BONG!
A DUCK?
PFRRRT
HEY! LOOK EVERYBODY! THAT KNIGHT'S A DUCK!

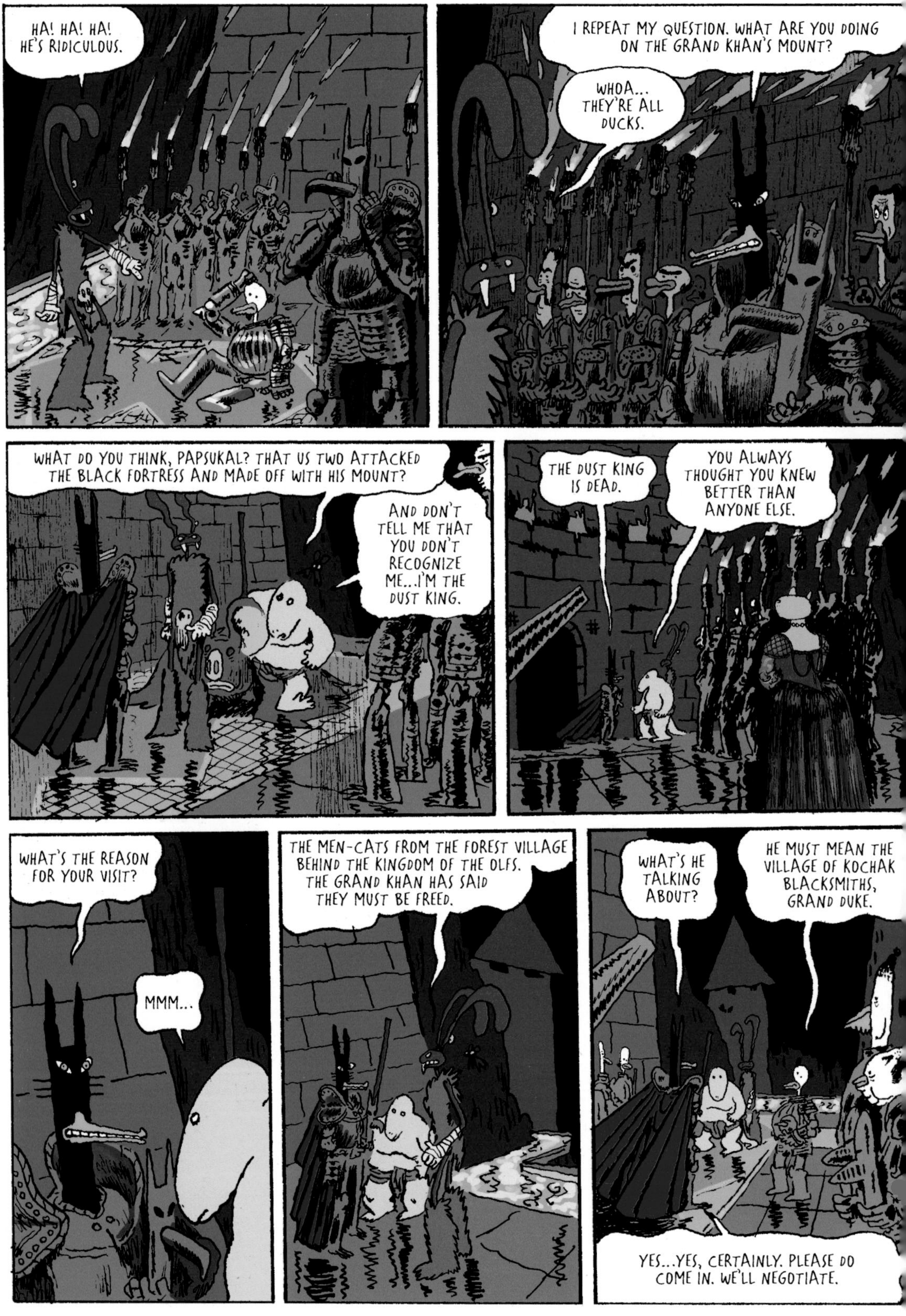
HA! HA! HA! HE'S RIDICULOUS.
I REPEAT MY QUESTION. WHAT ARE YOU DOING ON THE GRAND KHAN'S MOUNT?
WHOA... THEY'RE ALL DUCKS.
WHAT DO YOU THINK, PAPSUKAL? THAT US TWO ATTACKED THE BLACK FORTRESS AND MADE OFF WITH HIS MOUNT?
AND DON'T TELL ME THAT YOU DON'T RECOGNIZE ME...I'M THE DUST KING.
THE DUST KING IS DEAD.
YOU ALWAYS THOUGHT YOU KNEW BETTER THAN ANYONE ELSE.
WHAT'S THE REASON FOR YOUR VISIT?
MMM...
THE MEN-CATS FROM THE FOREST VILLAGE BEHIND THE KINGDOM OF THE OLFS. THE GRAND KHAN HAS SAID THEY MUST BE FREED.
WHAT'S HE TALKING ABOUT?
HE MUST MEAN THE VILLAGE OF KOCHAK BLACKSMITHS, GRAND DUKE.
YES...YES, CERTAINLY. PLEASE DO COME IN. WE'LL NEGOTIATE.

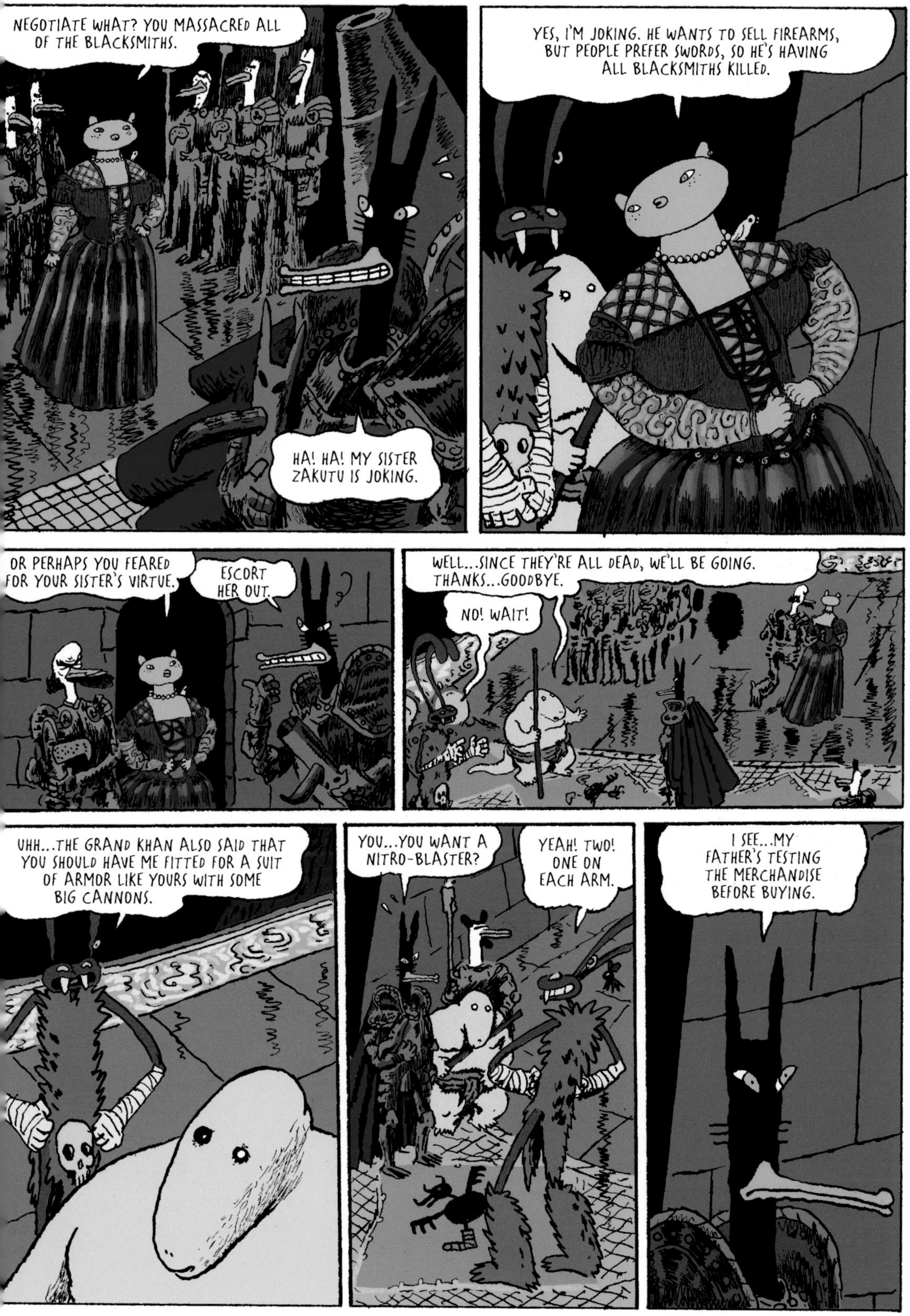
NEGOTIATE WHAT? YOU MASSACRED ALL OF THE BLACKSMITHS.
HA! HA! MY SISTER ZAKUTU IS JOKING.
YES, I'M JOKING. HE WANTS TO SELL FIREARMS, BUT PEOPLE PREFER SWORDS, SO HE'S HAVING ALL BLACKSMITHS KILLED.
OR PERHAPS YOU FEARED FOR YOUR SISTER'S VIRTUE.
ESCORT HER OUT.
WELL...SINCE THEY'RE ALL DEAD, WE'LL BE GOING. THANKS...GOODBYE.
NO! WAIT!
UHH...THE GRAND KHAN ALSO SAID THAT YOU SHOULD HAVE ME FITTED FOR A SUIT OF ARMOR LIKE YOURS WITH SOME BIG CANNONS.
YOU...YOU WANT A NITRO-BLASTER?
YEAH! TWO! ONE ON EACH ARM.
I SEE...MY FATHER'S TESTING THE MERCHANDISE BEFORE BUYING.

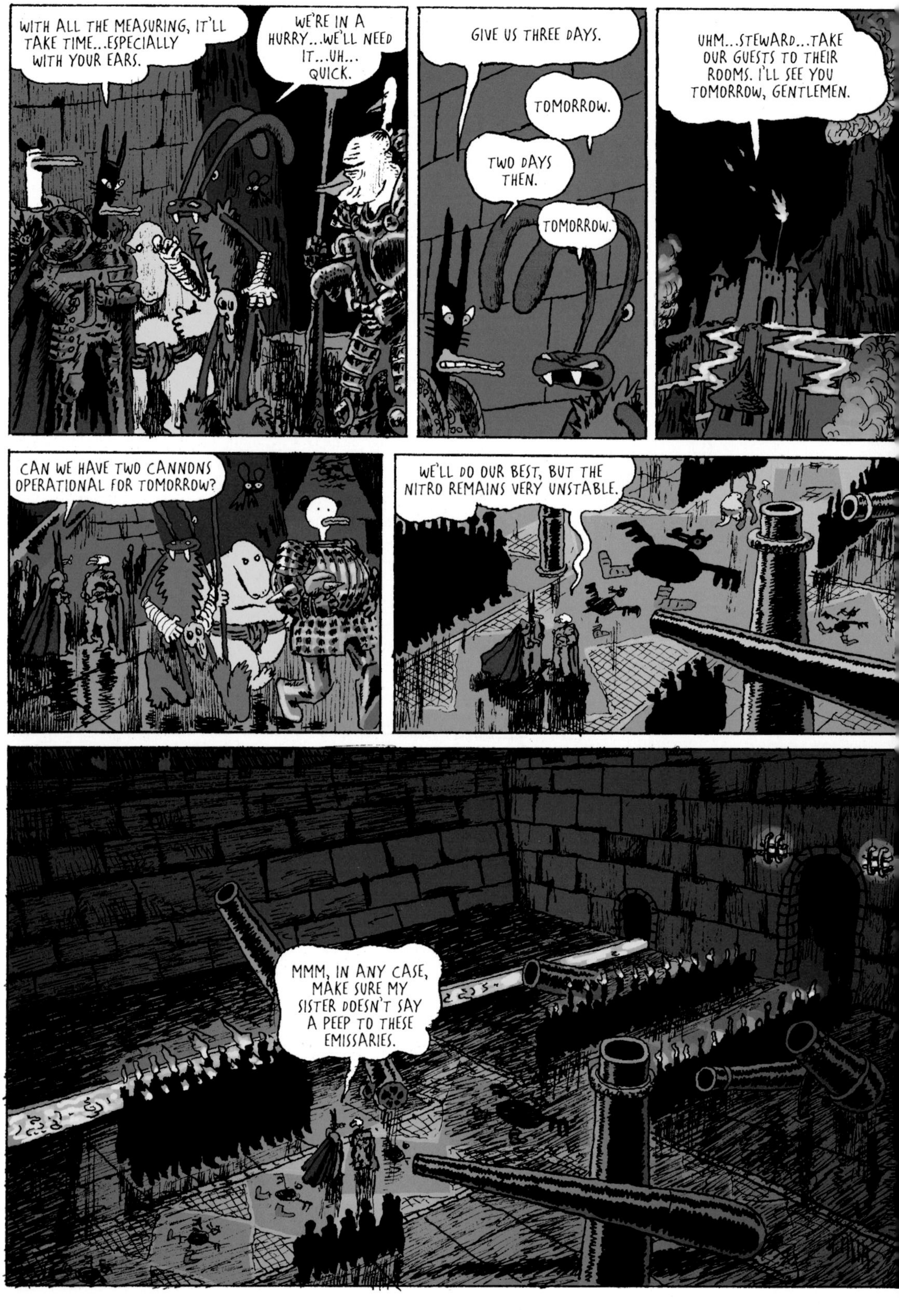
WITH ALL THE MEASURING, IT'LL TAKE TIME...ESPECIALLY WITH YOUR EARS.
WE'RE IN A HURRY...WE'LL NEED IT...UH... QUICK.
GIVE US THREE DAYS.
TOMORROW.
TWO DAYS THEN.
TOMORROW.
UHM...STEWARD...TAKE OUR GUESTS TO THEIR ROOMS. I'LL SEE YOU TOMORROW, GENTLEMEN.
CAN WE HAVE TWO CANNONS OPERATIONAL FOR TOMORROW?
WE'LL DO OUR BEST, BUT THE NITRO REMAINS VERY UNSTABLE.
MMM, IN ANY CASE, MAKE SURE MY SISTER DOESN'T SAY A PEEP TO THESE EMISSARIES.

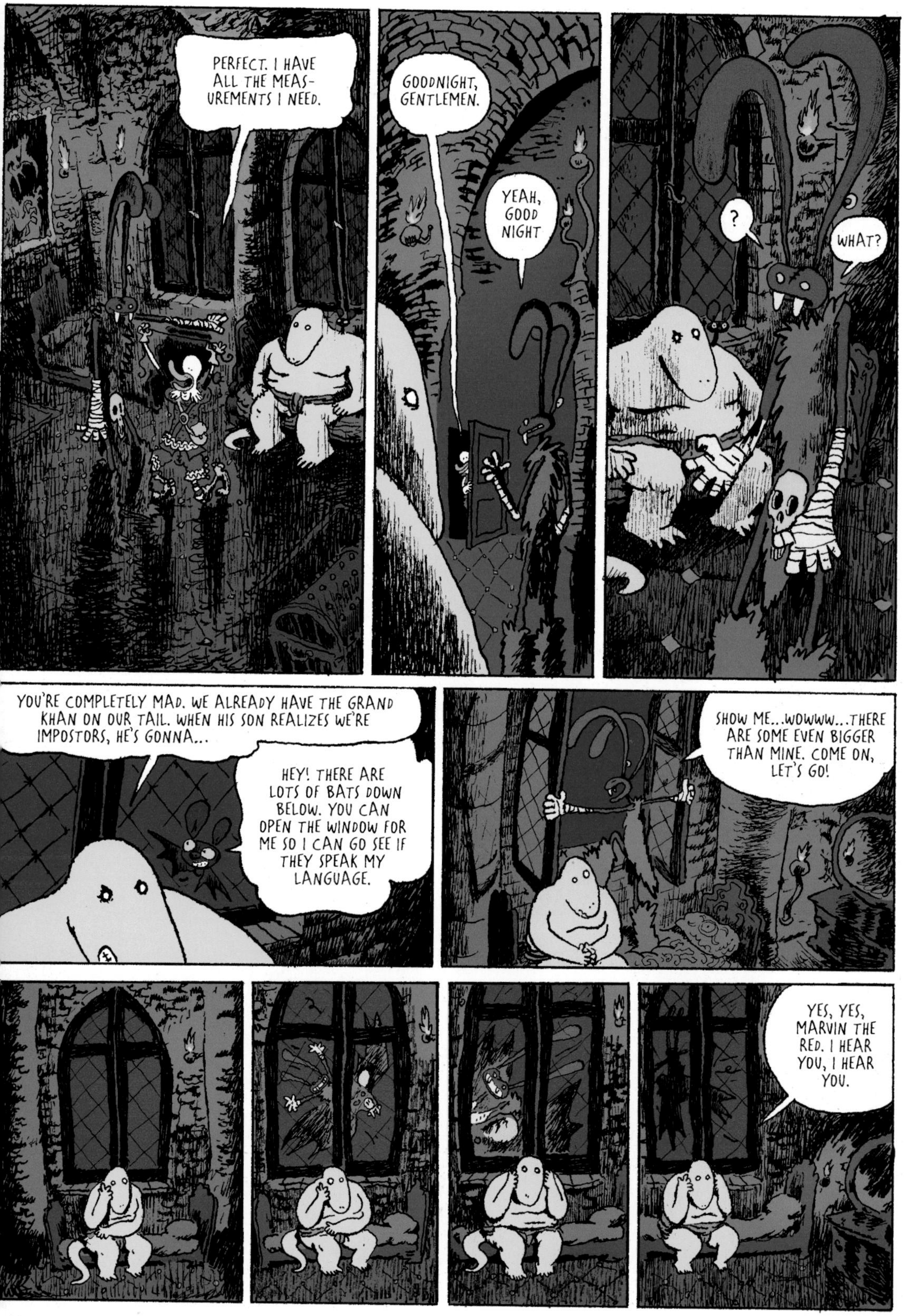
PERFECT. I HAVE ALL THE MEAS-UREMENTS I NEED.
GOODNIGHT, GENTLEMEN.
YEAH, GOOD NIGHT
?
WHAT?
YOU'RE COMPLETELY MAD. WE ALREADY HAVE THE GRAND KHAN ON OUR TAIL. WHEN HIS SON REALIZES WE'RE IMPOSTORS, HE'S GONNA...
HEY! THERE ARE LOTS OF BATS DOWN BELOW. YOU CAN OPEN THE WINDOW FOR ME SO I CAN GO SEE IF THEY SPEAK MY LANGUAGE.
SHOW ME...WOWWW...THERE ARE SOME EVEN BIGGER THAN MINE. COME ON, LET'S GO!
YES, YES, MARVIN THE RED. I HEAR YOU, I HEAR YOU.

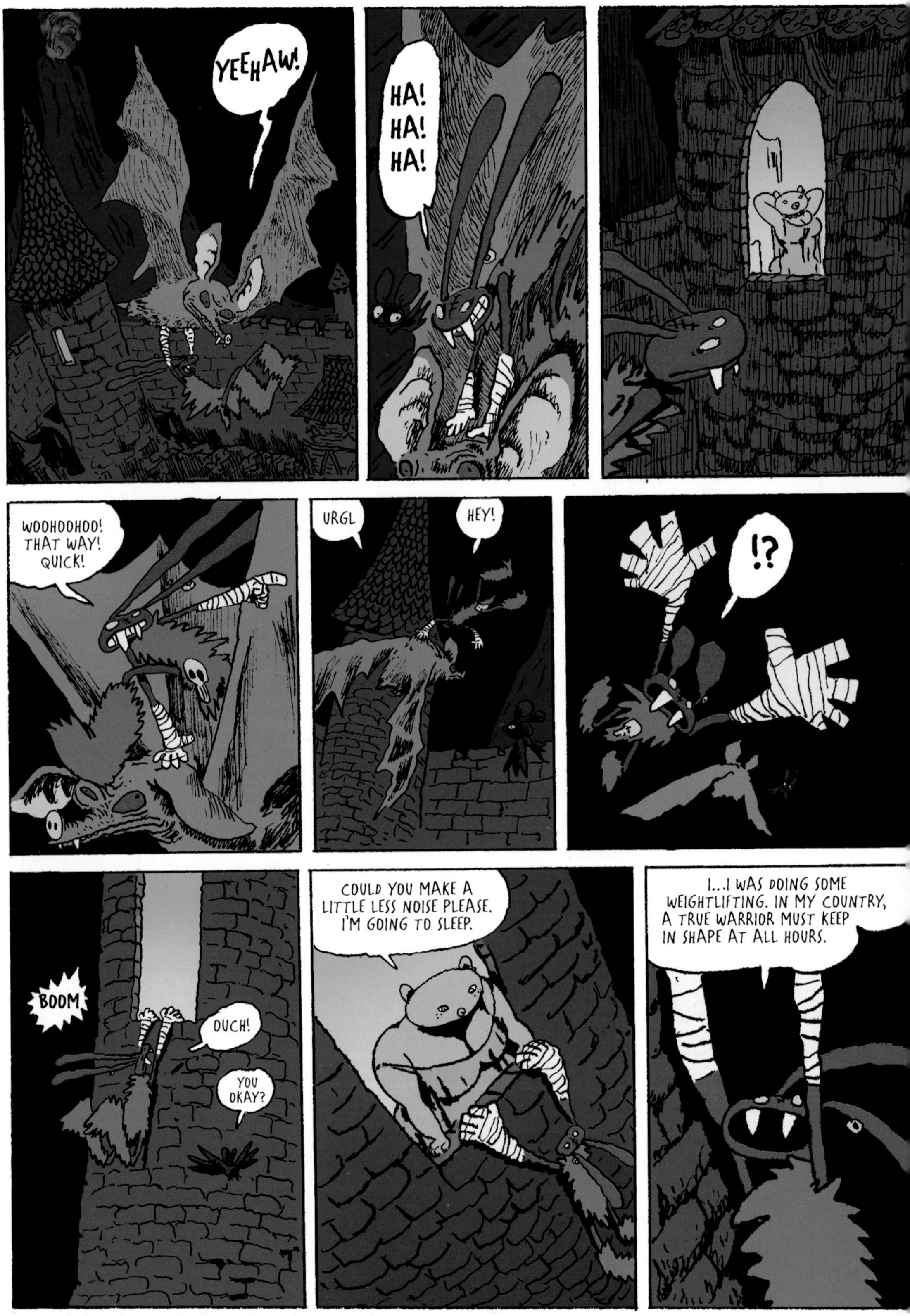
YEEHAW!
HA! HA! HA!
WOOHOOHOO! THAT WAY! QUICK!
URGL
HEY!
!?
BOOM
OUCH!
YOU OKAY?
COULD YOU MAKE A LITTLE LESS NOISE PLEASE. I'M GOING TO SLEEP.
I...I WAS DOING SOME WEIGHTLIFTING. IN MY COUNTRY, A TRUE WARRIOR MUST KEEP IN SHAPE AT ALL HOURS.

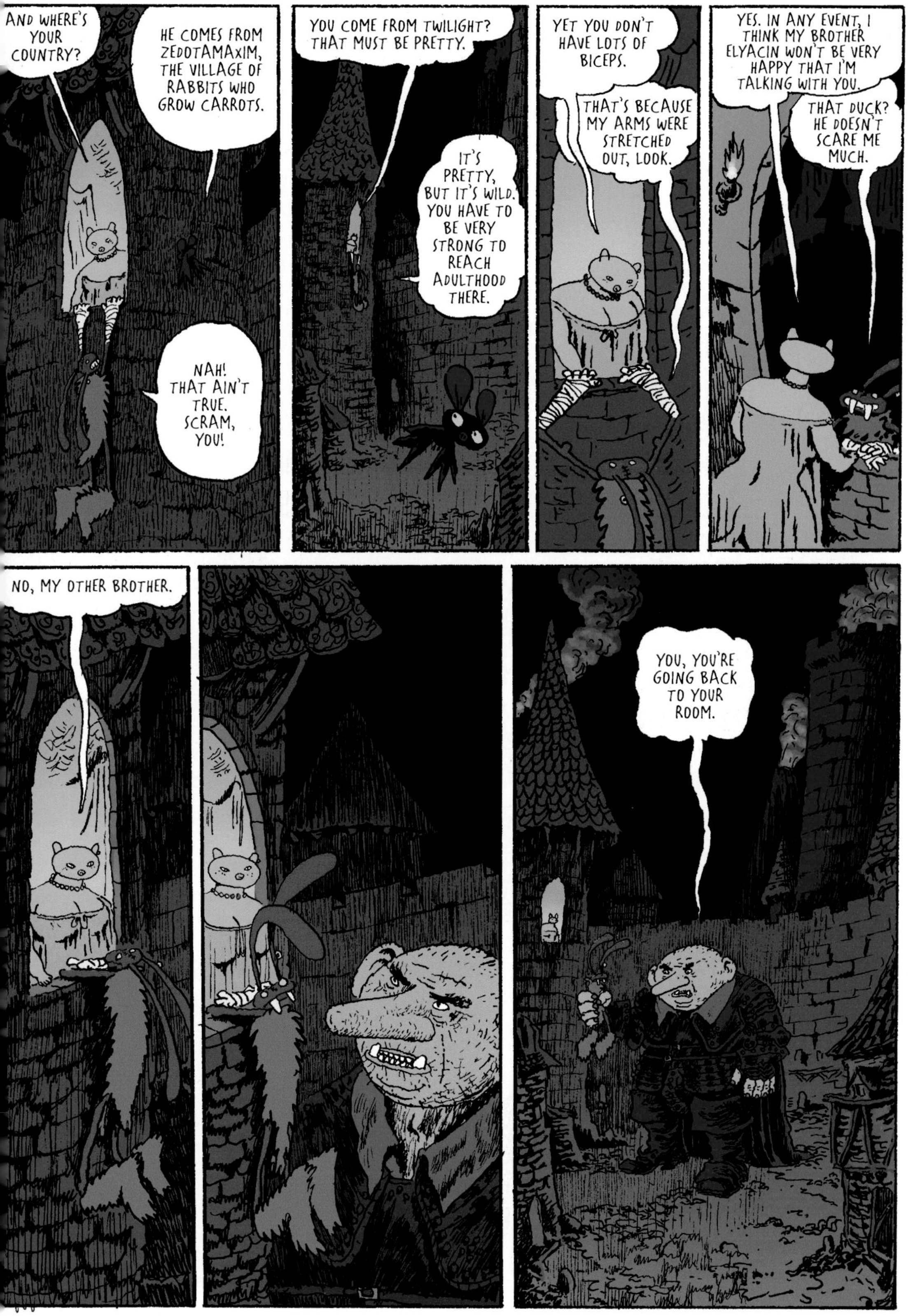
AND WHERE'S YOUR COUNTRY?
HE COMES FROM ZEDOTAMAXIM, THE VILLAGE OF RABBITS WHO GROW CARROTS.
NAH! THAT AIN'T TRUE. SCRAM, YOU!
YOU COME FROM TWILIGHT? THAT MUST BE PRETTY.
IT'S PRETTY, BUT IT'S WILD. YOU HAVE TO BE VERY STRONG TO REACH ADULTHOOD THERE.
YET YOU DON'T HAVE LOTS OF BICEPS.
THAT'S BECAUSE MY ARMS WERE STRETCHED OUT, LOOK.
YES. IN ANY EVENT, I THINK MY BROTHER ELYACIN WON'T BE VERY HAPPY THAT I'M TALKING WITH YOU.
THAT DUCK? HE DOESN'T SCARE ME MUCH.
NO, MY OTHER BROTHER.
YOU, YOU'RE GOING BACK TO YOUR ROOM.

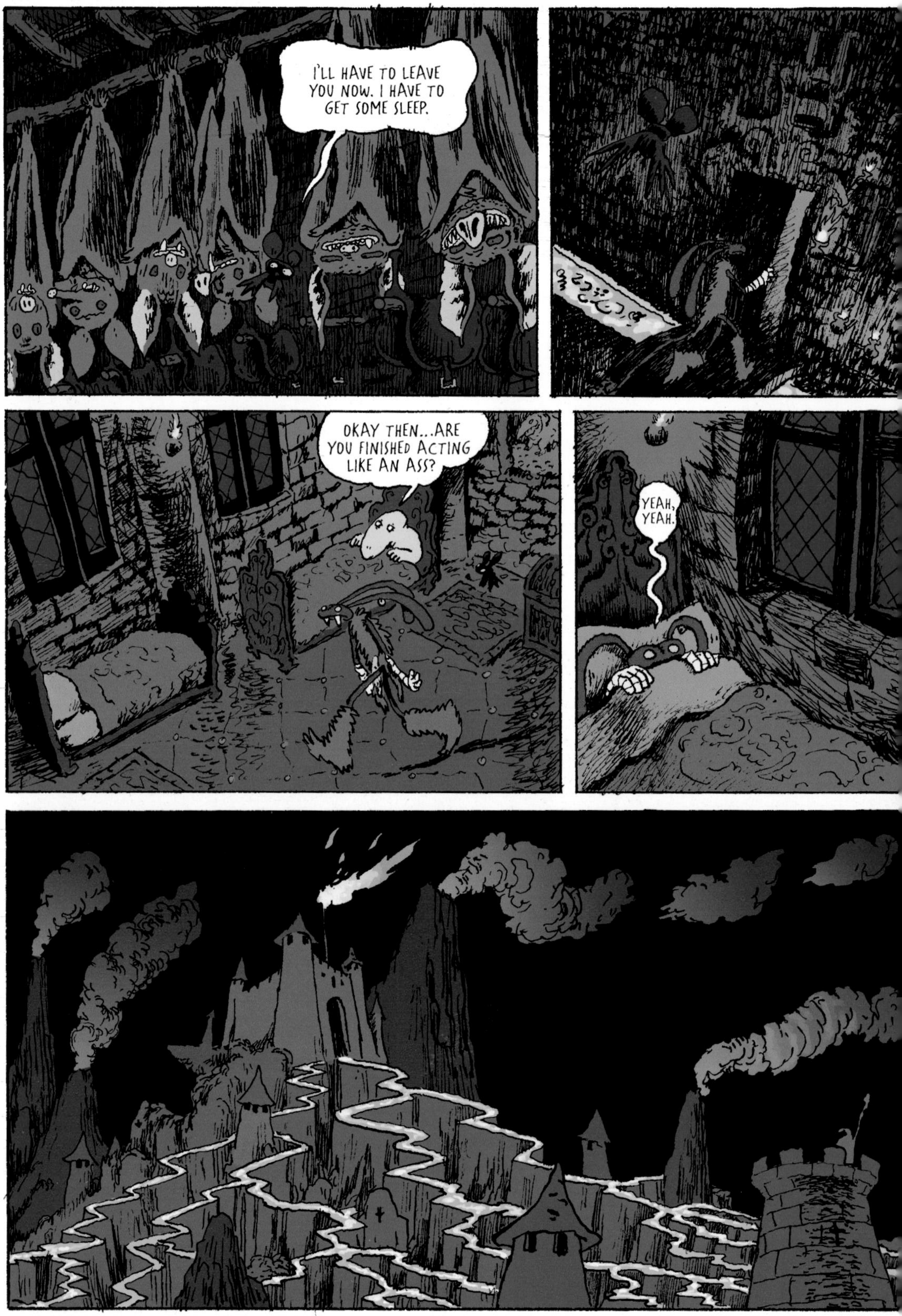
I'LL HAVE TO LEAVE YOU NOW. I HAVE TO GET SOME SLEEP.
OKAY THEN...ARE YOU FINISHED ACTING LIKE AN ASS?
YEAH, YEAH.

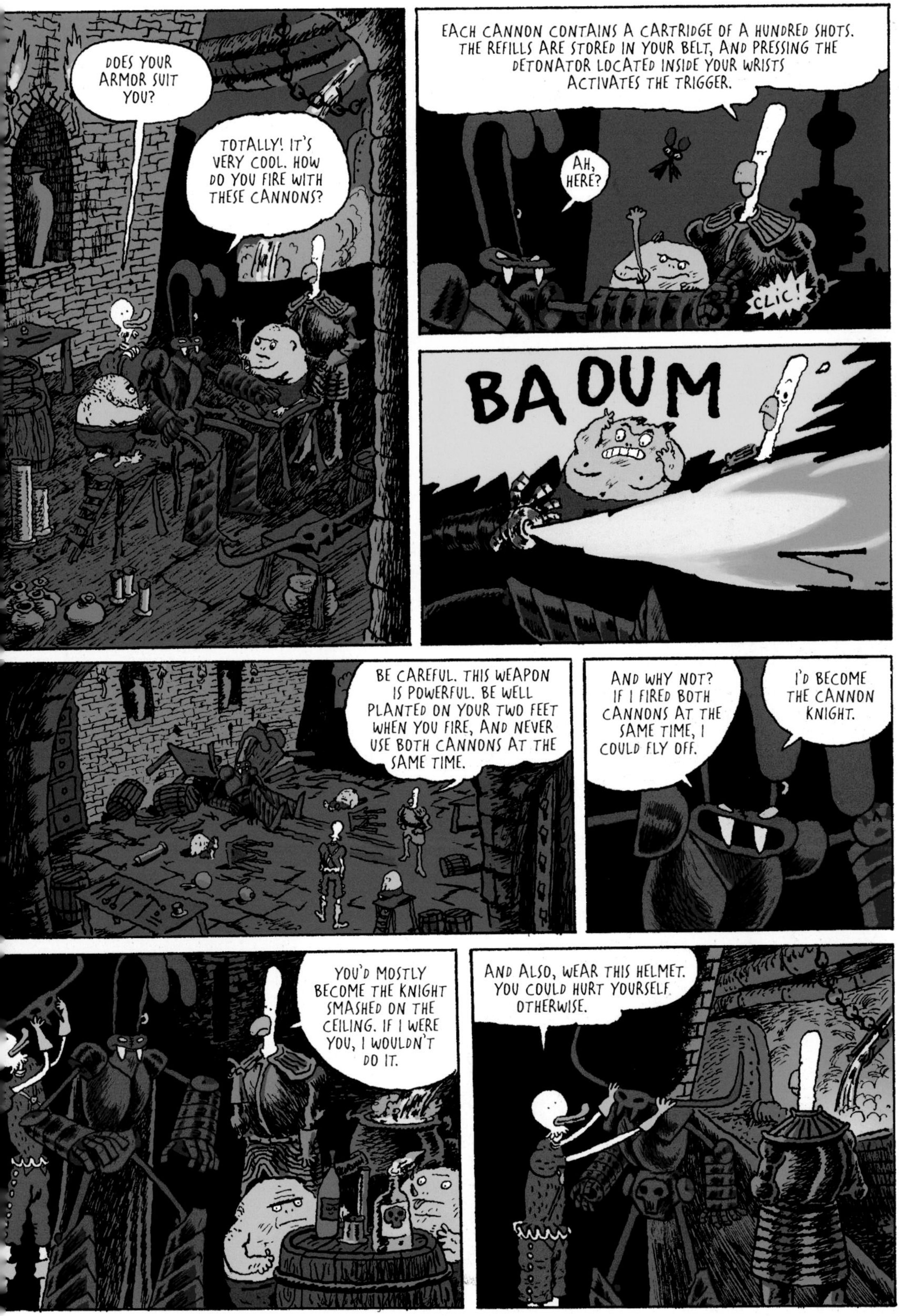
DOES YOUR ARMOR SUIT YOU?
TOTALLY! IT'S VERY COOL. HOW DO YOU FIRE WITH THESE CANNONS?
EACH CANNON CONTAINS A CARTRIDGE OF A HUNDRED SHOTS. THE REFILLS ARE STORED IN YOUR BELT, AND PRESSING THE DETONATOR LOCATED INSIDE YOUR WRISTS ACTIVATES THE TRIGGER.
AH, HERE?
CLIC!
BAOUM
BE CAREFUL. THIS WEAPON IS POWERFUL. BE WELL PLANTED ON YOUR TWO FEET WHEN YOU FIRE, AND NEVER USE BOTH CANNONS AT THE SAME TIME.
AND WHY NOT? IF I FIRED BOTH CANNONS AT THE SAME TIME, I COULD FLY OFF.
I'D BECOME THE CANNON KNIGHT.
YOU'D MOSTLY BECOME THE KNIGHT SMASHED ON THE CEILING. IF I WERE YOU, I WOULDN'T DO IT.
AND ALSO, WEAR THIS HELMET. YOU COULD HURT YOURSELF OTHERWISE.

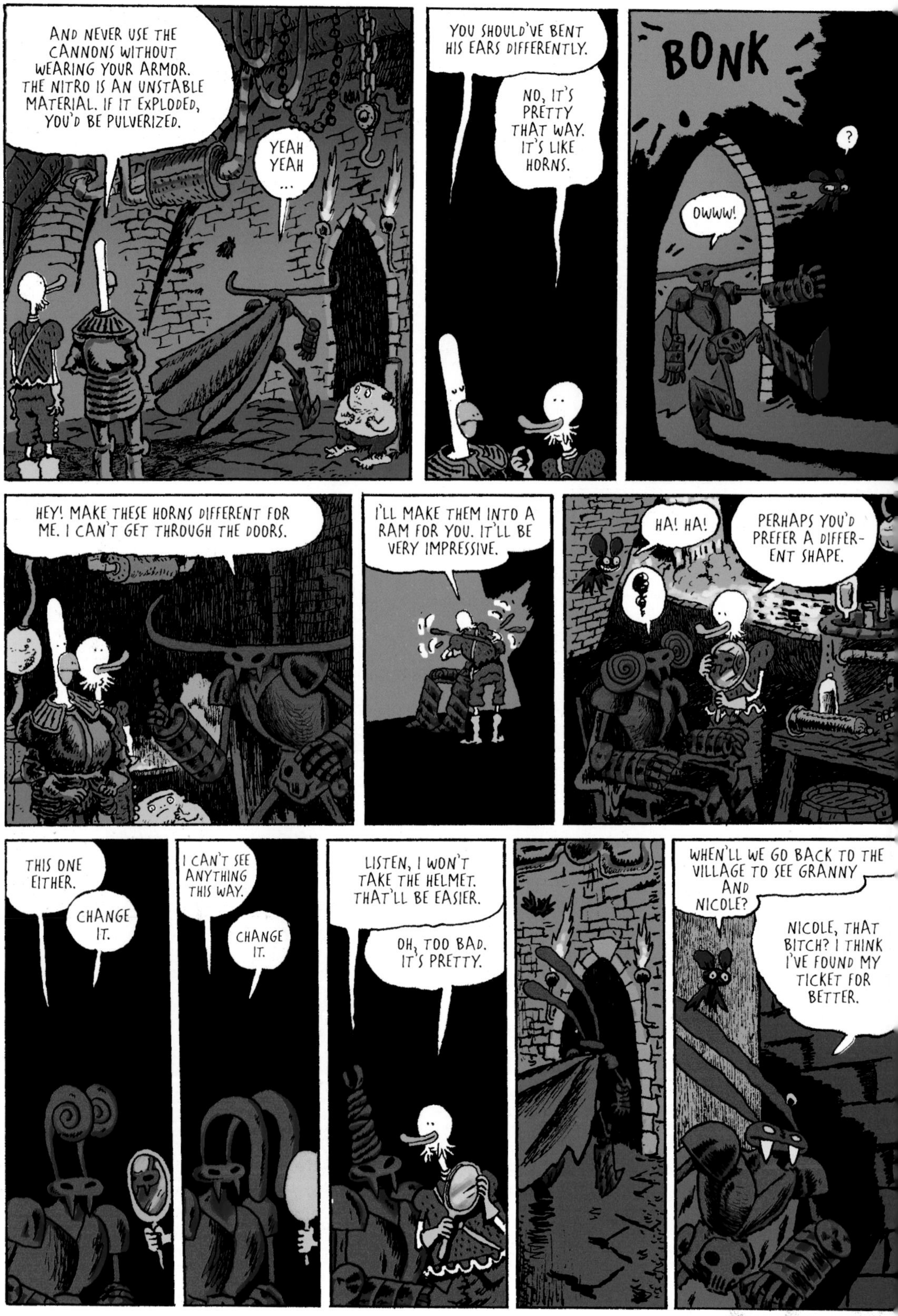
AND NEVER USE THE CANNONS WITHOUT WEARING YOUR ARMOR. THE NITRO IS AN UNSTABLE MATERIAL. IF IT EXPLODED, YOU'D BE PULVERIZED.
YEAH YEAH ...
YOU SHOULD'VE BENT HIS EARS DIFFERENTLY.
NO, IT'S PRETTY THAT WAY. IT'S LIKE HORNS.
BONK
?
OWWW!
HEY! MAKE THESE HORNS DIFFERENT FOR ME. I CAN'T GET THROUGH THE DOORS.
I'LL MAKE THEM INTO A RAM FOR YOU. IT'LL BE VERY IMPRESSIVE.
HA! HA!
PERHAPS YOU'D PREFER A DIFFERENT SHAPE.
THIS ONE EITHER.
CHANGE IT.
I CAN'T SEE ANYTHING THIS WAY.
CHANGE IT.
LISTEN, I WON'T TAKE THE HELMET. THAT'LL BE EASIER.
OH, TOO BAD. IT'S PRETTY.
WHEN'LL WE GO BACK TO THE VILLAGE TO SEE GRANNY AND NICOLE?
NICOLE, THAT BITCH? I THINK I'VE FOUND MY TICKET FOR BETTER.

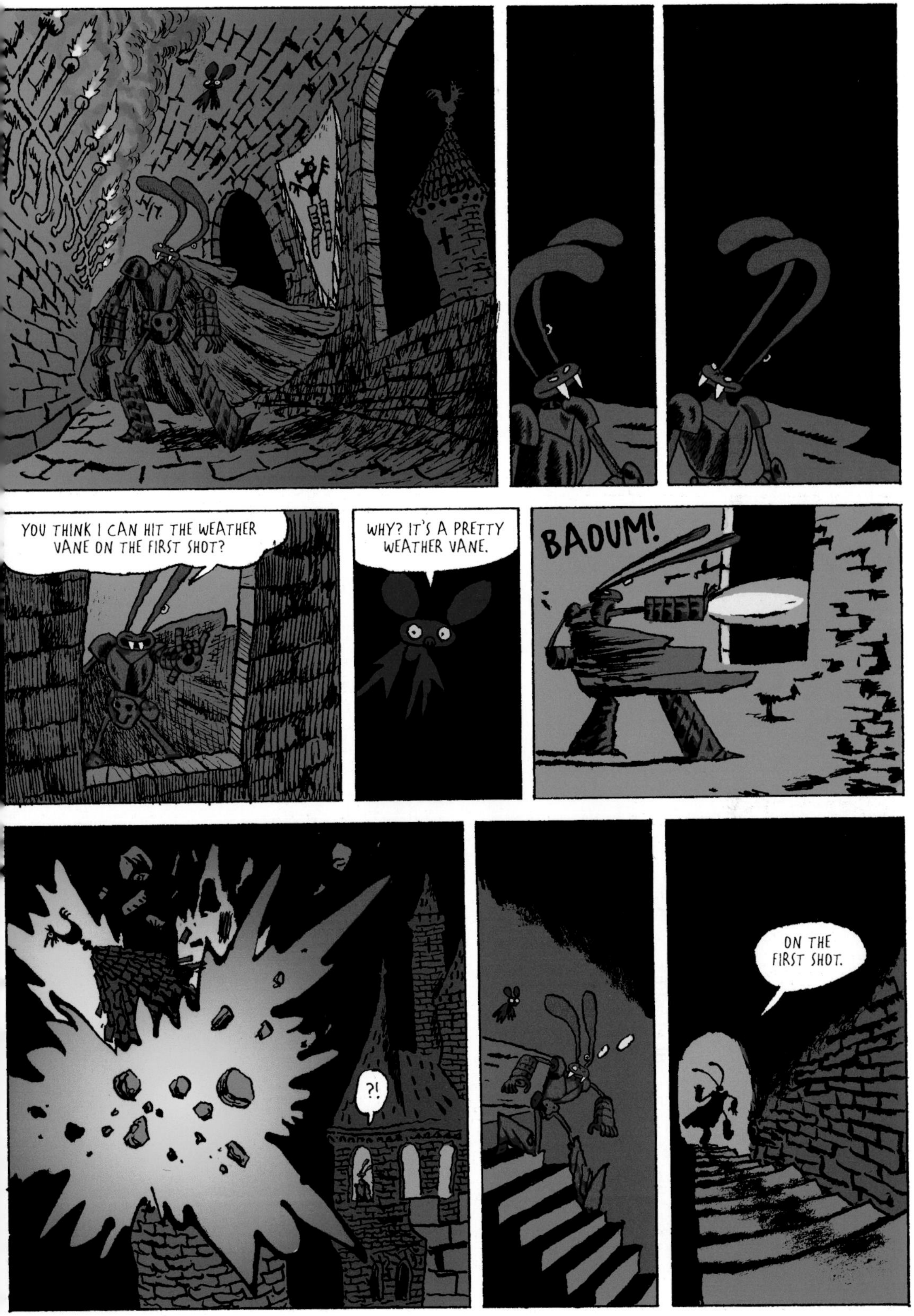
YOU THINK I CAN HIT THE WEATHER VANE ON THE FIRST SHOT?
WHY? IT'S A PRETTY WEATHER VANE.
BAOUM!
?!
ON THE FIRST SHOT.

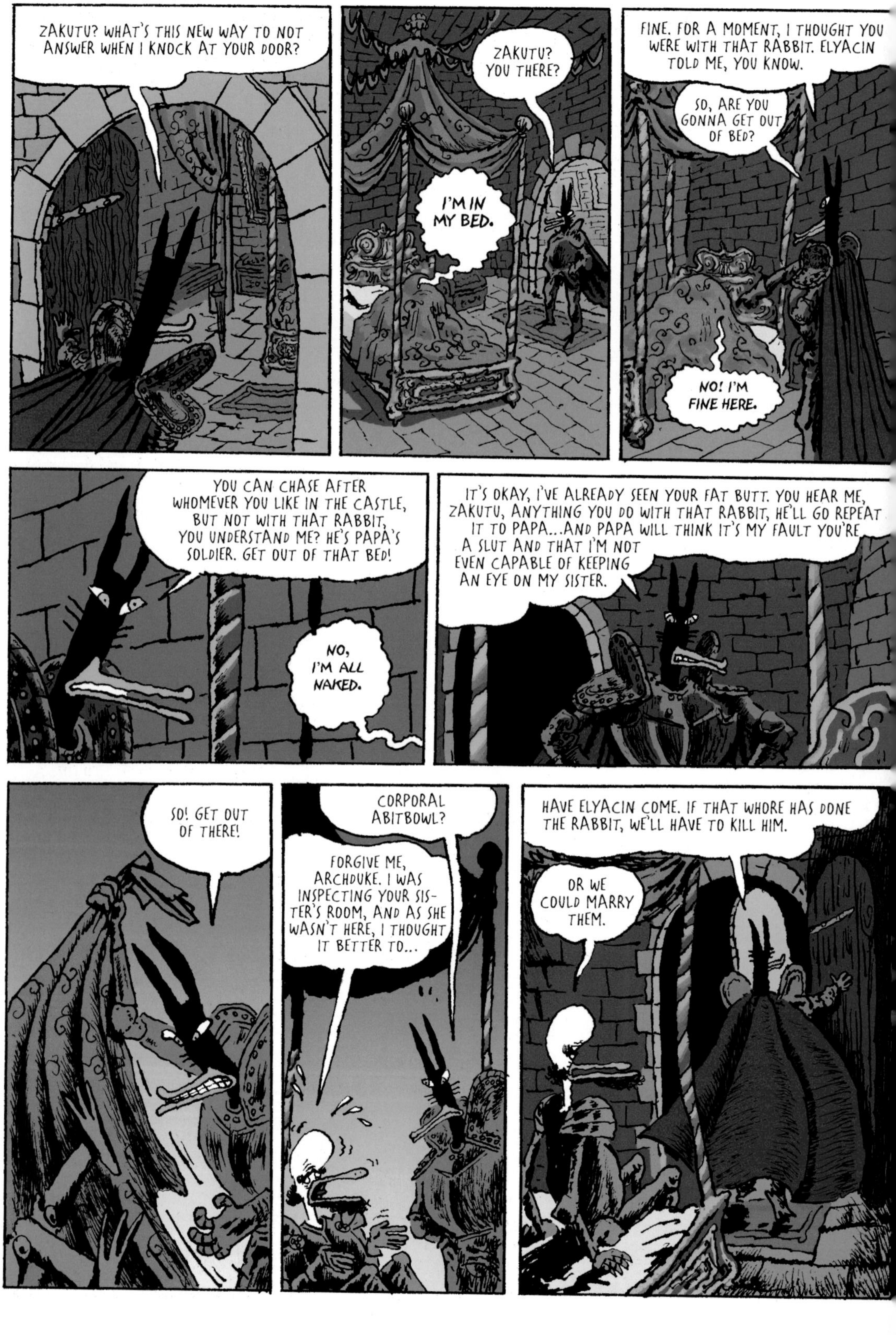
ZAKUTU? WHAT'S THIS NEW WAY TO NOT ANSWER WHEN I KNOCK AT YOUR DOOR?
ZAKUTU? YOU THERE?
I'M IN MY BED.
FINE. FOR A MOMENT, I THOUGHT YOU WERE WITH THAT RABBIT. ELYACIN TOLD ME, YOU KNOW.
SO, ARE YOU GONNA GET OUT OF BED?
NO! I'M FINE HERE.
YOU CAN CHASE AFTER WHOMEVER YOU LIKE IN THE CASTLE, BUT NOT WITH THAT RABBIT, YOU UNDERSTAND ME? HE'S PAPA'S SOLDIER. GET OUT OF THAT BED!
NO, I'M ALL NAKED.
IT'S OKAY, I'VE ALREADY SEEN YOUR FAT BUTT. YOU HEAR ME, ZAKUTU, ANYTHING YOU DO WITH THAT RABBIT, HE'LL GO REPEAT IT TO PAPA...AND PAPA WILL THINK IT'S MY FAULT YOU'RE A SLUT AND THAT I'M NOT EVEN CAPABLE OF KEEPING AN EYE ON MY SISTER.
SO! GET OUT OF THERE!
CORPORAL ABITBOWL?
FORGIVE ME, ARCHDUKE. I WAS INSPECTING YOUR SISTER'S ROOM, AND AS SHE WASN'T HERE, I THOUGHT IT BETTER TO...
HAVE ELYACIN COME. IF THAT WHORE HAS DONE THE RABBIT, WE'LL HAVE TO KILL HIM.
OR WE COULD MARRY THEM.

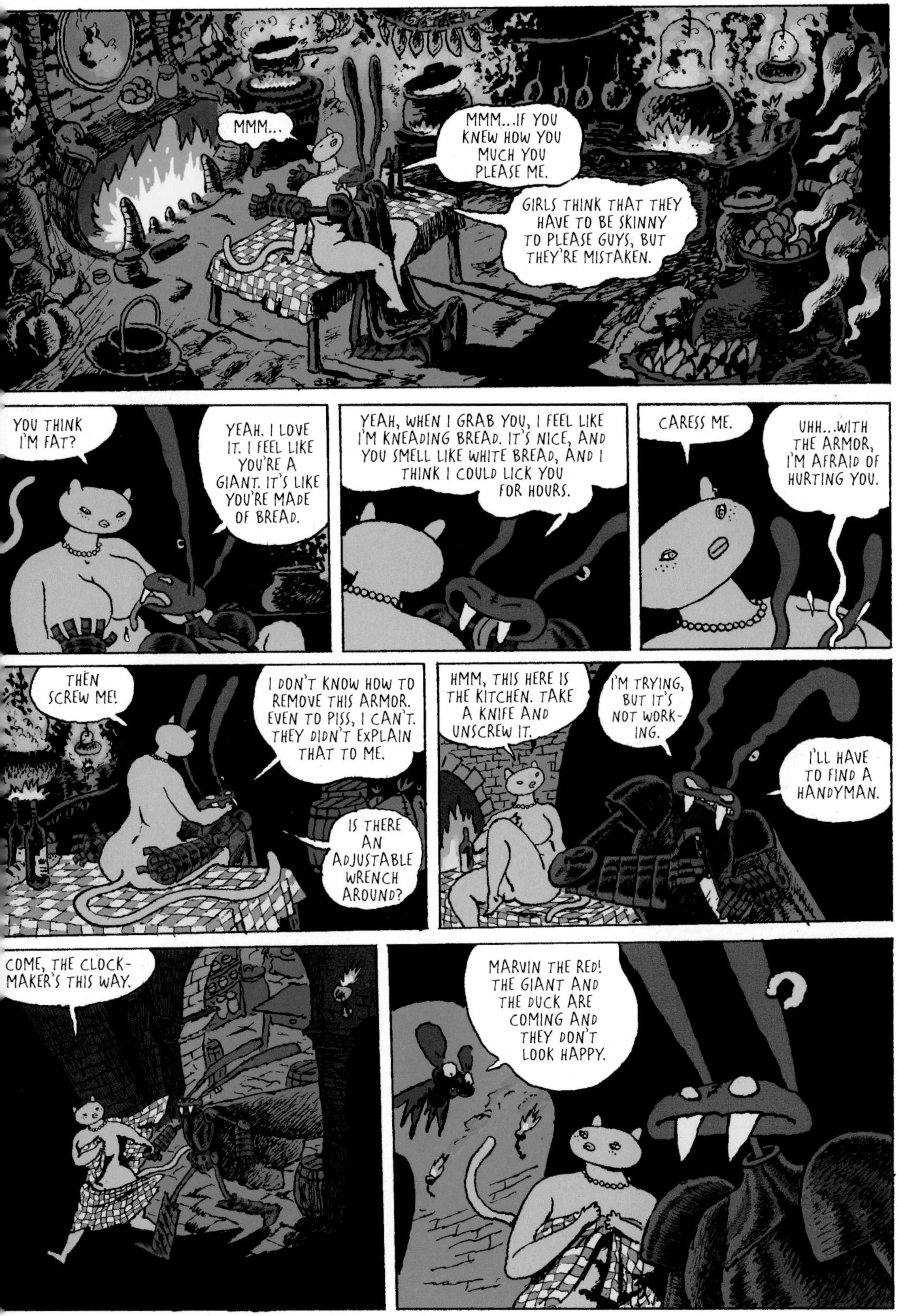
MMM...
MMM...IF YOU KNEW HOW YOU MUCH YOU PLEASE ME.
GIRLS THINK THAT THEY HAVE TO BE SKINNY TO PLEASE GUYS, BUT THEY'RE MISTAKEN.
YOU THINK I'M FAT?
YEAH. I LOVE IT. I FEEL LIKE YOU'RE A GIANT. IT'S LIKE YOU'RE MADE OF BREAD.
YEAH, WHEN I GRAB YOU, I FEEL LIKE I'M KNEADING BREAD. IT'S NICE, AND YOU SMELL LIKE WHITE BREAD, AND I THINK I COULD LICK YOU FOR HOURS.
CARESS ME.
UHH...WITH THE ARMOR, I'M AFRAID OF HURTING YOU.
THEN SCREW ME!
I DON'T KNOW HOW TO REMOVE THIS ARMOR. EVEN TO PISS, I CAN'T. THEY DIDN'T EXPLAIN THAT TO ME.
IS THERE AN ADJUSTABLE WRENCH AROUND?
HMM, THIS HERE IS THE KITCHEN. TAKE A KNIFE AND UNSCREW IT.
I'M TRYING, BUT IT'S NOT WORK-ING.
I'LL HAVE TO FIND A HANDYMAN.
COME, THE CLOCK-MAKER'S THIS WAY.
MARVIN THE RED! THE GIANT AND THE DUCK ARE COMING AND THEY DON'T LOOK HAPPY.

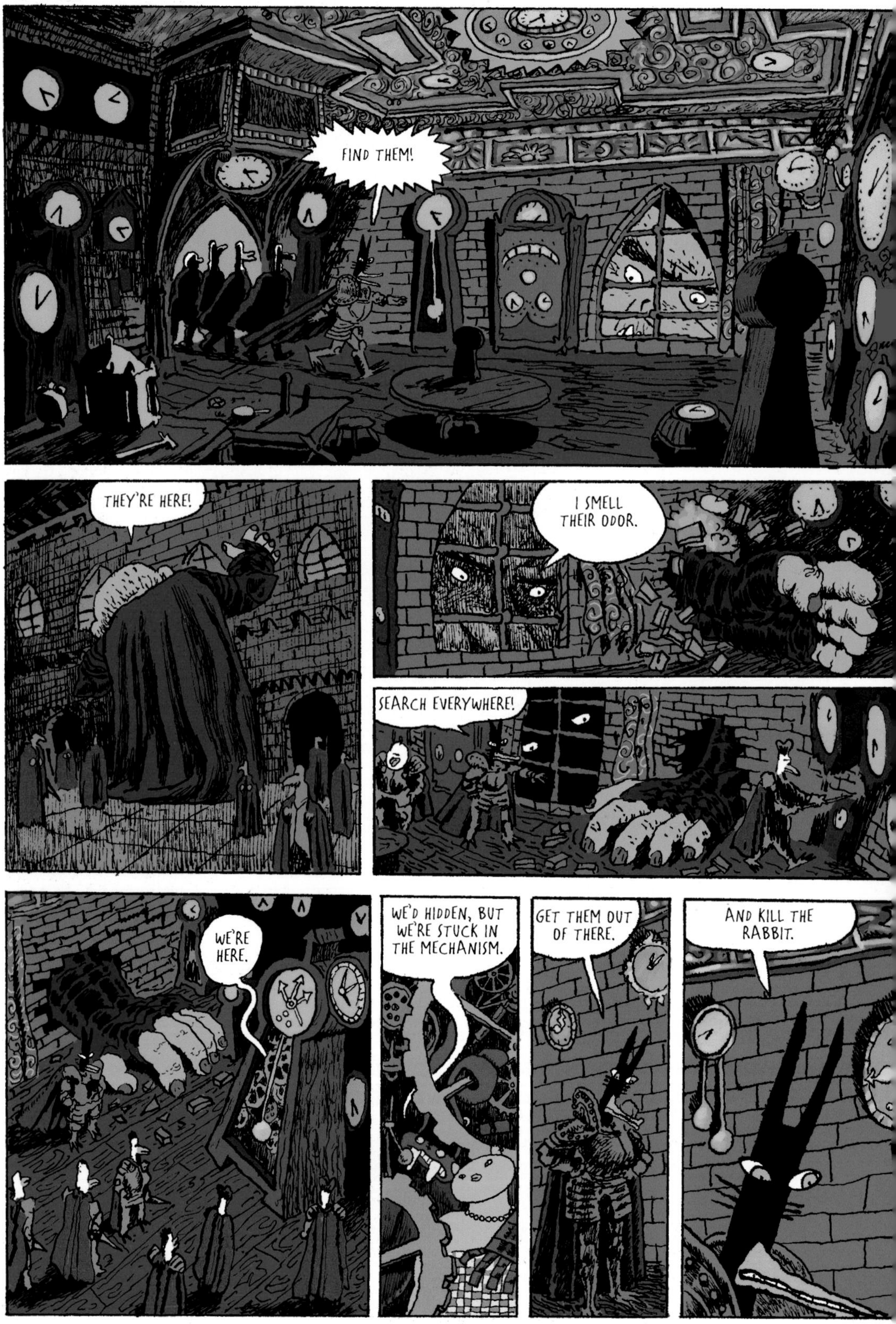
FIND THEM!
THEY'RE HERE!
I SMELL THEIR ODOR.
SEARCH EVERYWHERE!
WE'RE HERE.
WE'D HIDDEN, BUT WE'RE STUCK IN THE MECHANISM.
GET THEM OUT OF THERE.
AND KILL THE RABBIT.

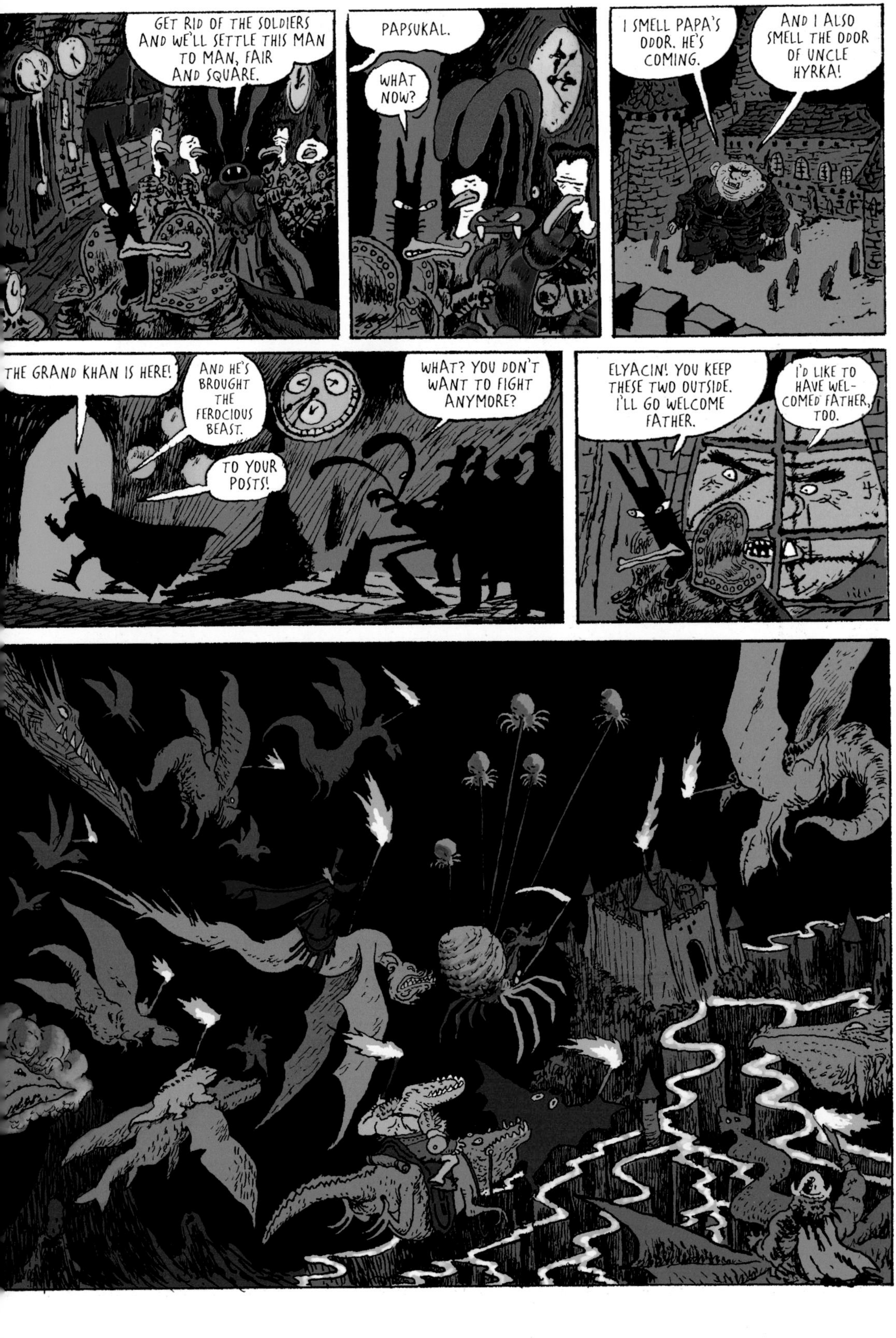
GET RID OF THE SOLDIERS AND WE'LL SETTLE THIS MAN TO MAN, FAIR AND SQUARE.
PAPSUKAL.
WHAT NOW?
I SMELL PAPA'S ODOR. HE'S COMING.
AND I ALSO SMELL THE ODOR OF UNCLE HYRKA!
THE GRAND KHAN IS HERE!
AND HE'S BROUGHT THE FEROCIOUS BEAST.
TO YOUR POSTS!
WHAT? YOU DON'T WANT TO FIGHT ANYMORE?
ELYACIN! YOU KEEP THESE TWO OUTSIDE. I'LL GO WELCOME FATHER.
I'D LIKE TO HAVE WELCOMED FATHER, TOO.

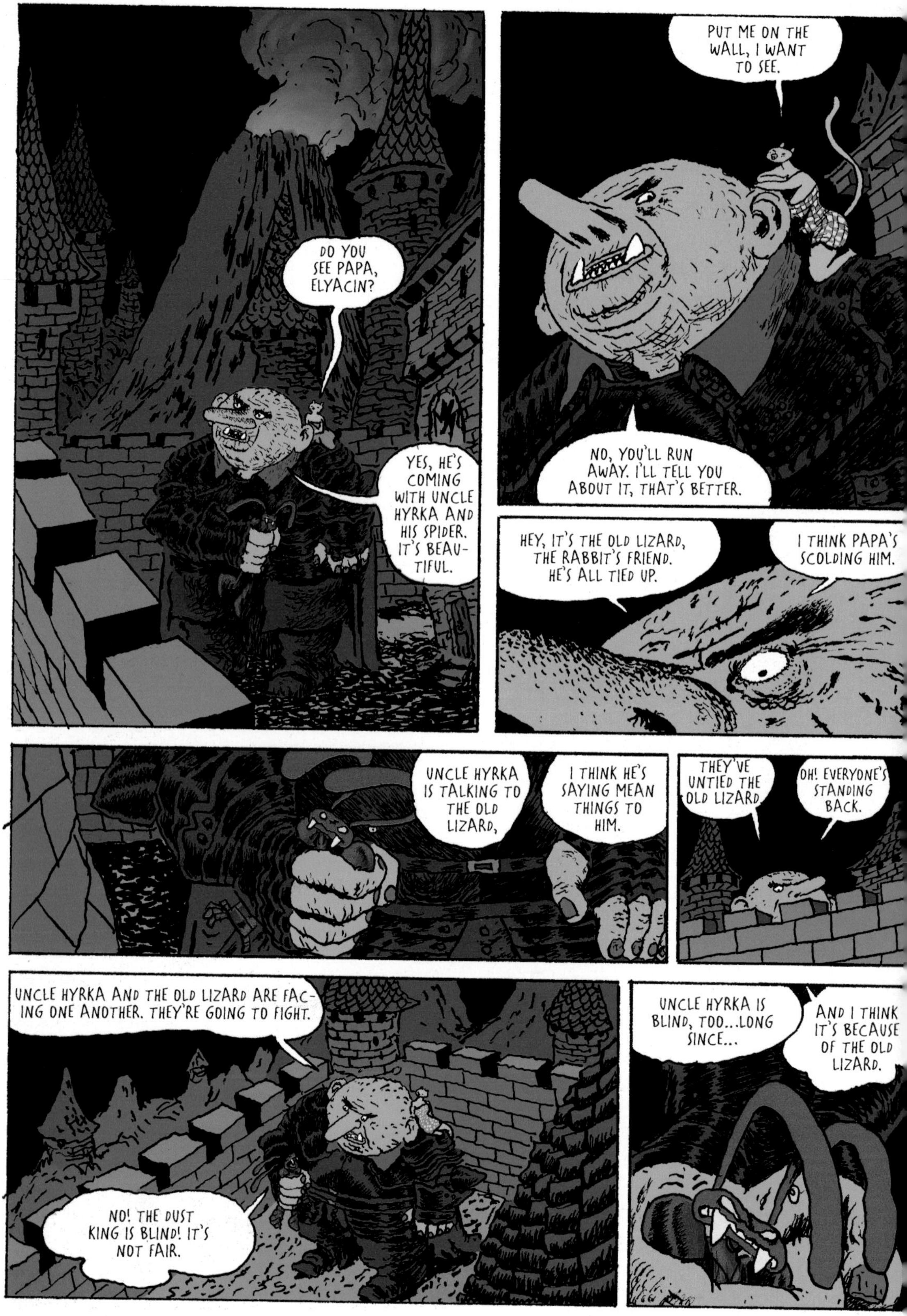
DO YOU SEE PAPA, ELYACIN?
YES, HE'S COMING WITH UNCLE HYRKA AND HIS SPIDER. IT'S BEAU-TIFUL.
PUT ME ON THE WALL, I WANT TO SEE.
NO, YOU'LL RUN AWAY. I'LL TELL YOU ABOUT IT, THAT'S BETTER.
HEY, IT'S THE OLD LIZARD, THE RABBIT'S FRIEND. HE'S ALL TIED UP.
I THINK PAPA'S SCOLDING HIM.
UNCLE HYRKA IS TALKING TO THE OLD LIZARD,
I THINK HE'S SAYING MEAN THINGS TO HIM.
THEY'VE UNTIED THE OLD LIZARD.
OH! EVERYONE'S STANDING BACK.
UNCLE HYRKA AND THE OLD LIZARD ARE FAC-ING ONE ANOTHER. THEY'RE GOING TO FIGHT.
NO! THE DUST KING IS BLIND! IT'S NOT FAIR.
UNCLE HYRKA IS BLIND, TOO...LONG SINCE...
AND I THINK IT'S BECAUSE OF THE OLD LIZARD.

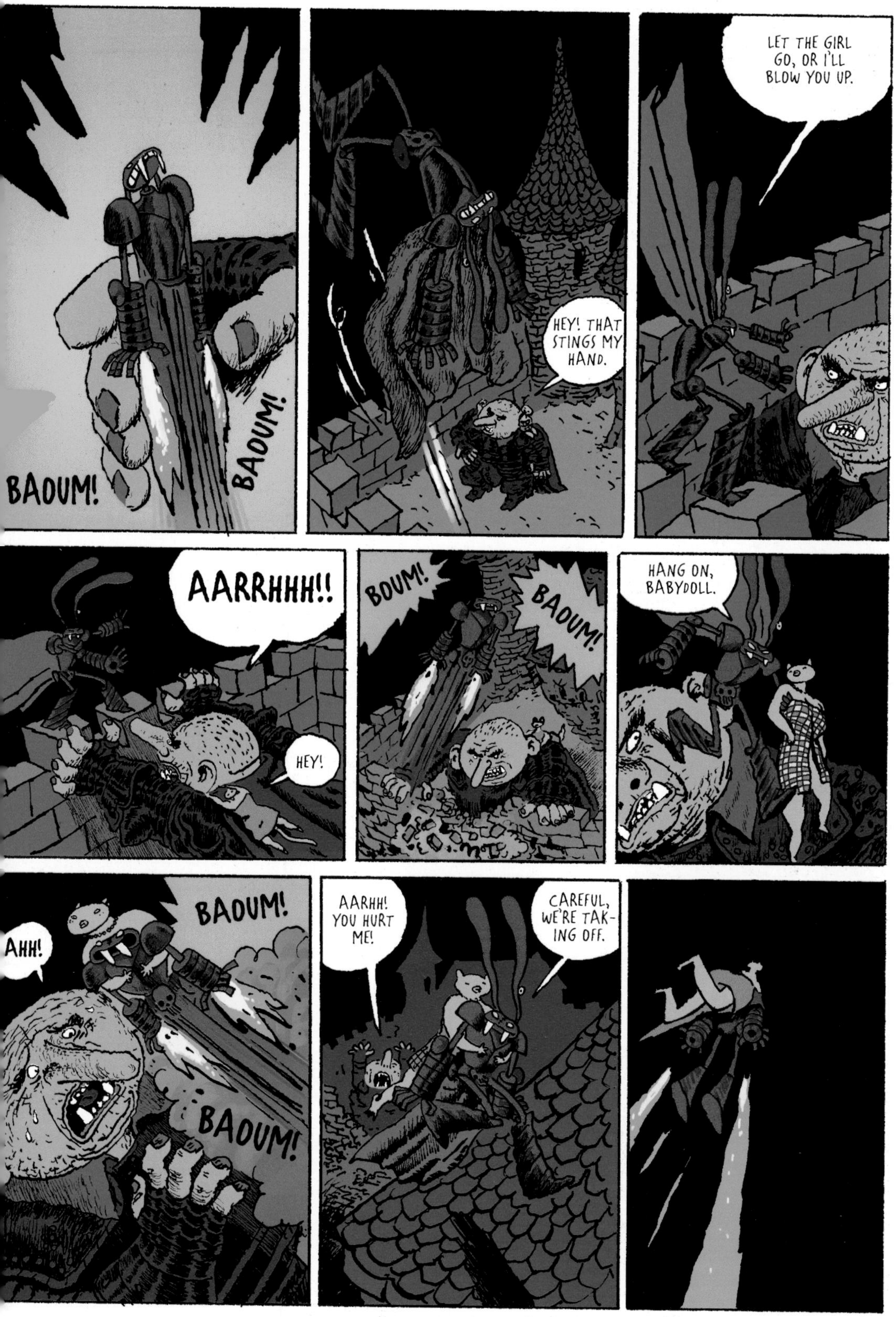
BAOUM!
BAOUM!
HEY! THAT STINGS MY HAND.
LET THE GIRL GO, OR I'LL BLOW YOU UP.
AARRHHH!!
HEY!
BOUM!
BAOUM!
HANG ON, BABYDOLL.
AHH!
BAOUM!
BAOUM!
AARHH! YOU HURT ME!
CAREFUL, WE'RE TAKING OFF.

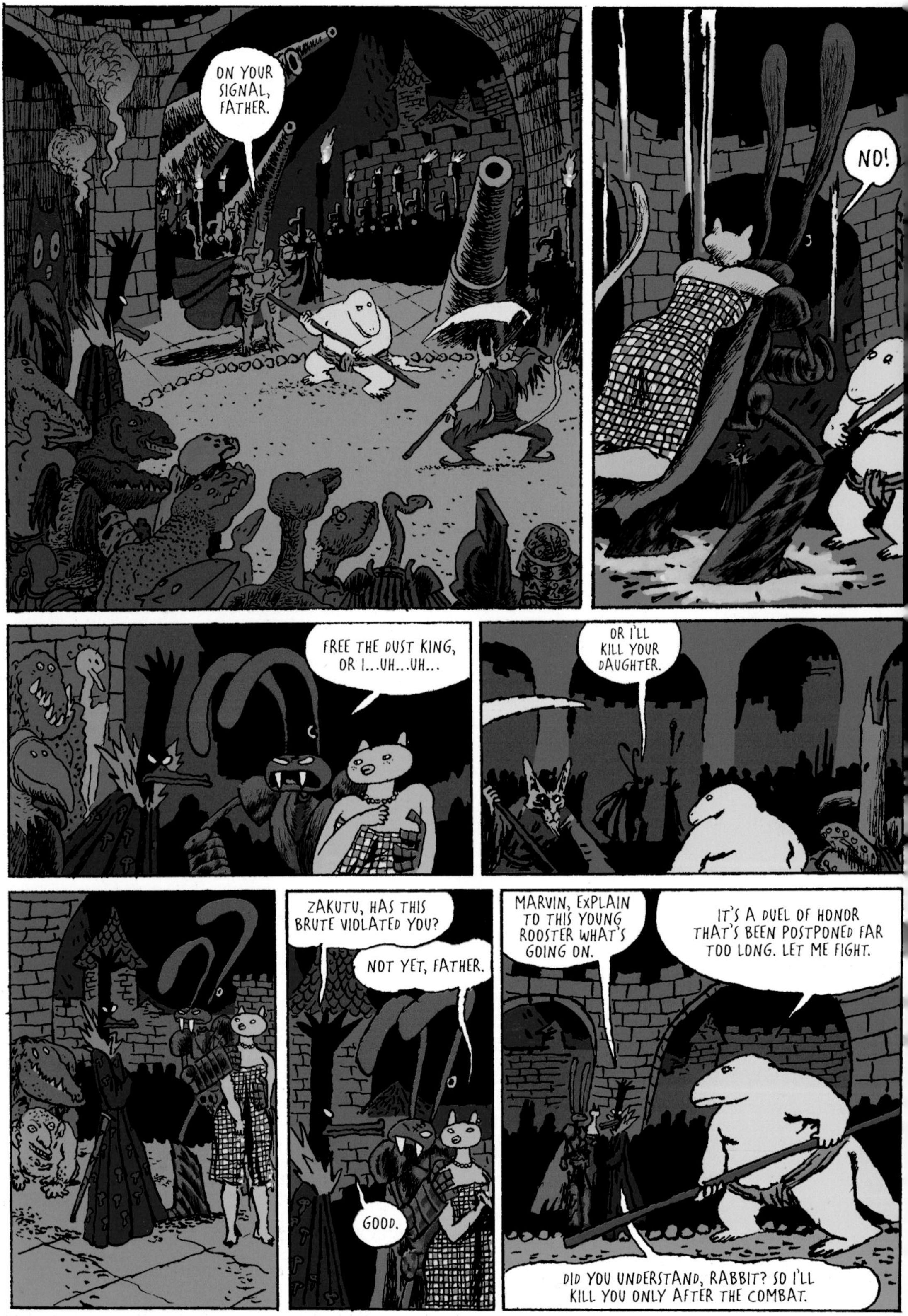
ON YOUR SIGNAL, FATHER.
NO!
FREE THE DUST KING, OR I...UH...UH...
OR I'LL KILL YOUR DAUGHTER.
ZAKUTU, HAS THIS BRUTE VIOLATED YOU?
NOT YET, FATHER.
GOOD.
MARVIN, EXPLAIN TO THIS YOUNG ROOSTER WHAT'S GOING ON.
IT'S A DUEL OF HONOR THAT'S BEEN POSTPONED FAR TOO LONG. LET ME FIGHT.
DID YOU UNDERSTAND, RABBIT? SO I'LL KILL YOU ONLY AFTER THE COMBAT.

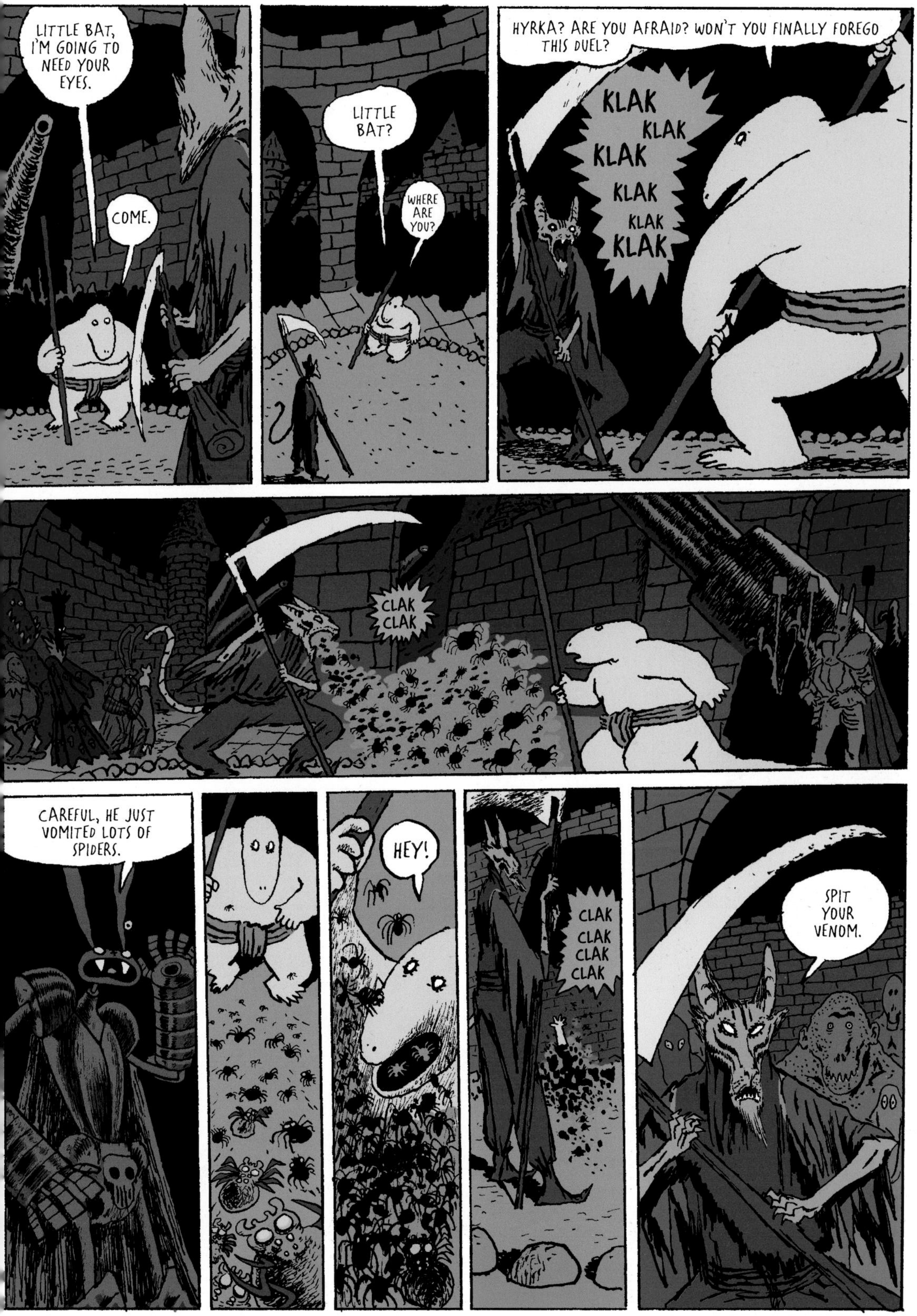
LITTLE BAT, I'M GOING TO NEED YOUR EYES.
COME.
LITTLE BAT?
WHERE ARE YOU?
HYRKA? ARE YOU AFRAID? WON'T YOU FINALLY FOREGO THIS DUEL?
KLAK KLAK KLAK KLAK KLAK KLAK
CLAK CLAK
CAREFUL, HE JUST VOMITED LOTS OF SPIDERS.
HEY!
CLAK CLAK CLAK CLAK
SPIT YOUR VENOM.

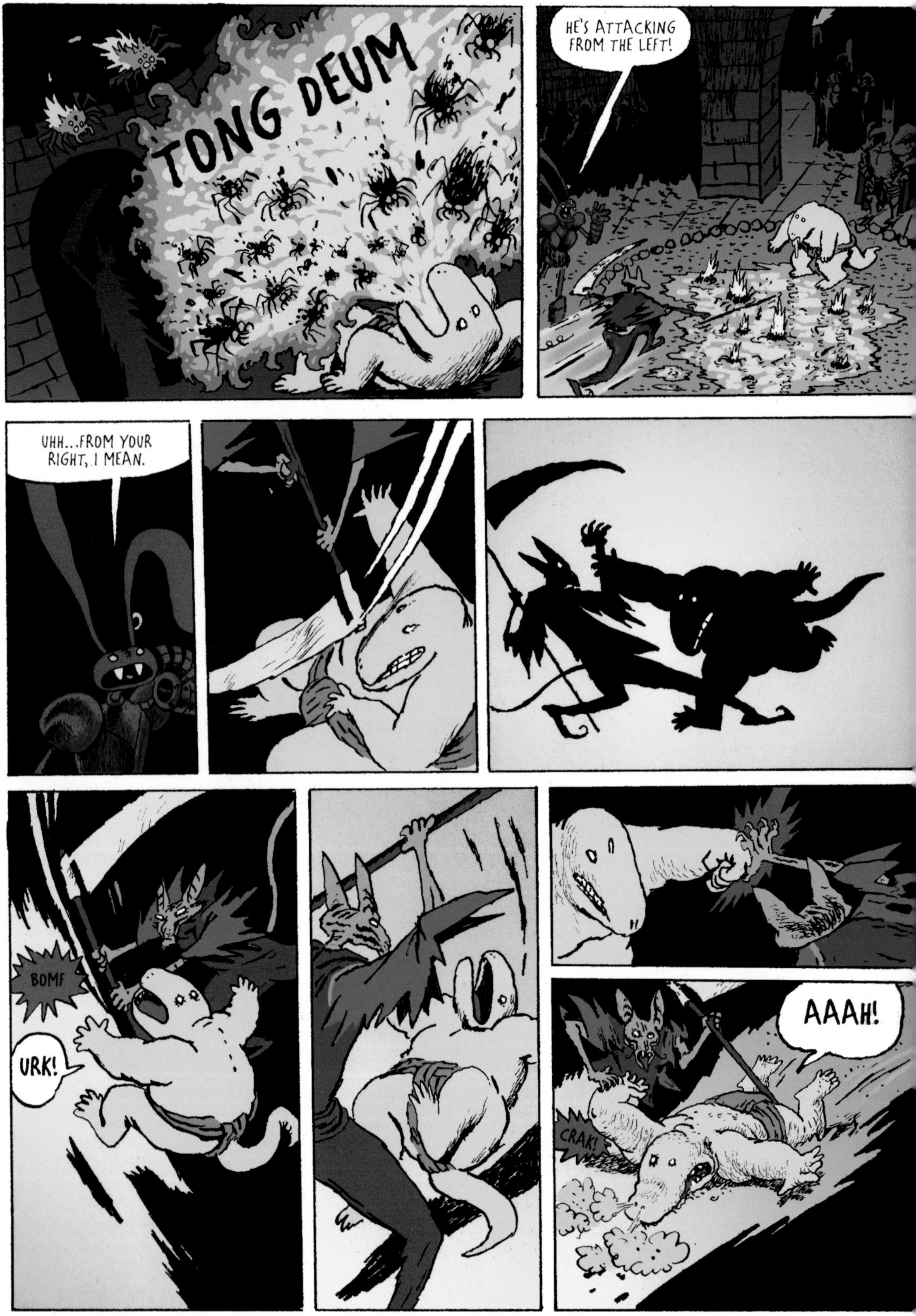
TONG DEUM
HE'S ATTACKING FROM THE LEFT!
UHH...FROM YOUR RIGHT, I MEAN.
BOMF
URK!
AAAH!
CRAK!

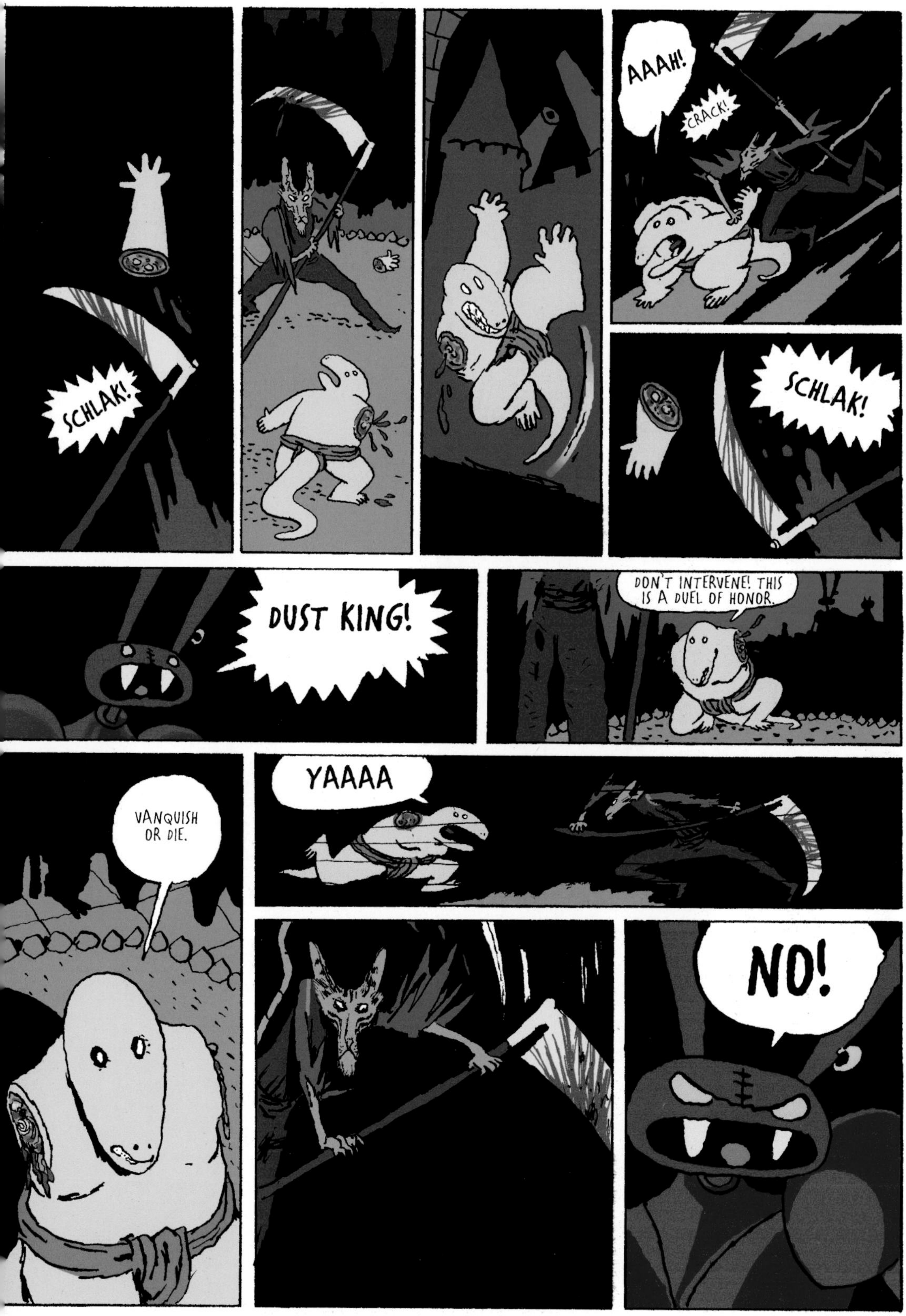
SCHLAK!
AAAH!
CRACK!
SCHLAK!
DUST KING!
DON'T INTERVENE! THIS IS A DUEL OF HONOR.
VANQUISH OR DIE.
YAAAA
NO!

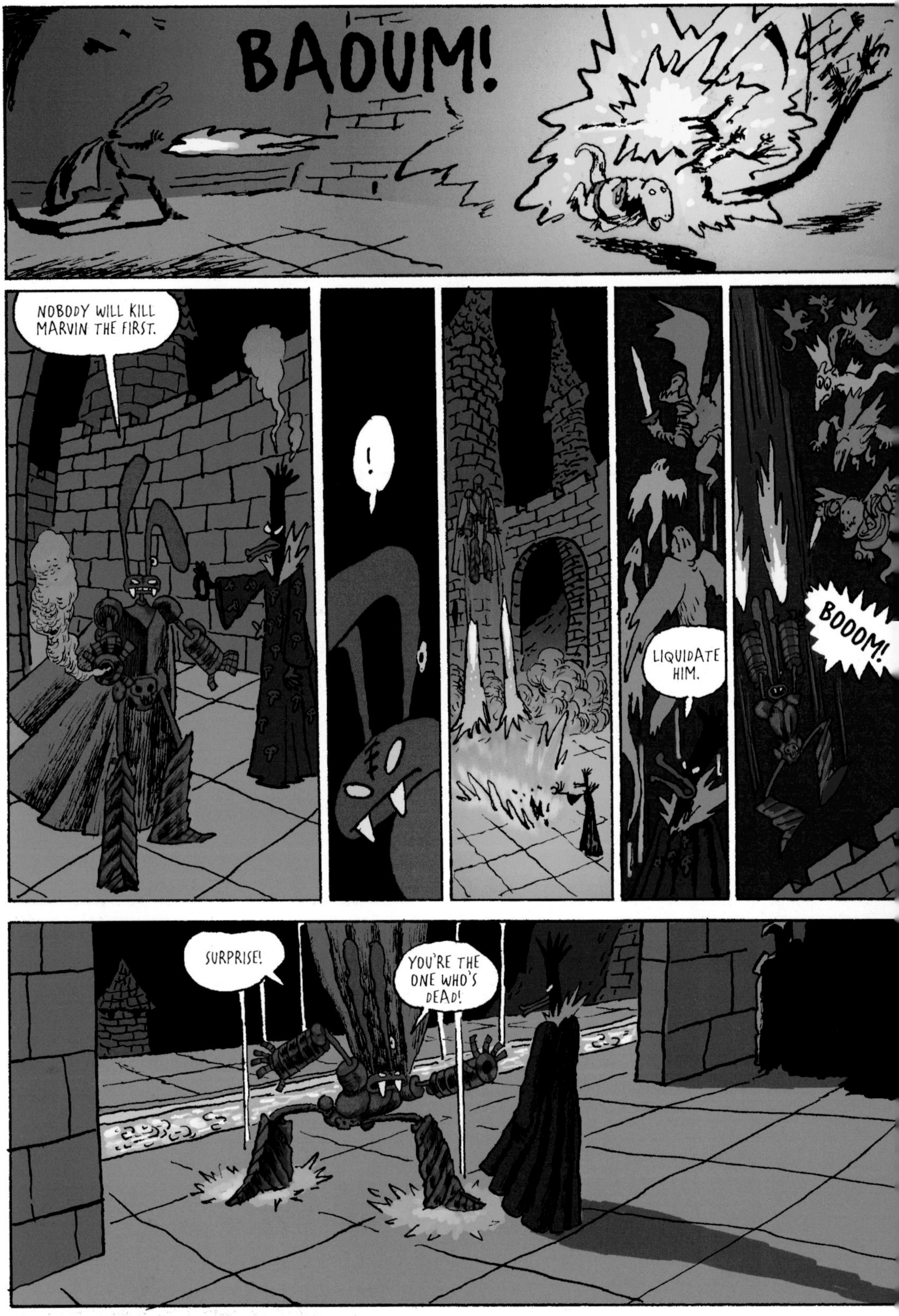

BAOUM!
NOBODY WILL KILL MARVIN THE FIRST.
!
LIQUIDATE HIM.
BOOOM!
SURPRISE!
YOU'RE THE ONE WHO'S DEAD!

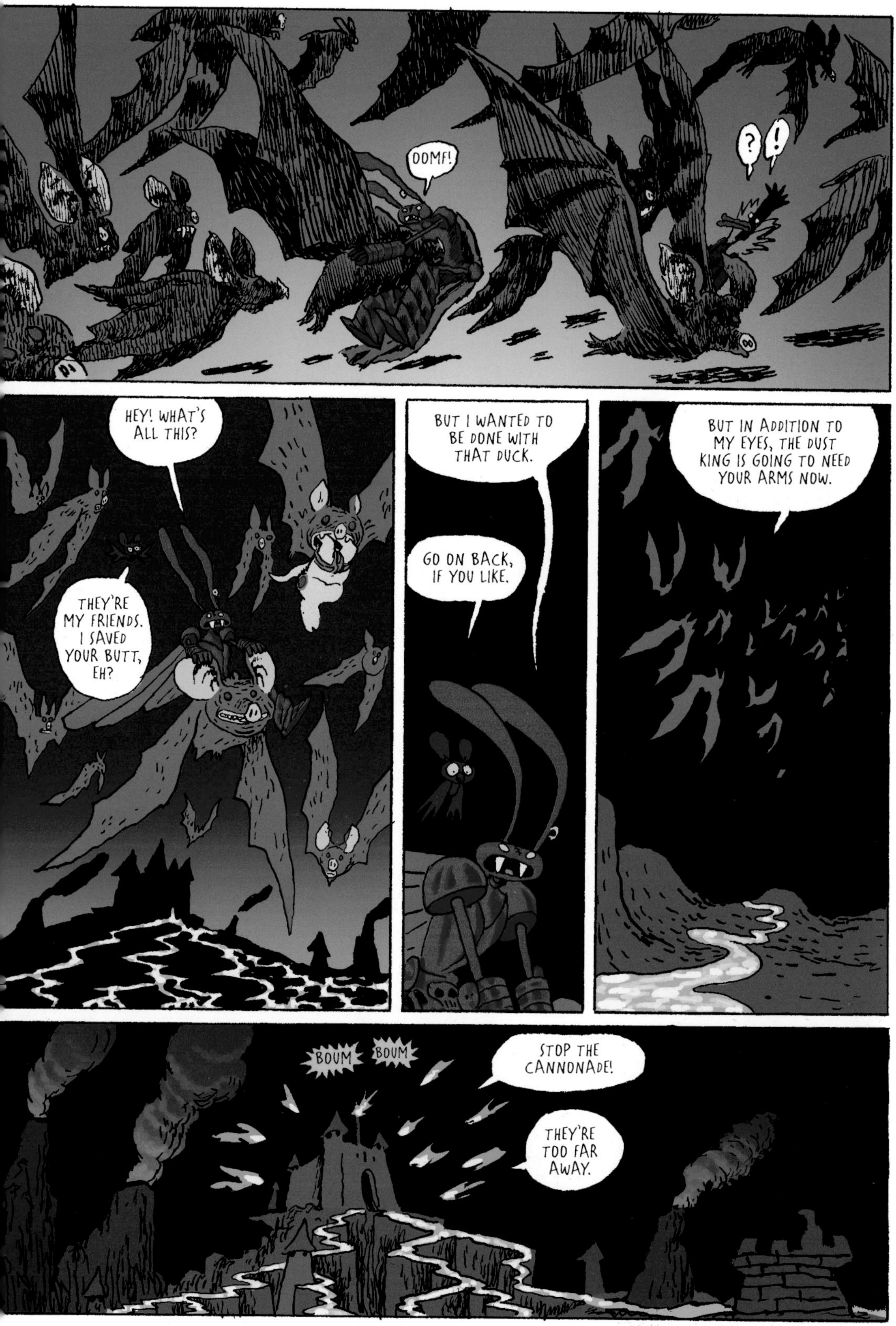
OOMF!
?!
HEY! WHAT'S ALL THIS?
THEY'RE MY FRIENDS. I SAVED YOUR BUTT, EH?
BUT I WANTED TO BE DONE WITH THAT DUCK.
GO ON BACK, IF YOU LIKE.
BUT IN ADDITION TO MY EYES, THE DUST KING IS GOING TO NEED YOUR ARMS NOW.
BOUM
BOUM
STOP THE CANNONADE!
THEY'RE TOO FAR AWAY.

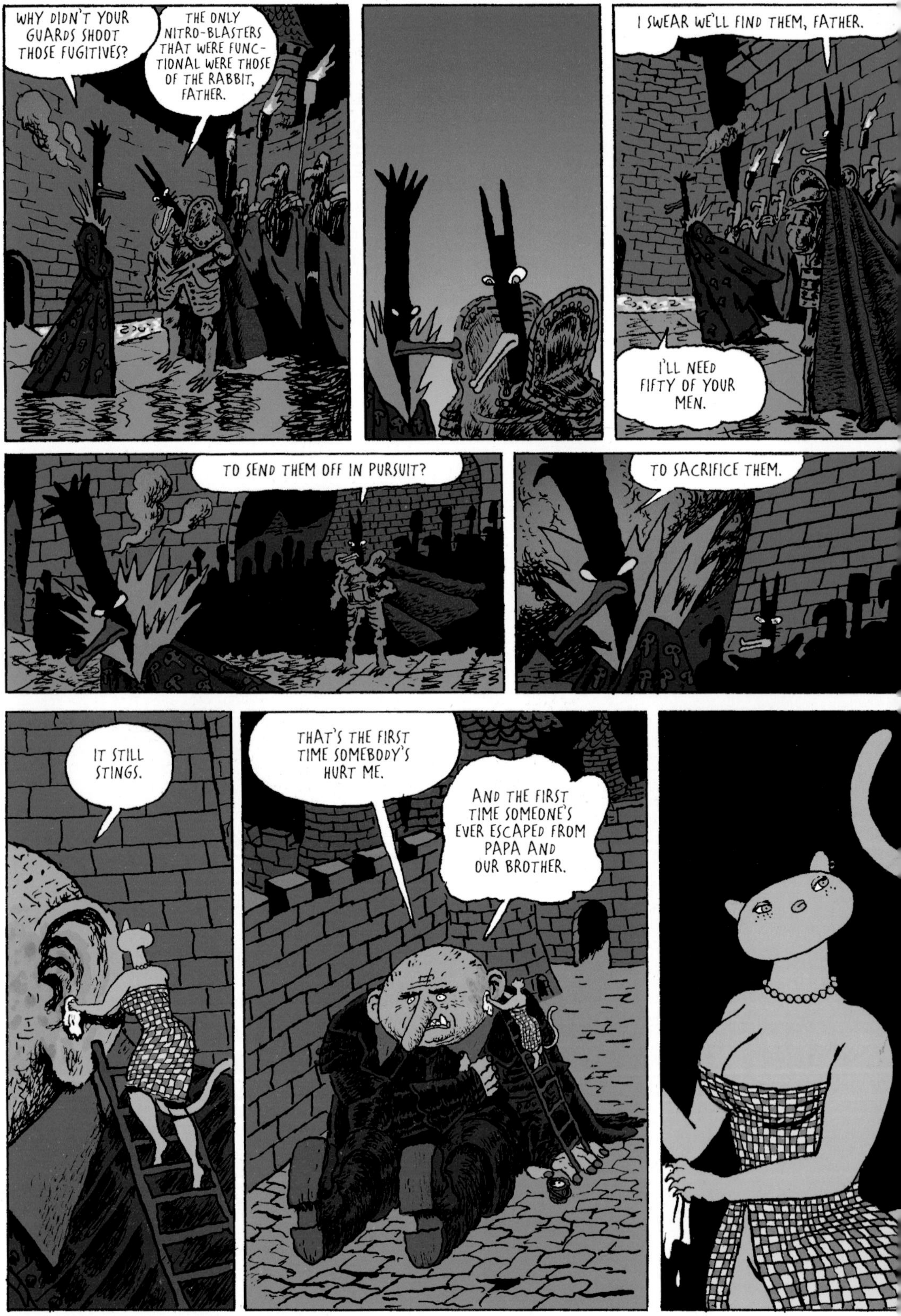
WHY DIDN'T YOUR GUARDS SHOOT THOSE FUGITIVES?
THE ONLY NITRO-BLASTERS THAT WERE FUNCTIONAL WERE THOSE OF THE RABBIT, FATHER.
I SWEAR WE'LL FIND THEM, FATHER.
I'LL NEED FIFTY OF YOUR MEN.
TO SEND THEM OFF IN PURSUIT?
TO SACRIFICE THEM.
IT STILL STINGS.
THAT'S THE FIRST TIME SOMEBODY'S HURT ME.
AND THE FIRST TIME SOMEONE'S EVER ESCAPED FROM PAPA AND OUR BROTHER.